Praise for MALCOLM GLUCK'S SUPERPLONK

'An impressive and accessible guide to what's really worth drinking'

Observer

'Gluck has a distinctively brash style which some love and others hate: his descriptive vocabulary is all his own, and some of his judgments turn convention on its head'

Time Out

'Reading Malcolm Gluck's introduction, it is easy to see why he is one of our most popular wine writers. If you're looking for a wine book that will tell you where there is value for the pound in your pocket, this is it'

Hampstead & Highgate Express

'For a clear and unpretentious guide to what is eminently drinkable on the supermarket shelf, there is none better than Malcolm Gluck's *Superplonk*'

Edinburgh Evening News

About the Author

Malcolm Gluck was first alerted to the profundity of wine on May 29th 1964 at 10.30 in the evening but had to wait until 1989 to write on the subject for the *Guardian.* He is now the newspaper's wine correspondent, writing a regular Saturday column, *Superplonk.* He writes three wine guides a year, each one fresh and fruity and unadulterated by anything but his own singular viewpoint. He presented his own BBC-TV wine series – *Gluck, Gluck, Gluck.* He is consultant wine editor to Sainsbury's Magazine, contributing a monthly wine diary. He has compiled a double-CD of classical music with wine for Deutsche Grammophon. Other major preoccupations are his children, dead authors, all styles of piano music, and relaxing in cemeteries.

Superplonk 1999

Malcolm Gluck

CORONET BOOKS
Hodder and Stoughton

First published in Great Britain as
a Coronet paperback original in 1998

10 9 8 7 6 5 4 3 2 1

'Loss' by Wendy Cope from *Serious Concerns*, Faber & Faber,
is reprinted by kind permission of the publisher.

The extract from *Pleasures Strange and Simple* by William Sansom
© 1953 published by The Hogarth Press, is reproduced by
kind permission of Greene & Heaton Ltd.

British Library Cataloguing in Publication Data

Gluck, Malcolm
Superplonk 1999
1. Wine and wine making – Great Britain – Guidebooks
I. Title
641.2'2'0296'41

ISBN 0 340 71311 9

Typeset by Palimpsest Book Production Limited,
Polmont, Stirlingshire
Printed and bound in Great Britain

Hodder and Stoughton
A division of Hodder Headline PLC
338 Euston Road
London NW1 3BH

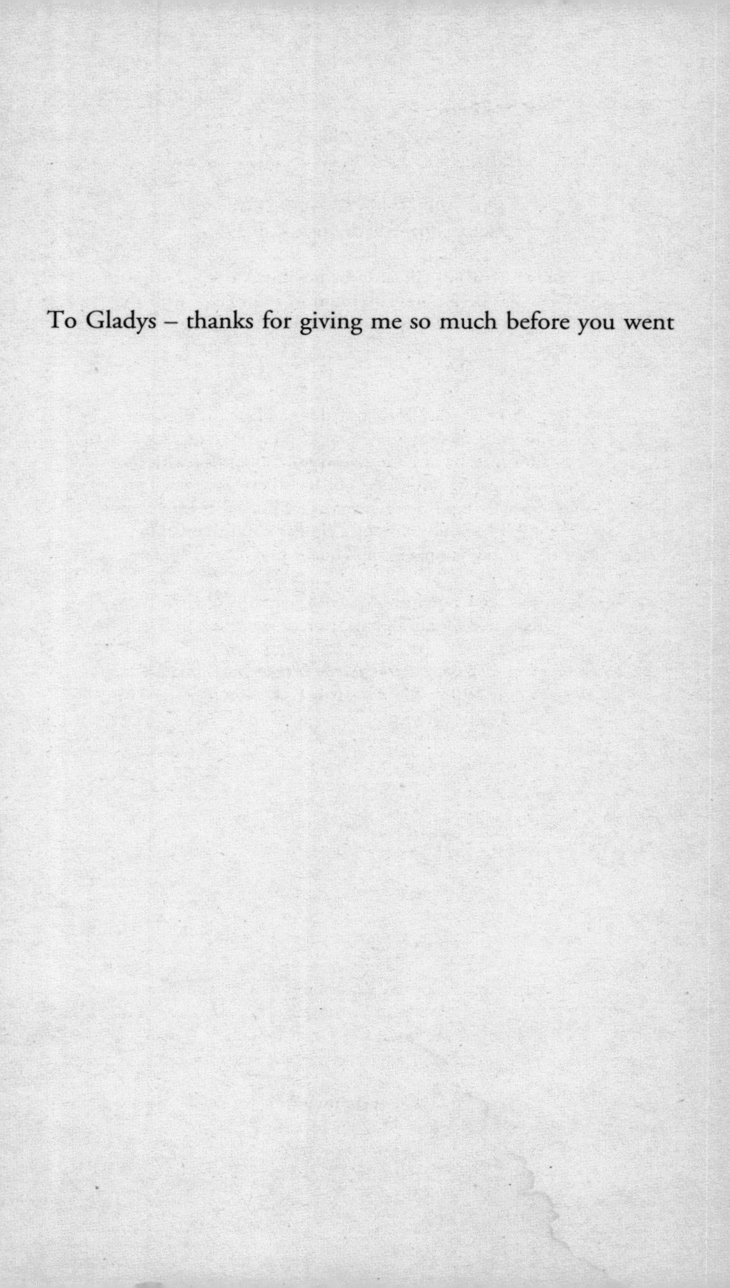

To Gladys – thanks for giving me so much before you went

'Have I not always had a great desire for confession, even when wine has not made me more expansive still?'

Italo Svevo, *Confessions of Zeno*

Superplonk 1999

CONTENTS

INTRODUCTION

Dear Diary doesn't sound right. (Regular readers will hardly need reminding that value for money is the object here not dearness.) Anyway, here's my journal as it assembled itself during my tour last autumn of the nation's new and old bookshops, radio & TV stations, restaurants, lesser hotels, supermarkets, railway carriages etcetera. It gives you, for one thing, an insight into the mental condition of this book's debauchee* of an author, surely of some value when he boasts of tasting seven or eight thousand wines a year** and rating them accurately, and it also provides, for another and arguably more useful thing, some idea, small but insightful, of the current state of supermarket wine retailing and drinking in this astonishing country of ours.

30th October 1997

As an irony lover (very good for the blood irony) I receive a massive but unsettling dose of it at my first signing of the 1997 season. It takes place in the Inner Temple, between the Thames and Fleet Street. The evening is designed not only to flatter the author but to raise money for Macmillan Cancer Relief. The attendees have each paid £20 to be instructed in wine tasting and to discover the delights of the 1998 editions of

* '*Words ending in -ee frequently give pleasure. Debauch ... comes from an old French word meaning "to turn away from the workshop"...*' Ivor Brown *A Word in Your Ear* – 1942.

** This is the figure provided by my computer. It equates with an average of 22 wines a day. I must say this seems modest. But then the computer does not take into account wines tasted in restaurants or tasted for a second or third time at home.

Superplonk and *Streetplonk*. It turns out rather an uneasy experience because a number of people insist on smoking cigarettes whilst sniffing at M & S's Alta Mira Cabernet Sauvignon, Safeway's Kleinbosch Young Vatted Pinotage and Somerfield's own-label Chilean Cabernet Sauvignon (amongst several other interesting wines), and do not cease even when I ask if they might, please, momentarily cease partaking of Monsieur Nicotine's innovation. Wine tasting and weed inhalation do not mix congenially and on top of this I am peculiarly susceptible to fag pollution. I am also struck by the thought that if these people, a minority of those present admittedly but a potent minority nonetheless, want to do something positive to relieve cancer they might give a care for what they shove in their lungs in the first place. Personally, I couldn't give the fleas in a monkey's armpit what all these tax-raising smokers do to their health as long as I don't have to share their filthy air. If only they could take it home with them.

4th November

An experiment: a wine tasting/book signing in a Sainsbury's supermarket coffee shop. But then this is Harrogate – town of health and wealth. The evening is a huge success. Harrogate once flaunted more springs than a Queen sized Dunlopillo. The Victorians wallowed in them and still died young. Water isn't always good for the health.

5th November

Edinburgh – and although due to do several things before I start the bottles rolling in the evening I get deflected all afternoon by, firstly, *panetella con salcicce paesano* (i.e. a sausage sandwich) and a half bottle of '93 Barolo Ascheri Giacomo at Valvona and Crolla's caffe – V & C are the UK's most delicious Italian wine specialist – and, secondly, a visit to a secondhand bookshop* I spot discreetly cowering in a basement opposite V & C (so

* '*How many cities have revealed themselves to me in the marches I undertook in the pursuit of books!*'

much more rewarding a museum than London's egregious V & A) which I have never before noticed in that city. I spend ninety minutes and £21.25p in this bookshop (it's called McNaughtan's and run by the handsomely cardiganed Elizabeth A. Strong who would call herself an antiquarian bookseller I fancy) and come away with *Life & Letters of Lewis Carroll* (pub. Nelson 1898) by Stuart Dodgson Collingwood £2, *The Worst of Love* (pub. Eyre & Spottiswoode 1931) by Hugh Kingsmill illustrated in b & w by Nicholas Bentley £2.50, *A Narrow Street* (Penguin 1947) by Elliot Paul £1, *Nettles* (pub. Faber & Faber 1930) by D. H. Lawrence 75p, *Some Principles of Fiction* (pub. Jonathan Cape 1953) by Robert Liddell £3, *A Last Diary* (pub. Chatto & Windus 1920) by W. N. P. Barbellion £4.50, and *Baedeker's Southern France* (pub, Karl Baedeker, Leipzig, 6th revised edition 1914) by Karl Baedeker £8.50. This last a unique gem in that it includes, held fast by the ingenious use of tiny adhesive stickers rather like the ones philatelists employ for the backs of their stamps, many newspaper and miscellaneous cuttings the original owner of the book took the trouble of inserting into the guide which were relevant to the various towns s(he) visited or, since we are talking about 1914 here, intended to visit. Events rather overtook the European traveller from August 1914. I hope my Baedeker's original owner was not one of its twenty million victims. The Elliot Paul is a rarity and I have another copy*. It was first published in 1942 in America and relates the American author's life in a narrow street, La Rue Etroite of the original title, in Paris between the wars. It is a treasure and it is destined to be a Christmas present for a much liked American neighbour. One whole pound! Who says I am not also a generous, nay profligate!, fellow at festive times?

Generosity is the order of the evening as I am taken out to Silvio's in Leith and treated to a bottle of 1967 Barolo Giorgio

*'*To a book collector, you see, the true freedom of all books is somewhere on his shelves.*' Both from Walter Benjamin's 'Illuminations' – Fontana paperback 1992.

Carnevale (with its soft anise/marzipan/licorice undertone) with tagliolini con tartufo and then, would you believe, a bottle of 1970 Barolo Altare Giovanni La Moura (which is superbly chocolatey) with a plate of tripe in the divine company of Claire Gordon-Brown and Jane Hughes who will, if organisational talent, intelligence and personality count for anything in the world of supermarketing, be main board directors of their employer, J Sainsbury plc, by the turn of the century. Read the Barbellion before turning in. Now there *is* a diary for you . . .

6th November

Why this conspiracy of silence? Why was there no indication by the Thistle Hotel breakfast staff that I had no need to rush my kipper? Why didn't reception, smiling through her galaxy of Celtic freckles, laugh when I ordered the cab for 9.45 and ask if I wanted to reach Heathrow? Why didn't the concierge whisper a word when he told me the cab would be 2 minutes late (rare enough in Edinburgh)? Why didn't the cabbie ask why I was going to the airport? Why? Why did I have to reach the BA check-in desk, at precisely the 10.15 time indicated as advisable on my flight schedule, to discover the airport I wished to reach as ticketed was, in the check-in clerk's honeyed words, 'closed to all flights until this afternoon.' I should have read the (free) morning paper instead of my book. I might have learned something useful for a change. I enquire at another airline counter and find, for an outrageous £110, I can acquire a single ticket on Air-UK and fetch up at Stansted. Nearer London than Edinburgh, that's for sure. Though ludicrously Stansted claims to be a London airport, just like Gatwick and even Luton nowadays. Scandalous proximity to a damn lie rather than comfortable proximity to London. Still, I buy the ticket.

Linger for a moment in the airport bookshop. Pick up latest Jeffrey Archer. Read first page. Feel greatly satisfied. Replace book on pile and fight my way through the throng to the departure lounge. Francis Bacon put his finger on it as far as Jeffrey Archer is concerned when he said, 390 or so years ago, that 'some books are to be tasted, others to be swallowed, and some few to be chewed and digested.' Do I have to read the whole of an Archer novel to form an opinion of it? Do I have to eat a complete airline meal or every course at *La Cuillere Graisseux* to decide this is not to be further investigated? One taste, one *whiff*, is enough to give one the flavour of it.

7th November

I am asked, prior to being interviewed on Classic FM by John Brunning, when I will start to write next year's edition of *Superplonk*. I am able to reply I began it a week ago. Later, I enjoy the rare experience of drinking chasselas in a London restaurant (the excellent Snows on The Green in Shepherd's Bush London W6). Chasselas is not an especially well regarded grape variety, indeed the French outside Alsace seem mostly to regard it as a table grape, but the Swiss turn it into some silky wines and so does Bernard Schoffit in Colmar. His Schoffit Chasselas Vieilles Vignes Cuvee Caroline 1994 is utterly delicious, a curious combination of richness and refreshing minerality, and a second bottle is soon called for. If only more restaurants were brave enough to list uncommon, sensibly priced wines like Schoffit's chasselas, eating out at non-BYOBs would not only be less of an obscenely expensive business but also much more illuminating.

9th November

I am allowed to cook Sunday lunch, since even my wife recognises I need to relax after my first week on the road. I make pea souffles with asparagus sauce (which even the kids like in their individual pots), fresh tuna with spinach & olive sauce (but slices of swordfish for the kids and a less aggressive sauce), and prune, apricot and almond tart. My wife loathes the Von Kesselstaat 1991 Riesling I wish to drink and insists on 1996 Santa Carolina Chardonnay lying in the fridge. Just as well we don't trying cooking together, my wife and I. All those sharp knives . . .

10th November

The wine guides are officially launched at a party at the notorious Groucho Club. Booksellers turn out in force and even the odd wine writer – though only the odd wine writer would condescend to respond to the invitation. Mr Oz Clarke for instance; here is an individual singularly free of the rancour, jealousy, hatred, disgust, misapprehension and ignorance which bedevils many of his contemporaries when it comes to discussing inexpensive wine widely available. Public school and Oxford seem to have done him no harm whatsoever. He is an attractive advertisement for both. Mr Clarke is one of the few wine scribes who does not live in a house which, like all these blessed bores' residences, is called 'The Snotteries.'

11th November

Interviewed on Radio-5 Live. Don't feel alive I must say. Walk in to Euston station afterwards and encounter Ms Mandy Wheeler walking out. Ms Wheeler is the only person in this country I know of who can direct a radio commercial. Such people are rarer than first-rate white burgundies. She also has other rare qualities and she has been sharing them with students at my old college, an institute for the vaguely insane which, for a very short time many years ago, was my stab at tertiary education. My time there had its memorable moments. One of which was the Head of the Art School, panting with excitement on the second or third Monday after the start of term, telling us all we had to catch this amazing new TV programme he'd clocked over the weekend. It was called 'That Was The Week That Was.' Is it any wonder my younger son thinks I'm so old I went to school by chariot? Actually, he's not far wrong. The coal, milk, and bread were all delivered by specially trained horses when I was a toddler. Our next door neighbour used studiously to pick up all the malodorous souvenirs with a shovel and pack them around the bottoms of her rose bushes. You wonder I turned to wine drinking.

Travel to Chester via Crewe. The journey begins with the

usual cabaret announcement: 'I'd like to apologise to customers. There is no catering service on the train today. This is due to problems with the catering firm.' Not, you note, a problem remotely to do with the company running the trains. Turn to my pile of readers' problems. (Sometimes, I feel like an agony uncle.) Amongst the letters requiring an answer, which I dictate into my little handheld gizmo thus doing my bit to counteract the shrilling mobile phones the traveller using Intercity express train 1st class carriages is perpetually menaced by, is one which does not demand a response but which good manners recommends should get one. It is a copy of a letter sent to Mr V. G. Gale, a *Superplonk* reader in Bideford Devon, by Mr David Howse, communications manager of Thresher. Mr Gale had originally written to me expressing his displeasure at his inability to acquire certain Thresher wines when I clearly stated that these were widely and rudely beckoning on Thresher's shelves. I replied that I was astounded at this since my Saturday *Guardian* column is ruthlessly checked by Ms Linda Peskin, my administrative guru, prior to submission to the paper. I sent a copy of Mr Gale's letter to me and my reply to him to Mr Howse asking what, in this single instance, had gone wrong. Mr Howse assuaged Mr Gale's irritation, and was generous in making restitution, but, it was the first paragraph of Mr Howse's reply which most warmed my cockles.

Wrote Mr Howse: 'Dear Mr Gale, I am writing to you because I have received a copy of a letter written to you by Malcolm Gluck. May I firstly reassure you that Mr Gluck and his *Superplonk* team are fastidious, almost to the point of causing distress to the likes of me in the wine trade, in checking and rechecking the facts behind where and when a wine will be available. The process seems to be as thorough as that which Mr Gluck undergoes to choose the wines for his column in the first place.' In nigh on ten years of doing this job, that paragraph gives me more pleasure to contemplate that any number of fatuous wine writing awards or favourable newspaper reviews of my books. I have never seen my work as simply one of having a high old time boozing at someone else's expense with my readers jolly lucky to find a recommended wine at an out-of-the-way merchant's with an ordinance survey map in one hand and the steering wheel of a 4-litre four-track in the other. My commitment is to widely available, terrific value wines, the odd wondrous bottle at small merchants excepted, and I insist that those wines will be on the right shelves at the right price when my weekly *Guardian* column is published. True, with a book like this, particularly if it is being utilised after its initial November publication date (with Spring buds beginning greenly to poke through) by a reader expecting to find extant examples of that incredibly inexpensive 18.5-point red, then nothing is guaranteed. Wine, the great bargains particularly, enjoy only a short life and we must possess them when we can. In truth, it seems to me, such wine's brevity of availability is a paradoxical measure of the inordinate length of time they are capable of providing unforgettable pleasure once purchased. We cannot truly possess bricks and mortar, or our car (or bicycle), our books, or even our children; we only enjoy them for a period of time before they pass into other's hands. But a wonderful bottle of wine is possessed utterly. We drink it. Our digestive system absorbs it. Our memory can replay the distinct pleasure of it, that lazily luxurious texture, that ineffably rich and multi-stranded fruit, for as long as we live. We have uniquely and utterly possessed that wine. Sorry. I seem to have strayed off the point somewhat. Where was I? Oh yes . . . mumbling into my Philips Pocket Memo Voice Tracer 191 . . . goodness . . . what a hush has stolen over the carriage . . .

Chester book signing is at another Sainsbury's. Other wine writers are often critical of the fact that I write for Sainsbury's magazine but what they don't appreciate is that I am freer to write, and say, what I like than many of them are. The magazine, though only on sale at Sainsbury checkouts, is independently published and is pleased to print exactly what I wish to write (except it sometimes asks me to cut out libellous references). No other magazine, especially wine magazine, would give any journalist such width of approach to wine and depth of freedom in which to write about it. Is this why I am pleased to turn up at so many Sainsbury's to do book signings and tasting? Curiously, no. It is because the supermarket organises the events so well (at branch management level as well as head office) and because I enjoy encouraging supermarket shoppers to make more courageous decisions where wines are concerned. And of course there are the wines themselves. Among this evening's line-up: Vouvray (yum!), La Baume Chardonnay, Casillero del Diablo Cabernet, the extraordinary own-label Aussie chardonnay, a couple of pinotages, Leasingham Shiraz – I could go on. These tastings are worth my doing. Innovative wines, innovative wine makers.

Can't claim much innovation at dinner afterwards. Order my usual bottle of Alsatian wine (at a fancy joint called Crabwell Manor.): Clos des Capucins Riesling Theo Faller 1990. New world specimens apart, Alsatians seem to be the affordable standby when I eat at 'posh' restaurants – that is to say where the women diners wear pearls and the men ties. My throat is conspicuously absent of both externally, but a jewel of a wine certainly travels down inside it.

The cabbie who brought me here from the Sainsbury's is bubbling over with indignation over the Louise Woodward case – the English nanny from Cheshire alleged to have killed a baby in America. The cabbie said she knew Louise Woodward 'never killed that baby'. 'Plain as the nose on your face the girl is innocent. I should know,' she spits out, 'I live in the village next along from hers.'

12th November

My schedule, thanks to the ruthless efficiency of Hodder's Ms Katie Gunning, reads as follows: Depart Chester 10.56am, Arrive Manchester 11.55am, Depart Manchester 12.12pm, Arrive Leeds 13.14pm, Depart Leeds 13.29pm, Arrive Harrogate 14.04pm. I arrive in a philosophical mood (egged on by a degree of hunger since no edible food was offered en route). What is one's moral responsibility towards a spent match? I discovered one nestling between the handles of my overnight bag whilst boarding the TransPennine Express from Manchester Piccadilly's Platform 13 to Leeds. Then I remembered the man I brushed past at Chester Station whilst walking swiftly to catch the Manchester train. He had just lit a cigarette and his arm was finishing a discarding gesture. Was this the source of my gift? Had it lain on my bag the whole 55 minutes of my first rail journey today? I am usually only happy with a spent match in my hands when I have lit the gas hob, the automatic igniter having failed to start, and flame spurts under something wonderful-to-come like a pot of mussels done the Thai way with lemon grass, chillies and ginger. The evocative qualities of a spent match!* What do I do with such a sliver of wood on Piccadilly Station? I cannot cast it away on Rail Track property as its original ejector had attempted. I would be as careless of good manners as he. When the Scarborough train pulls in, which goes past Leeds, I still have the object in my hand. But I am also reading a book, Italo Svevo's *Confessions of Zeno*, and at this precise moment I read '. . . some curious advice had been offered to me to help me give up smoking . . . sometimes it was quite enough if one lit a match and threw away both match and cigarette.' Interesting coincidence. I feel grateful to the litterbug smoker on Chester station. We have now travelled fifteen minutes to Stalybridge, where the station clock is the fattest in the county and the platform buffet has handsome sash windows with the uppers in stained glass of art deco design, and the match, now snapped in two involuntarily by my fingers at the surprise of the coincidence in my book, lies on the table. I don't suppose the railway police will apprehend me if I leave

* In Elias Canetti's breathtaking book, *Crowds & Power* (Penguin 1973), there arises the compelling imagery of the match box as the container of a forest and the matches as a forest fire. Walter Benjamin, the German critic, has also commented evocatively on the invention of the match in the middle of the nineteenth century; as the initiator, via one brisk motion of the hand, of a complex process of numerous parts. Did Benjamin's writing (specifically the essay on motifs in Baudelaire) inform Canetti's own ideas in some way?

it there. And I will be leaving it there. Haven't I already given it a free ride from Chester? My original question still remains however. The answer: my moral responsibility is the same as its original owner's. I must dispose of it responsibly. Slowly, I get up and take the two pieces of wood to the litter bin three seats along. I have done my duty. The carriage is unaware of the clown in its midst.

As Svevo has his character Zeno reflect: 'Fancies which spring from wine are as real as actual events.' And, later: 'Wine is a great danger not because it brings the truth to light; but, on the contrary, because it reveals what is past and forgotten and plays no part in one's present conscious will . . . our whole life-history is written there and wine proclaims it abroad, regardless of the emmandations of time.'

I check in at Harrogate's marvellously quaint White House hotel, a copy of Eliot's collected poems (1909–1962) once owned, so the title page tells me, by one Jennie Forster by the bed, and lying in the well-worn, concave-bottomed Lloyd loom chair by the window an old sheep, a stuffed toy, with a purple bow tie. It has a message affixed: 'If you do not wish to be disturbed place me outside your door'. There is nothing, however, in the room for me to place outside the door if I wish to indicate the opposite. Surprising lapse for a hotel so eccentric. It was once the Mayor of Harrogate's residence.

Already my values are changing in these luxurious conditions. Here I am in Harrogate and I'm contemplating buying a Rolls Royce and 1966 claret. The Rolls – vintage '55 at a guess is a Dinky toy in a junk shop. The claret is part of a cache of dusty bottles in an antique emporium. But I need food. The Chinese takeaway across the street looks promising. 'The Perfect Restaurant' it says in elegant unhurried script 'Chinese Food to Take Away.' Classy, but I want to sit down.

I tear myself away and plump, downtown, for a late tea of Alsace pinot noir with leek sausages and roast potatoes at Betty's, a Harrogate landmark.

Then it's time for my annual fund raising wine auction at

Morrisons, the supermarket chain which until recently was a strictly northern manifestation. But Banbury Oxon is opening and Erith in Kent is up and running. Does Erith, famous for bricks and being the birth place of the great Kentish poet Wendy Cope, know what it's in for? Morrisons is pleased to sell wines, good wines, very inexpensively indeed. Mr Purdie and Ms Smith do the buying. No supermarket gives me more pleasure to visit – all those single figure price tags. And no supermarket event gives me more pleasure to conduct than this annual fund raising. We raise £4000 for the cancer nurses. And I get to drink a wine like the red Cotes de Saint Mont, with its rich tannat grape (plus cabernet), for a mere £3.69 – but this is Morrisons remember (Oh Erith! You lucky bricks!). However, if you were to buy four bottles of it, three quid gets knocked off the aggregated price. You'd be pushed to buy a red this good in a Calais hypermarket for the equivalent of £2.94 a bottle. No wonder Morrisons figured they could open in Erith. Maybe they should open further down in Kent, like Dover.

13th November

Leave Harrogate, go to York, leave York, get to Kings Cross, and realise I have an hour and half to kill before Steve Wright grills me on BBC-radio. Find Zeno Consini is really getting on my nerves. Can fictional characters dictate real emotions to readers? I don't mean being swept up with the sentimental grandeur of the sentimental fictional moment – I mean real douleur setting in or rich elation. What a crepuscular, dank mean little world signor Corsini inhabits in late 19th century Trieste! I turn gratefully to *The Language Web*, the book of Jean Aitchison's 1996 BBC Reith Lectures, which she kindly sent me. Professor Aitchison is hugely entertaining – not a quality many people would attach to an Oxford don especially a Professor of Language and Communication – because not only does she write limpidly and free of jargon about a technical subject but she draws on a wealth of learning and reading in other disciplines with an open mind and a hungry intellect.

I sneak in to Nico Central, state the urgency of my hunger, and they agree to feed me Shin of Veal and Chips and a bottle of Los Vascos Cabernet Sauvignon 1995 and see me off the premises by 1.20. Of course such a lunch is always conducted in a spirit of research. The man at the next table, grey suited and an employee of a major clothes retailer, black moustache hanging on grimly as he masticates, says 'great' on receipt of mineral water and 'wonderful' on being given a peppergrinder. Interesting how language develops (I will not say becomes corrupted) when phrases in current usage in one sphere of activity – and great and wonderful are simply synonyms for thanks in the rag trade – become translated to another. The young French waiter who brings both water and peppergrinder and who speaks very little clear English is receiving a confusing education.

Later, at the BBC, I provide the wines for a Christmas on air lunch: Cava to start, Chilean own-label reds for the turkey (Sainsbury, Safeway, Tesco, Morrison et al), Rhone reds for the cheese, and Moscatel de Valencia for the pud. The interviewer is Steve Wright plus Lisa, who, so she says, 'embraces Portuguese wine.'

Get home to a message on the machine: can I write three articles for September publication by Monday midday? I say no. It doesn't conflict with the *Guardian* and the fee is excellent. But it's Friday and I need my children's company.

In the evening it's Waterstone's in Richmond. Someone takes great exception, on racist grounds, at my calling the French frogs. Kathy, who I haven't seen for seventeen years, turns up.

14th November

10.15 to Didcot reading *Le Petit Prince* for light relief from Zeno Consini's infidelities. I espy a notice stuck by the carriage window. It says, 'This carriage has been reserved for customers who require a quiet environment. Therefore for the convenience of your fellow passengers, we ask that you do not use mobile telephones and personal stereo equipment within this carriage'.

Just as one feels crushed like a grape on its way to the fermenting tank, along slithers the yeast of commonsense to raise one's spirits!

Didcot is where I break the world book signing record: 1990 copies in 1 hour 59 minutes. Didcot is the home of Bookpoint, wholesalers, and I am assisted in my triumphant scribbling by three stalwart assistants. The first lays open the book at the right page, the second whisks the signed copy away and hands it to the chap who packs it in a box for despatch, and in those few seconds the first guy plonks down another book in front of me. What do we talk about for these two hours? Football.

In the evening I go to a champagne tasting at Richard & Emma's house. Always a treat, that. Though this time, since the evening revolves around a champagne and sparkling wine tasting (since R is an *Independent* food and drink writer), the treat, to begin with at least, is somewhat lessened by my having to work – and in company, a thing I never usually do. But it all works out right in the end: champagne, one example aside, gets the thumbs down and sparkling wines win the prize.

18th November

Book signing at 6.30 in the upstairs demonstration kitchen at the Books for Cooks bookshop. It passes uneventfully. I point out that the UK is the third most important wine market in the world in volume terms behind France and the USA, but in terms of image the UK is by far the most prestigious (with not only the world's largest wine merchants, Tesco and Sainsbury, but also an abundance of wine styles from every wine growing country in the world – with the possible exceptions of Madagascar and Egypt). A member of the small and perfectly formed audience yawns. Yes, well. I can't tell jokes all the time.

19th November

An elderly woman on the tube from Royal Oak to Kings Cross has legs freckled like one of those photographs of deep space taken by the Hubble telescope. For all we earthlings can learn of life on galaxies millions of light years away and composed of billions of stars, we might just as well train a cockroach with a magnifying glass to tour old lady's legs.

I am bound for my favourite city in Britain (my home town apart). I am reading '*Species of Spaces*' by Georges Perec. It is the sort of oddity which encourages introspective acerbity. Hence, perhaps, my feeling – uncomfortable, rancid, competitive, alien, abrasive, crowded yet eavesdrop-ational. To travel in the first class carriage of an Intercity Express nowadays is to step inside Corporate Britain (note the caps). All those correct white, grey and blue shirts. All those overdecorated yet indecorous ties striving so hard to tell the world that the wearer is creative when the very opposite is perfectly plain. Do I care to hear about everyone else's telephonic commercial derring-do's and don'ts, their evening arrangements, all those 'darlings' who constitute their telephonic wives (married to mobile phones as much as men)? I don't think I do. Thank God the little computers, lying closed like unloved stamp collections, are silent.

I see clearly that I do not write a wine guide. I write and publish an annual record of a man's drinking. One ambition of Perec was to 'write the sort of books that are devoured lying face down on a bed.' I am disqualified from this canon. *Superplonk* is the sort of book which is best devoured standing upright in front of a shelf of supermarket wines.

A cultivated attachment to misnomers. Surely this is a sign of an unrefined mind?

Several words requiring further research: engological, maientics, effevent, aleatory (meaning depending upon the throw of a die), sonorities, artene, *comme parterre*, tetanus as a spasm, Pelage, Samuel Foote, the phenomenon of the 1st World War being closer to us than the Gulf one, Hamlet's and Wittgenstein's 'the rest is silence', Sir Thomas Browne's poetry, Dorothy Richardson's 'Tunnel' pub. in 1919, cobwebs as mops, urtication as a property of sauvignon blanc wines.

I can't be the only reader who gets pissed off by the names in Russian novels.

What a great pity we can't film a meeting between Nicholson Baker and Georges Perec! Just let the camera run . . . with hours of film . . . Insomnia cure?

Can one swallow words and spice the food? Or is it the other way around?

Wines must be accorded the measure of doubt we grant to people. Did you drink the same wine as me? Did you meet the same disagreeable misanthrope? Or did we merely encounter the same bottle/person in a different mood?

Joyce in *Ulysses* wrote well of reading on the loo, and the male pleasures to be gained thereby. Just before Bloom goes to the funeral, I think. A writer naturally accumulates piles (books, press cuttings, readers' letters, never-to-be-published poems, ideas, dream-novel openings, recipes).

Of course, the eskimoes couldn't get by with a single word for ice. Between the fact of semi-liquid slush and solid frozen water a dozen or more shades of iciness must exist for the natives of such a landscape. (Not an original thought, this.)

Reach my destination deliberately early so that I can explore the Newcastle Bookshop before going to Dillons (old books being more interesting than new ones) only to find the place closed! I push open the imposing black iron gates which front the alleyway the bookshop hides in. A young person, a bright pumpkin in the lit doorway of the rear entrance of the fish and chip shop which has a side door on the alley, stirs himself. Only sign of life in the alley. It begins to rain. Find solace in the Fox Talbot Café and sip a large expresso in a glass cup. Haven't put my lips to glassed coffee since 1966! Are you old enough to remember all those steamy cafés? And those far-from-steamy exchanges between the sexes?

Stroll up to Dillons and discover the lie in the last paragraph. Certain new books are altogether as interesting as old ones; waiting in the second floor of the shop for readers/drinkers to arrive I discover Noel Malcolm's *The Origins of English Nonsense* (pub. Harper Collins 1997) and buy a copy (or rather I buy *the* copy). On the evidence of the first half dozen pages read whilst waiting, this will be more than adequate recompense for my failed gamble. I had assumed that I did not need to take a book with me when leaving my hotel for companionship over dinner since I was bound to find something original at the second-hand shop. Mr Malcolm is a find.

Much wine drunk at the evening, only one irrelevantly drunk customer. Someone brings all *Superplonk*s published since 1993 for me to sign. Questions, as always with Novocastrians, are forceful, intelligent, unpretentious.

Part of the reason I like Newcastle is 21 Queen Street, the name and the location of an interesting restaurant. The Alsatian Pinot-Blanc 1994 goes with ham hock terrine with peas pudding and walnut oil salad to start and pheasant chou-croute to follow. It is brilliant German influenced cooking of a very high and imaginative standard. With my sticky date pudding I have a half-bottle of 1990 Chateau de la Genaiserie Les Petits Houx (App. Coteau-du-Layon Saint-Aubin Controlee) a superb Loire white, 14.8% alcohol, from the village of St. Aubin-de-Lignere (and available solely from Aquitane Wines, Kilburn, Yorks, Tel: 01347868612). Houx is holly in French, the sommelier tells me. The wine certainly sticks in the throat.

20th November

Durham today. But breakfast has to be faced first. A kipper is hoped for ('Hope is a good breakfast, but a poor supper' said Francis Bacon). I'm not allowed to grill kippers at home because of the smell. Staying in a hotel, then, is a treat if there's any on the breakfast menu. The Malmaison Hotel opposite the station has a handsome breakfast room in a mildly camp, gothic way but awful bedrooms, the shower circa. 1950 army camp, no shaving socket, and bad tempered breakfast staff. 'Earl Grey!!?' Big roll of the eyes as if I'd asked for poached inner thigh muscle of breakfast waitress. Much apologies. Staff bring Earl Grey 'didn't know we did it.' Kipper barely edible, swimming in butter, but it is reminiscent of the fish.

Take taxi to face one of my favourite interviewers on the

local BBC radio station. Do the usual hatchet job on Beaujolais nouveau which is just being released. Take taxi to Newcastle Bookshop and buy a pile of *Vogue*s of the 1953/1954 vintage for my daughter. Eat lunch in the Cafe Chinois in the old Barclays Bank building. Crap wine list. But 6 native oysters at £7 isn't bad ('We do not recommend the drinking of spirits or an excess of other alcohol with oysters or clams'). Do these people know who they're dealing with here? When I was much younger, and before I rammed a poisoned one down my gullet, I would eat twelve dozen oysters with two bottles of Chablis for supper. But then Chablis was a drink, like Beaujolais Nouveau, in those days too. My lunch is a curious and not altogether harmonious blend of west and east: crispy Chinese duck and Mediterranean salad. Enjoy a large glass of La Fontina Merlot (£3.50) in a huge glass, big bowled, almost half full. What a world on a single diner's table! Approve of: 'Please refrain from smoking in the dining area.'

Read Noel Malcolm over lunch. Discover interesting things: 'taffeta' as a term for nonsense also fustian; Farce = from French farce = stuffing = bombast from a padding used by tailors. Spend 2 hours in Cafe Chinois with Malcolm. I accost the waiter.

Me: Excuse me. Can you tell me how long you've been opened as a restaurant?

Him: Two hours.

Me: No, no. Not how long since you opened up this morning. I mean how long has the restaurant had been going . . . as a restaurant.

Him. I told you sir. Two hours.

It is a bit unnerving being in a restaurant with groups of extremely young '60's hippies who are wandering about dressed in 'I was Lord Kitchener's Valet' castoffs of the Beatles early days. There is ten times more staff in the place than customers. Early days yet. Ms Anne Pickering, who lives in Durham, greets me and says she'll see me in Durham later. Writing this book, you meet a very high quality of reader.

The Chinese manager, bringing my bill, has the wits to ask

me why I hadn't drunk the expresso I ordered. I told him it was a feeble imitation. He asked me to show him how to make it properly and we went over to the machine. I showed him and drank the proceeds.

Take the train to Durham. Meet Alastair Gilmour, *Northern Echo* journalist (and candidate for a Beer Writer of the Year award – which he subsequently wins). We drink tea and he records my comments.

Signing later at Waterstones is a delight. Much jollity and high spirits (and ripe wine). I try to hide the fact that I've never felt so jaded. The year is beginning to tell on me. Take myself off to dinner at Bistro 21 and gorge myself on spiced Thai mussels (a mountain of coconut-edged/chilli mussels whilst Elvis Presley circa 1958 screams on the speakers 'don't you step on my blue suede bivalves . . .'). Polish off hare and chips with a bottle of Vacqueyras Domaine Le Clos des Cazaux Cuvee Des Templiers 1994. Is my life a long sentence of severe parataxis?

Consider my note book. When Elvis became too strident I put Malcolm aside and looked at some of my notes made over the past few weeks. All nonsense: Earl Archimbaud-Vache, 'a spade is a spade' – is Cecily Cardew given a borrowed simile?, 40 years is only the same separation as Vera Lynn and Berlioz, mascarpone sorbet with black pepper is not an uncivilised idea.

21st November

Sleep some way out of Durham as hotels all full due to conference. Come down to breakfast at 8.22 am to see the sun like a benediction blessing every vivid executive tie in the room. A waitress grumpily nods at my good morning and shows me to the table I have asked for, which is by the window.

Me: 'Goodness me! What a wonderful day!'

Her: 'Wasn't earlier . . . rainin' 'n that . . .'

Me: 'But it's a lovely day . . . now.'

Her: 'Humph! Sun tryin' to shine I s'pose . . .'

Me: 'Trying? There's not a cloud in the sky.'

Her: 'Humph! Just you wait. It'll change.'

Welcome to the breakfast room of the Eden Arms in Rushyford. Kipper adequate. Noel Malcolm is a lively and contentious breakfast companion.

Taxi to station, driven by a lunatic – Mr Dodds by name. He drives as if late for a crucial meeting, overtaking everything. He plays loud pop music in my left ear. My kipper, I begin to feel, might soon rejuvenate itself over the back of his cab. It will be a suitable tip to leave the young tearaway.

Notice on Durham station (among other things):

'Welcome to Great NorthEastern Railway.

Our aims:

1) To run trains on time

2) To give you accurate information about the times of trains.'

I pause to listen to voice over tannoy. 'The 09.59 service to Newcastle will be 5 minutes late.'

Two minutes later the tannoy cuts in again. 'The 09.59 service to Newcastle will be 27 minutes late.'

Well that's clear then. Item number two is in brilliant shape. It's item number one that's going to take a little sorting out.

Durham, another notice informs me, is 259 miles from London. 20,000 railway electricity masts further south (a statistic I work out from yet another notice). Reminded – don't ask why – of something someone said of Molière – '*il fit rire, mais il n'ait pas.*' Hmm.

Train arrives on time. I settle down to consider the entries so far received in the Screw-Cap competition I set in the *Weekend Guardian.* I must say, in spite of so many interesting poems and the suchlike, it is the down-to-earth idea of Mr Leo Baxendale which keeps nagging at me as being the best. Why do wine retailers not, he writes, put a symbol on wines sealed with plastic corks, or screw-caps, so that customers knew? This is such a good idea and, passing Darlington (I think), I feel inclined to mount a campaign around the idea that all plastic corked wines should carry a symbol and a message 'GUARANTEED HEALTHY

CORK'. Put a rocket up the cork industry. However, what effect would a rocket have on the congenitally moribund?

24th November

Travelling to North Cheam for the evening book/booze event, the car goes down Trinity Road in Wimbledon and passes an off-licence called Dionysus. Nothing odd about this, but it also has a large sign in the window: 'Dry Cleaning'. The Greeks had a god for most things, from wine to silence, but who was the one for laundry? I am tempted to ask the driver to stop so I can investigate, but the traffic is horrendous.

This morning my mother-in-law died. This evening my previous mother-in-law drops in at the wine tasting.

25th November

Cycle to BBC for another local radio interview (Thames Valley radio). There seems to be a new arrangement to the reception area and a more modern air to the place. I go up to the smart new reception desk and announce my name. The receptionist nods, consults a piece of paper, smiles.

Receptionist: 'Would you like a cup of tea?'

Me: 'Cup of tea? No, I don't think so, thank you. Goodness, the Corporation is changing isn't it?'

Receptionist: 'I said WOULD YOU GO TO STUDIO 1T.'

Me: 'Oh. I see. One Tee. Of course. One Tee.'

Exeunt author – feeling foolish.

Later that afternoon, I find myself discussing the Icarus myth with my 11 year-old daughter. She has begun classics at her secondary school. How is that one so young can grasp allegories so well? Is it because she's female? I don't think we men get a grip on allegory until it's too late to put the lesson to any practical use. We are quicker at getting a grasp of metonyms (corkscrew = sexual power, that sort of thing).

Do an evening signing at Burpham in a flash Sainsbury store with low level lighting, pastel colours (subdued greens and blues), self-scanning facilities, and a freezing cold coffee shop. Get a touch pissed in order to warm up. Several customers join in. Baileys Old Block Shiraz 1994 is the last wine we drink. Drive home with Mike. Get home late, head buzzing.

26th November

6.45am – woken by 8 year-old son excited by previous night's handwriting homework which my absence prevented him from dazzling me with at bed-time. Are these really legible and correctly-spelt sentences? They wriggle like snakes before my burning eyes. He follows me into the lavatory and points out certain distinguished aspects of his calligraphy. What would family life be without moments like this?

3.15pm – train to Bath for evening signing/orgy. The bloke opposite, in Bristol accent, spends 15 minutes on his mobile phone discussing 'moving parts'. Perhaps if he was a well-known actor in conversation with his agent about a forthcoming melodramatic role he might be worth listening too. 'Okeydoke Bill' he signs off. This is theatre of a very low entertainment value. And it hugely interferes with Noel Malcolm's train of thought.

3.35. How wonderful! The ticket collector has turned up and turfed the mobile telephonist out of the carriage. This one it seems is for civilised passengers only. Open notebook to see large sign therein: GET DOWN TO ANSWERING READERS' LETTERS. I dutifully obey. I am in receipt of the letter below and need to respond to several readers on the topic it raises.

'21st November 1997.

Dear Malcolm,

Thank you for your forbearance, and your generosity in allowing Safeway an opportunity to reply before voicing your "angst" in print.

On behalf of Safeway I apologise unreservedly to all

Superplonk readers who have found price discrepancies between your published prices and our retail prices for wine. But an apology is not enough, the company would like to go further.

In recognition of the time and frustration you and your readers have suffered, not to mention your lobbying on readers' behalf – Safeway undertake to honour the prices you quote in your column until further notice. If customers can show a copy of your article in any of our stores, our staff will be briefed to match YOUR quote if any discrepancy arises between it and our current retail.

It is also possible to offer you much greater certainty than recently that prices will not alter after you have checked them. Some administration changes have now been made which should make changes highly unlikely.

Without in any way wishing to belittle your readers' complaints, I couldn't help reflecting ruefully (but happily!) that since the introduction of our PRICE PROTECTED scheme there will certainly be vastly more readers than those who have written in who will have found prices cheaper than they expected. And thank goodness!

May I say again how much I appreciate your assiduous handling of your readers' complaints and the admirable way you balance your prime loyalty to them with careful attention to your professional relationship with supermarkets – and to your relationship with Safeway in particular. It is one that I personally value very highly.

With kindest regards

Yours sincerely

Elizabeth Robertson MW'

Is it any wonder I often feel like some kind of unofficial ombudsman? Isn't it enough that wine growing is so imperfect a science? Does supermarket wine retailing also have to be imprecise? Is it really in keeping with our *fin-de-siecle* age of computer technology that a supermarket giant cannot offer a 100% perfect pricing policy? I am mystified.

6.30am. Arrive early at Milsom Street Waterstones. Watch a young tramp let his emaciated alsatian shit in the middle of the street. Prefer my emaciated Alsatians in a glass, chilled. I sign lots of copies for the shop's stock and retire to an unheated attic to read Norman Lewis on his adventures in Timor I find on a shelf.

Lovely crowd of people turn up for the evening. We drink loads of wine from plastic cups. Several doctors contest my pronouncements on male/female alcohol absorption. Richard le Parmentier, ex-star fleet captain (see *The Empire Strikes Back*) turns up with his two young daughters – they used to play in the same London street as my two.

Guy Woodward, local legal eagle and old family friend, whisks me off in his impressive BMW to Park Lane, where he lives with his wife Irene and two children, one a schoolboy and one a peripatetic professional magician who, after our Delia-inspired Moroccan Chicken with St Emilion, does amazing tricks with a pack of cards. Ben Woodward's dexterity and ingenuity defy belief. He recalls my own father when he lived in Bath, taking him and other children out and treating them to chocolate. Then Irene remembers how her mum and my mum met via the latter's first husband on the tram in 1930's Lambeth. 'Probably' says Irene 'your mum was suffering from post-natal depression'. Don't blame me. Blame my older brother.

27th November

8.45 am. Breakfast by the fast-running Avon looking down at the shops on the Pultney Bridge. The view is reminiscent of that of the Arno and the shops on the Ponte Vecchio when breakfasting at the Lugarno, borgo Sant'Jacopo. However, the Florentine hotel does not offer black pudding, bacon, grilled tomatoes and Earl Grey tea as does the remarkably ugly concrete excrescence in Walcot Street in Bath called the National Hilton.

9.40 am. Buy two bunches of flowers. Drop off one to thank Irene for dinner and the magic show. Drop the other, stem by stem, into the little round holes in the vase designed for floral tributes which is set into my parents' grave. On the drive to the station, I note a sign in a newsagents: 'Person required for early morning paper round – must have own car'. Such is the standard of living (and dying) in Bath, it is surprising to discover that local paperboys' jobs don't come with a company car. My cab driver is living proof of how high these standards are. He tells me he's getting married on New Year's Eve, and then jetting off to Agra and then Goa for the honeymoon.

Cabbie: 'Do you travel much in your job?'

Me: 'A bit. Here and there. You know.'

Cabbie: 'This year I've been to Oporto, Vienna, the Algarve twice and the Czech republic. After India, I've got Cyprus booked for the spring.'

Me: 'Blimey! You travel more than I do!'

Cabbie: 'Like travelling.'

Me: 'Good business, then, in Bath? Running a taxi?'

Cabbie: 'I'll say so.'

Reach station with some time to spare before the Paddington train gets in, so I explore a local bookshop. I buy nothing. I think this is a record (first time I've taken a record from a bookshop – sorry, bad joke).

There's something indecent about all these mobile telephonists. Platform No. 2 Bath Spa echoes as some charcoal-suited passenger, waiting for the same train as I, cries into his handset . . . 'Ma . . . tell me what to do!'

It's as if we no longer have clothes to hide behind or masks to wear. All these naked electronic intimacies. Why do the rest of us have to endure this theatre? The next step will be portable commodes, which the peripatetic can pocket and erect to save time.

I consult my notebook and ruminate on past notes. 'For the analysand on the couch the rose on the analyst's ceiling is like the watermark on the blank sheet of paper the confessor places into the typewriter.' That's a rum scribble. Where could I have cooked (or stolen) that one up from?

Extract from conversation overhead in station buffet:

'Is this a stirrer? I'll have a hot chocolate.'

'That's a stirrer, yes.'

'Knitting needle, is it? You know, I left my anorak in Birmingham.'

'No hot chocolate. You can't have one. We have cold. Can do you a cold chocolate. The expresso machine's not working proper.'

'Cold? Nope. Where do I find platform nine?'

'Platform nine is over the footbridge.'

To think. Pinter (and Beckett) made their names listening to exchanges like that. Maybe station announcers should add a bit of theatre to their stuff. 'The train at platform eleven will call at a selection of first and second division football teams plus one extinct: Preston, Burnley, Blackpool, Accrington. The driver's name is Stan. Nice bloke. His hobby is collecting bootlaces.'

Nabokov – pornstar & pawnstar.

28th November

4.50am. Woken by sense of impending doom. Read Betjeman. Too frivolous. Sue makes tea. Consult Donne. Is one of his obsequies appropriate for me to read at funeral next week? Settle on Wordsworth. Son lands on bed looking hollowed eyed. Saw him win his judo red belt last night. Never realised the little bugger was so difficult to knock off balance.

7.45am. Taxi to Heathrow takes over an hour. Why is it called Rush Hour when this is the precise time of day when anyone who wishes to rush cannot? Must be British sense of irony. Impending doom mood deepens.

9.00am. Eat sausage next to a young insurance executive of Indian extraction who asks me if Scotland will be very cold. I tell him, with all the aplomb of someone who is an expert on such things, that he is perfectly dressed (and very finely so as it happens but I feet it impertinent to compliment him).

10.00am. Vast queue for taxis at Edinburgh airport as I stride out. Impending doom mood drops to its lowest level. But it is misplaced. Ms Karen Geary, a person I am always glad to see, is at the very head of the queue and so I queue jump legitimately and she gives me a ride into town. Ms Geary is another reason for any author to wish to be published by H & S.

11.10am. Note the gorgeous tang of fino sherry, as in saline air blown up from Leith, as I enter Volvona & Crolla. I go to the back and sit in the Caffe bar and Carina Contini brings me a stomach-settling glass of Santa Costanza Vino Novello 1997 – an Italian of 11% alcohol made from sangiovese grapes in Tuscany. It is everything Beaujolais Nouveau no longer is – fresh, full, perfectly balanced weight of alcohol, and with a lovely pert, earthy edge. It costs £2.39 a glass, £7.99 a bottle – steep, yes, but mightily attractive. £5.99 a bottle in the shop.

1pm. I eat lunch, or bits of it since I'm saving my appetite for the flight back, and talk to Edwina Currie who sits adjacent. We discuss smoking bans (an area of acute concern for her when she was a government minister); the delights of living in the Loire; the shortcomings of Mohamed al Fayed; Balzac's industry. She knows how to point score – women who have been successful politicians learn the rules of fighting in a man's arena – but few men display such a subtle, subcutaneous sense of mischief.

1.45pm. Though I, eager to plug my book, stick rigidly to my allotted twelve minutes, Edwina, here to plug her book, talks for fourteen hours and Tony Bullimore, here to plug his book, for three days (slight exaggeration here but it conveys my frustration pretty well as I had to catch a flight at five – at one point in the Bullimore peroration I fell asleep which made me feel very guilty as he'd just got to the bit about him standing up to his neck in water and his little finger being chopped off). I killed myself to sign people's books as the taxi impatiently huffed and puffed outside but I made the flight with eight minutes to spare. Bullimore told me before I left that he once stayed in a hotel in Crete with a bathroom sink with three taps marked hot, cold and wine. What ones for tall stories these yachtsmen are!

29th November

Treat family to lunch at Kensington Place restaurant. I arrive fifteen minutes early and am invited to sit down with chef and *Guardian* columnist Mr Rowley Leigh (now defected to the *Telegraph*) and drink Barbaresco from Conterno. Sue loathes the wine when she arrives so I enjoy this wonderful specimen all to myself (although I do share it with my fois gras terrine and bollito misto). The food here is outstanding and the customers a mixture of the mildly raffish and the demonstrative yet sober – which goes for the waiters and waitresses as well.

30th November

Attempt to make a large net for a wolf-catcher – my son's part in the school play. I fail. Equally dismal is the attempt by my taxi driver to get me to Heathrow for the flight to Guernsey. Do it with 20 minutes to spare.

Air UK offers no thrills, spills or frills. 'Something to eat?' says the harridan masquerading as a flight attendant. As I express polite interest a cellophane-wrapped brown roll with bacon and mayonnaise on it is dumped in my lap. The air traveller often asks himself why he patronises airlines so politely when he receives little back unless the destination is Bangkok and the airline equally exotic. Luckily, the traveller who travels with William Sansom in his pocket at least has some relief from the frost. Just his first sentence alone (as I munch my roll – no evidence of bacon, just mayonnaise squirting all over my new green chenille sweater – £30 blued at M&S) is worth the quid I paid to rescue the book from its languish in a charity shop. This sentence is a particularly glorious 150-word encapsulation of London's most notoriously louche area and it reads thus: 'So Ho! So Ho! – the huntsman's cry setting the hare across the fields . . . And then Sir Francis Compton staking out his land from those same declining grasses: Monmouth's great mansion in the Square: Thomas de Quincey collapsed and near death on a cold doorstep, receiving life and a warm drink from his sweet prostitute: Mozart at 51 Frith Street: Hazlitt dead of a disordered stomach along at No 6: King Theodore of Corsica garreted not far away and holding court from a chair set on his pauper's bed – these and many others are the ghosts that stalk that amorphous part of Central London, never quite definable within exact street limits, rather an atmosphere than a district, where once the hare was hunted and now the gourmet and in seamier streets the greenhorn form the prey, and which to-day we still know roughly by its nickname of former years, Soho.'

Land in Guernsey. No one to greet me (as promised). No reservation at Duke of Richmond (as arranged). Guernsey is . . . yes! that sums the place up. Guernsey just *is* . . . this minor syntactical impression is not enhanced by the positively delicious Couly-Duteil Chinon 1989 I drink with a packet of crisps to cheer myself up in the hotel's ante-room. What in God's name possessed the Germans to bother with this place in the last war? Is it merely a place to fish from – with some highly useful banking arrangements on the dockside? I take myself to the marina, fail to gain entry to the old castle, tour the museum, note the French signs. Go back to the hotel and have another glass of Chinon. Is the etymology for the island's name, one wonders, from the French for *hardly*?

Then Tony Carey, who has organised tomorrow's literary lunch (sponsored by The Royal Bank of Canada) at which I shall speak, turns up and whisks me off to dinner at Nello's where with local sea bass we drink Ascheri Barbaresco Bricco 1993. The peculiarly anise edge of Barbaresco (not as rich or as alcoholically pugnacious as cousin Barolo) is to be recommended with sea bass. It is a pleasant evening. Barbara, Tony's wife, reveals her father went to school in Northern Ireland with Samuel Beckett. 'Difficult person even then' she comments wryly.

1st December

I discover the Priaulx Library (eponym: Osmond de Beauvoir Priaulx 1805–1891) round the corner from the hotel. If I were to be permitted to bring along bottles with me, I could spend a week, a month even, in this curious private library (book loans to Guernsey residents only). The library is in Candie House, which began life as a house in 1780 and it has some indomitable lush touches of the Georgian.

I make my lunchtime speech in which I am able to compliment the chef and Safeway. I don't think any donation of wine to a lunch by a retailer has ever been so perfect for the food. The '97 Australian Colombard was a wow with shrimps, the '97 Chilean Cabernet Sauvignon was a hit with the chicken, and the pudding was Laurel to the Hardy of the '95 Moscatel de Valencia. Safeway can be proud. Pity there is only one branch on the island. The great thing, for this audience, was the fact that all the wines cost under four quid. For some of the tax exiles in the room, and there were well over a hundred people present, I suspect it was the first time in their lives an under four quid wine had touched their lips. The fact that every set of lips in the room was smacking with relish, made me feel I was doing pioneering work. The fact that the august nature of the occasion had made me don a tie, a silk floral extravaganza dug out of my wardrobe and last worn in 1987, did not unnerve me in the slightest.

Before I flew back to London, I was given a tour of the local wine merchant Bucktrout & Co. A name to inspire confidence; a firm of the highest repute, as Lady Bracknell would have said. Bucktrout bricked up a part of the cellars before the Germans arrived, painted over it, hung a few pictures, and the wine behind the facade were the only things in Guernsey to develop for the better during those bellicose years. Mr Tom Castledine, the man who runs the shop, generously treated me to several glasses of 1996 Aloxe-Corton Latour before I left.

Arrive back home too late to make the Residents Association Meeting at the street's new Disability Centre.

2nd December
5.00pm. Train to Manchester Piccadilly for charity wine tasting/book signing for the Manchester Jewish Federation. The oddest question I have to deal with concerns alcohol levels in wine and one individual's insistence that height in this area is an indicator of quality. Mr Andrew Singer presents me with a bottle of malt whisky afterwards. Take myself to Nico Central – a new addition to the Holiday Inn and eat boudin noir with a ½ of Trimbach Gewurz. followed by casserole of winter veg with a ½ Chateau Carone 1983. The latter wine is beginning to show wrinkles, but I don't send it back. It isn't faulty but age is catching up with it fast.

Will Nico Ladenis one day be up there with Ronald Macdonald one wonders? The most enigmatic and reclusive of our chefs is also the most human and sincere – and vulnerable; the Wordsworth of the professional British kitchen, and here he is opening branches (× 3, small start but even McDonalds was once just a single outlet). Of course, Nico is tougher than any poet; he's a fabulous survivor. Poets aren't legendarily tough (Graves perhaps apart . . . and Ted Hughes, I guess). Rilke pricked his thumb on a rose thorn and died, Brooke got massacred by a mosquito, British Gas did away with Plath, Wilde died of disgrace, Byron took salt water, Keats passed away from an excess of blushing, Pope fell apart early ravaged, Larkin was stricken by lifelong melancholy, and . . . it goes on . . . Peter Reading, the least prissy of modern poets, seems tough enough (though so alert to the foulnesses of the human race there is the suspicion of a soft side).

3rd December
6.30pm. Hammick's Maidenhead. An hour of book signing. Pleased to introduce several paraplegics to the delights of cheap wine.

4th December
6.30pm. Signing at my local Waterstone's, Notting Hill Gate.

Linda P. drops in and gives me a copy of *The Seven Pillars of Wisdom* for Christmas. Chat mostly to Peter Gordon, the Sugar Club's chef, who is there signing copies of his own book.

5th December

4.45pm. Hammick's in Barnet. The mince pies with the wine don't go, but who cares?

6th December

7-something pm. Enter the lecture theatre of the Royal Society of Arts and give a talk on matching food with wine. Don't sell many books, but someone asks me to autograph the CD.

12th December

Drink a rare 18.5-point wine: Comtes Lafon Meursault Clos de la Barre 1991. Its rarity is enhanced by it being, of course, a white burgundy. But then Comtes Lafon is, so they say, a miraculous producer of the stuff. First time I've heard the truth and a white burgundy producer coincide. The place at which I drank the bottle was the Cherwell Boathouse Restaurant in Oxford. It was chosen by my companion over lunch, Gaetane Carron, the remarkable travelling French wine conjuror. The wine cost £38. It was a bargain. It's doubtful if wine merchant Morris & Verdin still has the odd bottle tucked away somewhere but the telephone number in London to find out is 0171-357 8866.

13th December

9.50am. The BBC car picks me up. When the BBC producer first telephoned, however, I was luke warm. Would I appear on the new BBC-TV 24-hour live news channel on a Saturday morning and discuss English wine? I didn't think so. Saturday morning is swim-with-the-children time. But then the aquatic monsters pointed out that Alexi and Simone, the babysitting Katz sisters ('Who's looking after your kids tonight?' 'The Katz of course' 'You're kidding? The cats?' 'That's right. They're beautifully trained'), wanted to take them to lunch – so could the customary Saturday swim be shelved? So it was that I found myself tasting a range of mediocre English wines whilst a man called Roy Cadman, who is very keen on the bland fruit of the UK vine, waxed lyrical and kept claiming greatness for the bottles he had brought along. At one point, failing to put his own words into my mouth, he called me a 'traitor'. But my loyalty is to my readers, not to the makers of feeble wine whoever they might be and whatever country they might live in. Until English wine grows up and stops being so empty of character and charm, then people like me, and I would guess the majority of my unsentimental readers, will continue to be unable to take it seriously. Mr Cadman kept comparing his wines, reds, whites, sweet and sparkling, with old French types – as if these were anyone's points of comparison any more. The poor chap was not going to change my mind about English wines on the basis of the specimens he had brought along. Frankly, with the exception of a very few east and southern English vineyards and the odd West country one, the majority of the 400-plus vineyard owners in the UK with their pitifully tiny 2500 acres of vines should either make sweet white wine to go with our excellent local blue cheeses or create young whites to go with fish and chips (national dishes both). I wish that all the energy certain people put into trying to persuade us of the virtues of third-rate wine was transferred into pushing the excellence of English apples – fruit we *can* crow about *and* claim superiority to the French specimens. I don't get upset about English wine having such a poor image because it has some relation to reality but I do get exercised about the English apple, in so many of its native varieties, being so unsung, undersold, underrated, and not available as widely as they ought to be in British supermarkets. Indeed, let's dig up English vines and plant more apple orchards. We have smoked salmon, malt whisky, cheeses, elderflower cordial, hams, cod and mackerel, various root vegetables, lamb, and wonderful apples, amongst many other terrific native foods and drinks in these islands of ours, and it is these culinary excellences we should trumpet and consume regularly ourselves. English wine? Well, it could certainly be turned into acceptable vinegar to sprinkle over our fish and chips (and with many examples hardly any effort would be required to hasten it to this condition of tartness). But in a wine glass English wine is largely, I am compelled in all honesty to point out, a waste of everybody's time, endeavours, space, and energy.

16th December

Lunch with Majestic's delightful Emma Davis and drink my first Indian red wine at an Indian restaurant (the Malabar, Uxbridge Street, London W8). The food is terrific. The wine, Anarkali Reserve 1994 from the Sahyadu Valley in western Maharashtra near Bombay, is perfectly vile. The 1994 Australian shiraz quickly ordered to replace it goes brilliantly with the array of rich and spicy foods it embraces.

17th December

5.00am. Write urgent *Superplonk* column for *Guardian.*

7.15am. Man arrives in large car to silently purr me to the South Bank to be grilled on GMTV – a breakfast TV company – about Christmas wines. I forget the name of the interviewer, but the producer, Misba by name, is unforgettably dishy, lively, and interesting. I get the distinct feeling she is a fan of E.M. Forster, always a mark of a refined mind where a woman is concerned (rarely a man). What seems to amaze everyone, when wine is discussed, is that the sixteen wines on the table are all under a fiver each. Waitrose's La Mejanelle Coteaux du Languedoc 1995 (16.5 points) is the star red, Kwik Save's Domaine Boyar Chardonnay/Sauvignon Blanc the star white – at £2.89 the price seems a misprint.

4.45pm. My last booksigning of 1997 beckons and promptly, as beautifully ordered by Ms Katie Gunning of Hodder & Stoughton (by the way that is not pronounced STOUT-ON but, less felicitously, as STOAT-ON – a fact I learned after 40 years of mispronouncing the firm's name), Mr Mike Lawson turns up in his Jaguar to whisk me off to Walthamstow, a London suburb at the end of the Victoria line famous for its reservoirs and being the postal-code eponym of a pop group (E17). I am beginning to like strong silent types behind the wheel. It makes a great change from railway carriages where mobile telephonists plague the ruminative traveller, and tannoy announcements from the rail staff (who, as they announce the next stop, always sound like the MCs of seedy Soho nightclubs whipping up enthusiasm for the next stripper or transvestite comedian) menace the quiet dreamer. Well I never, I hear you expostulate: when did *he* last visit a seedy Soho nightclub? Actually, it was 1959. Seedy nightclubs knew how to be seedy in those days (it was the Blue Angel in Windmill Street) and, of course, I was a fresh-faced virgin only five years out of short trousers. Alas, the long ones I *did* wear were never removed, as I had hoped, by any of the young women who did take their clothes off and apart from being shocked that I was permitted to become a member at my age (17) I was also disappointed my virginity stayed firmly intact. In fact, it stayed limply intact; but that is because I never felt remotely excited by the place: I only felt I *ought* to be excited by it. I think I was most excited by the thought of what my parents would say if they had the remotest idea of their middle son's location. And what of my old school chums? They would never have believed my membership possible let alone my attendance (three visits in three weeks before the boredom, and the expense, got to me and I've never been in such a place since – I discovered very quickly, shocking admission I know, that women were more exciting as people rather than as objects of lust and nothing else – but anyway I've strayed off the subject somewhat). Where was I? Oh yes, on my way to Walthamstow. This is the way to travel! True, I cannot read as I can on my beloved puff-puff. And I cannot draw gasps of admiration from bus passengers as I overtake the number 7 on my bike. But what I can do in a perfect state of unmolestation is listen to audio tapes and the one which accompanies me to E17 is the divine Alan Bennett reading his two-hour story 'The Clothes They Stood Up In.' Ah Bliss! My next step is to investigate whether Mr Lawson will introduce a refrigerator into his Jaguar. A small one is sufficient to take a couple of bottles of lightly alcoholic, but old, German riesling and then I can sip/read. I wonder if Hodder & Stoaton will wear that one? We shall see. Next year, November/December 1998, will bring yet another round of signings and, surely, wouldn't such a *responsible and civilised* publisher wish its author to arrive at each bookshop in as fighting a fit state as possible? Wish me luck, dear reader . . . and see you next year (liver permitting, that is).

Health Warning!

Health Warning is an arresting phrase. I hope by employing it I may save you from working yourself up into a state. Let me explain.

I get a few letters a week from readers (both column and book) telling me that a wine which I have said is on sale in a certain supermarket is not there and that the wine has either sold out or the branch claims to have no knowledge of it; I get letters telling me that a wine is a bit dearer than I said it was; and I get the odd note revealing that the vintage of the 16-point wine I have enthused about and which my correspondent desperately wants to buy is different from the one listed.

First of all, let me say that no wine guide in the short and inglorious history of the genre is more exhaustively researched, checked, and double-checked than this one. I do not list a wine if I do not have assurances from its retailer that it will be widely on sale when the guide is published. Where a wine is on restricted distribution, or stocks are short and vulnerable to the assault of determined readers (i.e. virtually all high rating, very cheap bottles), I will always clearly say so. However, large retailers use computer systems which cannot anticipate uncommon demand and which often miss the odd branch off the anticipated stocking list. I cannot check every branch myself (though I do nose around them when I can) and so a wine in this book may well, infuriatingly, be missing at the odd branch of its retailer and may not even be heard of by the branch simply because of inhuman error. Conversely, the same technology often tells a retailer's head office that a wine is out of stock when it has merely been completely cleared out of the warehouse. It may still be on sale on certain branches. Then there is the fact that not every wine I write about is stocked by every single branch of its listed supermarket. Every store has what are called retail plans and there maybe half-a-dozen of these and every wine is subject to a different stocking policy according to the dictates of these cold-hearted plans.

I accept a wine as being in healthy distribution if several hundred branches, all over the country not just in selected parts of it, stock the wine. Do not assume, however, that this means every single branch has the wine.

I cannot, equally, guarantee that every wine in this book will still be in the same price band as printed (these bands follow this introduction). The vast majority will be. But there will always be the odd bottle from a country suddenly subject to a vicious swing in currency rates, or subject to an unprecedented rise in production costs which the supermarket cannot or is not prepared to swallow, and so a few pennies will get added to the price. If it is pounds, then you have cause for legitimate grievance. Please write to me. But don't lose a night's sleep if a wine is twenty pence more than I said it is. If you must, write to the appropriate supermarket. The department and the address to write to is provided with each supermarket's entry.

Now the puzzle of differing vintages. When I list and rate a wine, I do so only for the vintage stated. Any other vintage is a different wine requiring a new rating. Where vintages do have little difference in fruit quality, and more than a single vintage is on sale, then I say this clearly. If two vintages are on sale, and vary in quality and/or style, then they will be separately rated. However, be aware of one thing.

Superplonk is the biggest selling wine guide to such an extent that all the other wine guides' sales put together do not reach even a fraction of it. I say this not to brag but, importantly, to acquaint you with a reality which may cause you some irritation. When *Superplonk* appears on sale there will be lots of eager drinkers aiming straight for the highest rating wines as soon as possible after the book is published. Thus the supermarket wine buyer who assures me that she has masses of stock of Domaine Piddlewhatsit and the wine will withstand the most virulent of sieges may find her shelves emptying in a tenth of the time she banked on – not knowing, of course, how well I rate the wine it until the book goes on sale. It is entirely possible, therefore, that the vintage of a highly rated wine may sell out so quickly that new stocks of the follow-on vintage may be urgently brought on to shelf before I have tasted them. This can happen in some instances. I offer a bunch of perishable pansies, not a wreath of immortelles. I can do nothing about this fact of wine writing life, except to give up writing about wine.

Lastly, one thing more:

'*Wine is a hostage to several fortunes (weather being even more uncertain and unpredictable than exchange rates) but the wine writer is hostage to just one: he cannot pour for his readers precisely the same wine as he poured for himself.*'

This holds true for every wine in this book and every wine I will write about in the years to come. I am sent wines to taste regularly and I attend wine tastings all the time. If a wine is corked on these occasions, that is to say in poor condition because it has been tainted by the tree bark which is its seal, then it is not a problem for a bottle in decent condition to be quickly supplied for me to taste. This is not, alas, a luxury which can be extended to my readers.

So if you find a wine not to your taste because it seems pretty foul or 'off' in some way, then do not assume that my rating system is up the creek; you may take it that the wine is faulty and must be returned as soon as possible to its retailer. Every retailer in this book is pledged to provide an instant refund for any faulty wine returned – no questions asked. I am not asking readers to share all my tastes in wine, or to agree completely with every rating for every wine. But where a wine I have well rated is obviously and patently foul then it is a duff bottle and you should be compensated by getting a fresh bottle free or by being given a refund.

How I Rate a Wine

Value for money is my single unwavering focus. I drink with my readers' pockets in my mouth. I do not see the necessity of paying a lot for a bottle of everyday drinking wine and only rarely do I consider it worth paying a high price for, say, a wine for a special occasion or because you want to experience what a so-called 'grand' wine may be like. There is more codswallop talked and written about wine, especially the so-called 'grand' stuff, than any subject except sex. The stench of this gobbledegook regularly perfumes wine merchants' catalogues, spices the backs of bottles, and rancidises the writings of those infatuated by or in the pay of producers of a particular wine region. I do taste expensive wines regularly. I do not, regularly, find them worth the money. That said, there are some pricey bottles in these pages. They are here either because I wish to provide an accurate, but low, rating of its worth so that readers will be given pause for thought or because the wine is genuinely worth every penny. A wine of magnificent complexity, thrilling fruit, superb aroma, great depth and finesse is worth drinking. I would not expect it to be an inexpensive bottle. I will rate it highly. I wish all wines which commanded such high prices were so well deserving of an equally high rating. The thing is, of course, that many bottles of wine I taste do have finesse and depth but do not come attached to an absurdly high price tag. These are the bottles I prize most. As, I hope, you will.

20 Is outstanding and faultless is all departments: smell, taste and finish in the throat. Worth the price, even if you have to take out a second-mortgage.

19 A superb wine. Almost perfect and well worth the expense (if it is an expensive bottle).

18 An excellent wine but lacking that ineffable sublimity of richness and complexity to achieve the very highest rating. But superb drinking and thundering good value.

17 An exciting, well-made wine at an affordable price which offers real glimpses of multi-layered richness.

16 Very good wine indeed. Good enough for *any* dinner party. Not expensive but terrifically drinkable, satisfying and multi-dimensional – properly balanced.

15 For the money, a good mouthful with real style. Good flavour and fruit without costing a packet.

14 The top end of the everyday drinking wine. Well-made and to be seriously recommended at the price.

13 Good wine, true to its grape(s). Not great, but very drinkable.

12 Everyday drinking wine at a sensible price. Not exciting, but worthy.

11 Drinkable, but not a wine to dwell on. You don't wed a wine like this, though you might take it behind the bike shed with a bag of fish and chips.

10 Average wine (at a low price), yet still just about a passable mouthful. Also, wines which are terribly expensive and, though drinkable, cannot justify their high price.

9 Cheap plonk. Just about fit for parties in dustbin-sized dispensers.

8 On the rough side here.

7 Good for pickling onions or cleaning false teeth.

6 Hardly drinkable except on an icy night by a raging bonfire.

5 Wine with more defects than delights.

4 Not good at any price.

3 Barely drinkable.

2 Seriously – did this wine come from grapes?

1 The utter pits. The producer should be slung in prison.

The rating system above can be broken down into six broad sections.

Zero to 10	Avoid – unless entertaining stuffy wine writer.
10, 11	Nothing poisonous but, though drinkable, rather dull.
12,13	Above average, interestingly made. Solid rather then sensational.
14, 15, 16	This is the exceptional, hugely drinkable stuff, from the very good to the brilliant.
17, 18	Really wonderful wine worth anyone's money: complex, rich, exciting.
19, 20	A toweringly brilliant world-class wine of self-evident style and individuality.

Prices

It is impossible to guarantee the price of any wine in this guide. This is why instead of printing the shop price, each wine is given a price band. This attempts to eliminate the problem of printing the wrong price for a wine. This can occur for all the usual boring but understandable reasons: inflation, economic conditions overseas, the narrow margins on some supermarket wines making it difficult to maintain consistent prices and, of course, the existence of those freebooters at the Exchequer who are liable to inflate taxes which the supermarkets cannot help but pass on. But even price banding is not foolproof. A wine listed in the book at, say, a B band price might be on sale at a C band price. How? Because a wine close to but under, say, £3.50 in summer when I tasted it might sneak across the border in winter. It happens, rarely enough not to concern me overmuch, but wine is an agricultural import, a sophisticated liquid food, and that makes it volatile where price is concerned. Frankly, I admire the way retailers have kept prices so stable for so many years. We drink cheaper (and healthier) wine now than we did thirty years ago.The price banding code assigned to each wine works as follows:

Price Band

A Under £2.50	B £2.50 to £3.50	C £3.50 to £5
D £5 to £7	E £7 to £10	F £10 to £13
G £13 to £20	H Over £20	

All wines costing under £5 (i.e. A–C) have their price band set against a black background.

ACKNOWLEDGEMENTS

I owe this book to my family's indulgence and the back up of Linda Peskin. Sheila Crowley, Kate Lyall Grant, Katie Gunning, Jamie Hodder-Williams, Martin Neild, and Karen Geary at my dynamic publisher are also to be thanked. I am also grateful to Felicity Rubinstein and Sarah Lutyens, my delicious agents.

ASDA

DOUBLE BARRELLED NICK GOES! SINGLE BARRELLED RUSSELL IS THE NEW TOP GUN!

Although Asda's Archie Norman confirmed that he is to stay in his job as chairman of the company in spite of being elected Conservative MP for Tunbridge Wells (also becoming a vice-chairman of the party and a leading light in Willy Hague's attempts to modernise the Tories), this was not as important an event to wine shoppers at Asda as the decision by Nick Dymoke Marr to quit. Mr Dymoke Marr, as ruling wine buyer, had done much to make Asda a force in the world of supermarket wine retailing and his new Orbital Wines, will no doubt soon be a force in wine importing. The new man at Asda's wine helm is Russell Burgess.

As a result of this – or was it coincidence? – Asda this year changed its innovatory system of shelving wines by style rather than by country. It has reverted to the norm and in the process not only made the shelves more accessible to any wine guide buyer (SFX: grinding of axe) but put in a snazzy new shelving system as well. I have every confidence Asda's share of the wine market will rise. The wine buying team of Alistair Morrell, Adam Marshall and Chris Elmore can only be criticised for being all-male. They cannot help this. The department's maleness is, however, unique, I think. Fortunately, there is a wine marketing manager, Jane Fenwick, to leaven the air of unreality which gender imbalance in a commercial environment encourages. In this respect, it is also noteworthy that Asda also dispensed with the services of its wine PR consultant, Alan Compton-Batt, and hired the all-female set-up of Westbury Communications (Sue Harris, Sara Hately, Helen Cristofoli and Jane Baerselman).

All of the above appointments went unnoticed by the outside world, but in other areas Asda has been causing headlines. In the High Court, International Distillers & Vintners forced Asda to change packaging on four of its spirits brands which resembled such famous names as Jack Daniels and Malibu (the retailer had already been forced by United Biscuits to change packaging of its Puffin biscuits which looked like the Penguin brand). Asda was resolute. It is the only retailer which has not signed up to a code of conduct on lookalikes, maintaining that 'if customers can't taste the difference then why should they pay for the difference?'

The seldom-out-of-the-news Mr Norman made a noise about the value of fish and chips in Asda stores (£2.49) versus The Savoy (£22.75) – a most useful comparison for Asda shoppers. A wag at *Retail Week* magazine noted that with the £2 million he earned from Asda last year (down from £3.7 million the year before), Archie would be able to afford more than 900,000 portions of fish and chips from Asda, compared with only 98,590 from The Savoy. Asda was also in the news over the discounting of children's comics which had angered newsagents.

Asda also linked up with the Spice Girls in an exclusive deal for some 40 different items of merchandise. I have yet to see any sign of this splendid deal appearing on the wine shelves but . . . why not? The store already has the youngest customer profile amongst the supermarkets where wine is concerned. The same month as this story broke, there was news that Asda and Safeway had abandoned discussions about a £9 million merger.

Asda got seriously into the seasonal spirit, however, when it ran training courses for Father Christmases at its head office in Leeds. These gentlemen were the star attractions at Santa grottoes at 200 Asda stores. At the same time, Asda managed to lead the table of cheap champagnes with a pre-Christmas price promotion on Richard Lourmel champagne at £7.99. No news is available at time of going to press whether this promotion will be around for 1998.

Asda's delicious price cutting tactics continued unabated and it really got up perfumiers' noses when the retailer cut the prices of leading perfume brands by up to 75% in the lead-up to St Valentine's Day. This was no joke to the serious souls in the fragrance business and it is extremely unlikely that any of the less dour members of this business sector answered Asda's advertisement in *The Stage* for a new joke writer for its Christmas crackers. The standard of jokes in Asda's crackers needed, the store felt, improving.

Asda does possess a wonderful sense of corporate humour. I hope it permeates through to the Tory party. It simply can't resist cutting things. In January, it won the first round of a High Court battle with the Parma ham producers' association who had objected to Asda selling Parma ham which though authentically produced in the region had been sliced and packaged in Britain. The producers said Parma ham can only be authentic if it is prepared and packaged in the Parma region. How, one wonders, did Asda's Parma exporter manage to get the hams out of the region in the first place? Surely all the producer's association needed to do was blacklist Asda's supplier and local cafes to refuse to serve him his usual morning cappuccino. The case would never have come to court.

Rumours again resurfaced about the marriage between Asda and Safeway. Even the suggestion of similar nuptials taking place between Liz Hurley and Hugh Grant received shorter shrift. No truth in either, it seems to me.

Not much substance either, according to my palate at least, in the criticisms levelled by certain wine writers at Asda this year. The Tramontane southern French range was not liked and likewise Arius from California. Please refer to my own, somewhat different, view of these wines in the listing which follows.

But then we all have different tastes. Each to his or her own. 'Taste,' wrote Edmund Burke in 1757, 'has no fixed principles.'

What a shame old Ed was born too early to lay hands on a copy of *Superplonk.*

My taste has the fixed principle of a rating for every wine.

Asda Stores Limited
Asda House
Great Wilson Street
Leeds
LS11 5AD
Tel: 0113 243 5435
Fax: 0113 241 8146
e-mail www.asda.co.uk.

SEE STOP PRESS SECTION AT END OF BOOK FOR LAST-MINUTE ADDITIONS OR UPDATES TO THIS RETAILER'S RANGE.

ARGENTINIAN WINE RED

Argentinian Bonarda 1997, Asda 14 B

Fruit given a new halo of jamminess.

Argentinian Malbec 1997, Asda 15 C

Juicy and rich and truly brilliant as a warm, soupy glug.

Argentinian Merlot 1997, Asda 15 C

Great soft textured and ripe fruit. Youth and style all over your taste buds.

Argentinian Pinot Noir 1997, Asda 13.5 C

Has some cherried earth to it.

Argentinian Red 1997, Asda 14.5 B

Dare I say it hits the spot? Beautifully? Great texture and plumpness of fruit. Not Rubenesque perhaps but nicely fleshy.

Argentinian Sangiovese 1997, Asda 15 B

Gorgeous baked fruit with a hint of custard. Yummy stuff.

Argentinian Tempranillo 1997, Asda 15 B

So jammy and beautifully baked you can spread it on toast.

ARGENTINIAN WINE WHITE

Argentinian Chardonnay 1997, Asda 16 C

Lovely richness and lingering flavour here, classy, bright, modern, deep.

Argentinian Chenin Blanc 1997, Asda 13.5 B

Slightly smoky quality would make it good with crab cakes.

Argentinian White 1997, Asda 14 B

Good rich fruit, for food.

Santa Julia Argentinian Viognier 1997 14 C

Has some typical viognier apricoty qualities. Different sort of beat to the wine, syncopated and quirky. Good for rich fish dishes.

AUSTRALIAN WINE RED

Hardys Bankside Shiraz 1996 14 D

Has some ruggedness to its essentially easy-going character.

Hardys Nottage Hill Cabernet Sauvignon/ Shiraz 1997 14 D

From the rolling-in-fruit '97 vintage.

Hardys Nottage Hill Cabernet/Shiraz/ Merlot 1995 14.5 D

Free flowing and full of itself – but charming company.

Mount Hurtle Cabernet/Merlot 1995 14 D

Soupy, rich, soft, saved from soppiness by the touch of earth.

Mount Hurtle Grenache Shiraz 1996 14 C

Not every day you find an Aussie red so juicy and ripe yet so amenable to food costing under a fiver.

Penfolds Rawson's Retreat Bin 35 Cabernet/Shiraz 1996 13 C

Peter Lehmann Vine Vale Grenache 1997 14.5 C

Sticky fruit of great adhesive character where food is concerned. Hums with fruit.

Rosemount Estate Cabernet/Shiraz 1997 13.5 D

If you like your life frank and juicy, this wine is perfect for you.

South Australia Cabernet Sauvignon 1996, Asda 14 C

Got some character lurking under that juicy freshness.

AUSTRALIAN WINE WHITE

Cranswick Estate Director's Reserve Marsanne 1996 13 C

Getting long in the tooth.

Cranswick Oak Aged Marsanne 1996

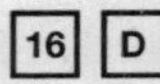

Superb food wine. I'd love it with crab cakes. It's got lushness yet finesse. An exciting wine of a noble grape.

Hardys Nottage Hill Chardonnay 1997

Ooh . . . ! It oozes with controlled richness yet calm, insouciant, relaxed fruitiness of inexpressibly delicious firmness and flavour.

Hardys Stamp Riesling Traminer 1997

Lovely exotic fruit hinting at fresh plump melon, a touch of pineapple, plus loads of personality.

Hardys Stamps of Australia Grenache Rose 1997

Mount Hurtle Chardonnay 1996

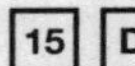

Good double act of zippy acidity and rich rolling soft fruit.

Penfolds Barossa Valley Semillon Chardonnay 1997

Love its richness and utter regality. It really lords it over other chardonnay blends.

Penfolds Rawson's Retreat Bin 21 Semillon Chardonnay Colombard 1997

Seemingly casually attired ar first meeting, it reveals some jazzy habiliments as it progresses from nose to throat.

Peter Lehmann The Barossa Semillon, 1997

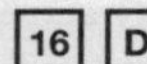

Gorgeous display of two-faced insidiously delicious fruit. Has a soft, exotic ripe fruit on one hand and a rippling mineral acidity on the other.

Rosemount Estate Semillon/Chardonnay 1997 15 D

Has some elegance and bite. Most attractive though it lacks the sheer pizzazz of certain other Asda Aussie whites.

South East Australia Semillon/Chardonnay 1997, Asda 16 C

Shows all the qualities of this brilliant vintage. A vivacious yet coolly elegant wine of great class. Really impressive structure.

BULGARIAN WINE RED

Bulgarian Cabernet Sauvignon 1996, Asda 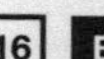

Brilliant tannins and rich earthy fruit. Absolutely stonking value here!

Bulgarian Cabernet Sauvignon, Svichtov 1995, Asda  

A quaffing bottle with real character – but the dry richness has a fruity tang on the finish.

Bulgarian Country Red, Asda  

Delicious quaffing here.

Bulgarian Merlot 1996, Asda 13.5 B

Bulgarian Oak Aged Cabernet Sauvignon, Svichtov 1993, Asda 15 C

Real maturity here; like a comfortable, much-loved old leather sofa, it simply and warmly enfolds you.

Svichtov Controlliran Cabernet Sauvignon 1993 13 C

BULGARIAN WINE WHITE

Bulgarian Chardonnay 1997, Asda 11 B

Bulgarian Oaked Chardonnay 1996, Asda 14 C

Good rich texture and gripping fruit. Terrific food wine.

CHILEAN WINE RED

Chilean Cabernet Sauvignon 1997, Asda 15 C

Has some dry tannins for character, and some soft fruit, for sheer fun. An amusing blend.

Chilean Cabernet/Merlot 1997, Asda 15.5 C

Oozes flavour and personality. Great glugging here.

Chilean Red 1997, Asda 14.5 B

Possibly the fruitiest of the Chilean reds on sale anywhere. It literally coats the taste buds, so liberally they weep.

Cono Sur Oaked Cabernet 1997 16 D

Superb dry edge gives the thrillingly soft, ripe fruit dignity and compelling richness.

Gato Negro Chilean Merlot 1997 15 C

Merlot as a juicy, friendly, cheeky chappie.

Pionero Chilean Merlot 1997 13.5 C

Juicy.

Rowan Brook Cabernet Sauvignon Reserve 1994 13 C

Terrifyingly ripe and juicy.

Rowan Brook Oak Aged Cabernet Sauvignon 1995 16 D

Deliciously minty and oaky yet very fresh and lively. Chile is effortlessly able to pull this trick off.

CHILEAN WINE WHITE

Chilean Sauvignon Blanc 1997, Asda 15.5 B

Classic hints of grass wrapped around a concentrated gooseberry centre. Real force, charm and character. Brilliant price for such wit. Trips over the tongue like an angel with clogs.

Chilean Sauvignon Blanc 1997, Asda 15.5 C

Superb richness and texture here. Loads of flavour, not overkilling or flush, but calm and well-tailored.

Chilean White 1997, Asda 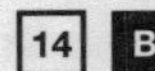

Great value quaffing here.

Pionero Chardonnay 1997 15.5 C

Creamy and nutty, very softly textured yet with a delicious hint of hard fruit on the finish.

Rowan Brook Chardonnay Oak Aged Reserve, Casablanca 1996 

Rich, woody, elegant, stylish, balanced, flavoursome, drinkable, good with food – what more can one say?

ENGLISH WINE — WHITE

Three Choirs Coleridge Hill English White 1996 

Almost terrific. Certainly one of England's better wines.

FRENCH WINE — RED

Beaujolais 1997, Asda 13 C

Quiet little Beaujolais – best chilled with a hotdog.

Beaujolais Villages 1997, Asda 

Remarkable! A Beaujolais which stings, not with the price, but with quality of the finish of the dry fruit.

Buzet Cuvee 44 1997 14.5 C

Best vintage yet!

Cabernet Sauvignon VdP d'Oc, Asda 15 B

Chateau de Parenchere Bordeaux Superieure 1996 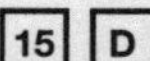

'Boiled sweet character', Asda wine buyer believes. I think it's a little more adult than that.

Chateau Fonfroide Bordeaux 1996 

Chateau Haut Plantey St Emilion 1995 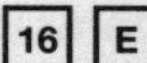

A wine to lay down for well beyond the millennium or to drink now – dry, rich, uncompromisingly clarety – with any sort of meat dish, especially grilled, pink, lamb.

Chateau Haut Saric, Bordeaux 1997 

Juicy on the finish and this jamminess slightly mars the tannins.

Chateau l'Eglise Vieille, Haut Medoc 1996 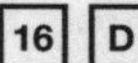

Classic dry claret with restrained richness, peppery tannins and real lingering vegetality and fruit. A superb food wine.

Chateau la Domeq Corbieres 1993 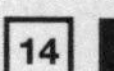

About as mature as a wine like this can be before its sappiness becomes sere. The tannins are on their last dregs and the fruit is sweet and mellow.

Chateau Peybonhomme les Tours, Premieres Cotes de Blaye 1996 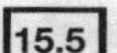

Experience its tremendous tobaccoey fruit with its evolved tannins.

Chateauneuf-du-Pape 1997, Asda 13.5 E

Great glugging. But at £4.99 not £8.99.

Claret NV, Asda 14.5 B

Remarkable value, quite remarkable. Genuinely chewy, bruised fruit with charcoal undertones.

Cotes du Rhone 1997, Asda 14 B

Terrific price for such friendly, soft fruit.

Domaine de Picheral Bin 040 VdP d'Oc 1997 (organic) 14 C

Soft and soupy, almost a touch Aussie.

Domaine Pont Pinot Noir 1996 13 D

Has a nice dryness to the finish: tannins!

Fitou 1996, Asda 13 B

Good price for adequacy.

Hale Bopp Merlot 1997 13 C

La Domeq 'Vieilles Vignes' Syrah 1996 16 D

A most compellingly flavoursome and vibrant syrah, with sunny fruit and earthiness but an underlying richness of great elegance.

Mas Segala Cotes du Roussillon Villages 1996

Good rich mix of earthiness and hedgerow fruitiness.

Merlot, Vin de Pays d'Oc 1996, Asda

Not rated as a poor imitation of merlot but as a terrific, fresh, fruity glug.

Montagne Noire Red NV

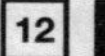

A simple companionable red – not rustic certainly but perhaps too polite.

Morgon Michel Jambon 1996

Touch expensive for the style.

Moulin a Vent Oak Aged 1997, Asda

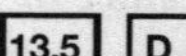

Oh, so close to being very good!

Oak Aged Cotes du Rhone 1997, Asda

Tramontane Grenache VdP d'Oc 1997, Asda

Lovely cherry/plum fruit with a vivid flush of beautifully textured ripeness.

Tramontane Merlot VdP d'Oc 1997, Asda

The most polished and rounded of the Tramontane range.

Tramontane Merlot/Syrah VdP d'Oc 1997, Asda

Earthy yet fresh. Terrific little characterful glugger.

Tramontane Red VdP de l'Aude 1997, Asda

Great glugging for the money.

Tramontane Reserve Oak Aged Cabernet Sauvignon VdP d'Oc 1996, Asda 15.5 C

Superb juiciness yet earthy characterfulness.

Tramontane Reserve Syrah VdP d'Oc 1996, Asda 16.5 D

Superb Aussie confidence shaker. From Aussies in the Languedoc this lovely rich, deep, aromatic, textured wine knocks many a homespun Aussie wine into a cocked hat.

Tramontane Syrah VdP d'Oc 1997, Asda 13.5 C

Rather juicy.

Tramontane Syrah/Merlot VdP d'Oc 1997, Asda 14.5 B

Juicy and ripe with a hint of cherried earth.

FRENCH WINE WHITE

Bin 042 Chardonnay, Mauzac 1997 (organic) 13 C

Chablis 1996, Asda 13.5 E

Decent enough fruit, not sure about the price.

Chablis Premier Cru Les Fourchaumes, 1995 14 F

Chardonnay, Jardin de la France 1997 14 B

Excellent value fish wine: fresh and keen.

Hale Bopp Bordeaux White 1997 13 C

Hale Bopp Semillon/Sauvignon 1997 14 C

Crisp yet full – rather engaging in its own quiet way.

James Herrick Chardonnay VdP d'Oc 1996 14.5 C

La Domeq 'Tete de Cuvee' Blanc 1997 14 C

Excellent food wine with its hint of dry earth. Fruity, yes, but has character and backbone.

Macon-Vinzelles Les Cailloux 1996 14.5 D

Montagne Noire Chardonnay VdP d'Oc 1996 13.5 C

Montagne Noire White NV 12 B

Muscadet 1997, Asda 13 B

Muscadet de Sevre et Maine sur Lie, Domaine Gautron 1996 12 C

Oak Aged Cotes du Rhone Blanc 1997, Asda 14 C

Great dry fish wine.

One Tree Hill Semillon 1997 13 C

Touch bare, this hill.

Pouilly Fuisse Clos du Chapel 1995 12.5 E

Pouilly Fume Les Corvets, Domaine Coulbois 1996 13 E

Has some pleasant mineral undertones.

Premieres Cotes de Bordeaux Blanc, Asda 14 C

Rose d'Anjou 1997, Asda 14 B

Brilliant richness and fullness. Hearty and heartfelt.

Sancerre Domaine de Sarry 1997 13 D

Unusually fruity and new-world tasting Sancerre.

St Veran Deux Roches 1997 16 D

Always one of the classiest white burgundies, the '97 shows creaminess, ripeness, devious interplay between the fruit and the acidity, and a superb finish. France can win the world cup with quality whites like this. (I wrote before they did).

Tramontane Chardonnay VdP d'Oc 1997, Asda 14 C

Solid.

Tramontane Chardonnay/Vermentino VdP d'Oc 1997, Asda 15 C

Fresh, perky, nutty, excellent balance.

Tramontane Oaked Chardonnay VdP d'Oc 1997, Asda 15.5 C

Creamy, perfumed, textured, lingering. Delicious.

Tramontane Reserve Oak Aged Chardonnay 1997, Asda 14 C

Rich flowing fruit, touch sticky.

Tramontane Sauvignon Blanc VdP d'Oc 1997, Asda 15 B

Brilliant grassy richness.

Tramontane Viognier, VdP d'Oc 1997, Asda 14 C

Good nutty fruit.

Tramontane White VdP de l'Aude 1997, Asda 13.5 B

VdP du Jardin de la France Chardonnay 1997, Asda 14 B

Fresh and perky.

Vin de Pays des Cotes de Gascogne 1996, Asda 14 B

Keen as a sushi chef's wit – plus fresh pineapple.

Vouvray Denis Marchais Hand Picked 1997 15.5 C

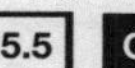

Chenin blanc in its dry honey and citric pineapple mode – lush yet fresh and bonny. Delicious aperitif.

Yves Grassa Chardonnay 1997 14.5 C

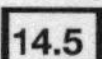

Curiously woody yet pineappley and ripe. Modern yet old-style at one and the same time.

GERMAN WINE — WHITE

Deidesheimer Hofstuck Riesling Kabinett 1997, Asda 11 C

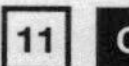

Devil's Rock Riesling Kabinett 1997 14 C

Good new vintage, maturing early. Crisp and clean.

Liebfraumilch Gold Seal 1997 13.5 B

Wild Boar Dry Riesling 1996 14 C

Really incisively dry yet not austere. Crisp, clean, correct.

HUNGARIAN WINE RED

Hungarian Cabernet Sauvignon NV, Asda 13 B

Hungarian Private Reserve Merlot 1997, Asda 13 C

River Route Merlot/Pinot Noir 1997 14 B

Juicy and fruity but great fun.

HUNGARIAN WINE WHITE

Gyongyos Barrel Fermented Chardonnay 1996 14.5 C

Now run by Germans after Australians and Englishmen had a go at making the wines, and the modernity of the fruit style shows. Woody and brightly fruity. Very classy, this vintage.

Hungarian Gewurztraminer 1997, Asda 12 C

Hungarian Irsai Oliver 1997, Asda 13 B

Hungarian Medium Chardonnay 1997, Asda 14 B

Excellent step up from Lieb! Not remotely sweet or soppy.

Hungarian Pinot Grigio 1997, Asda 13 C

Some dry, wry qualities to it.

Hungarian Pinot Noir Rose 1997, Asda 12 C

Not sure about the indecisiveness. Is it dry? Sweet? Or what?

Hungarian Private Reserve Sauvignon Blanc 1997, Asda 12 C

Hungarian Zefir 1997, Asda 13 B

Aperitif style.

Private Reserve Hungarian Chardonnay 1997, Asda 12 C

ITALIAN WINE RED

Amarone della Valpolicella Sanroseda 1993 (50cl) 15 D

Chianti 1996, Asda 12 B

Chianti Colli Senesi Salvanza 1996 13 C

Montepulciano d'Abruzzo Cantine Tollo 1997 14 B

Delicious bargain. Juicy but has hints of baked earth.

Rozzano Villa Pigna 1996 14 C

A lovely rich wine.

Sicilian Rosso NV, Asda 13.5 B

Fruity and fun and never soppy.

Valpolicella Classico 'Sanroseda' 1996 13 C

Valpolicella NV, Asda 13 B

ITALIAN WINE — WHITE

Cantina Tollo Rosato 1996 14 B

Work horse rose of great interest to barbecue cooks. Goes with anything – except conversation.

Due Bianchi Sauvignon/Pinot Bianco 1997 13.5 C

Frascati Superiore Colli di Catone 1997 13.5 C

La Vis Trentino Chardonnay 1996 13 C

Seems to need more fruit at this price.

Lambrusco Bianco, Asda 12.5 A

Lambrusco Rosato, Asda 12 A

Pinot Grigio Ritratti 1997 15 D

Real class here: richness yet quiet stylishness and pace.

Sicilian Bianco NV, Asda 14.5 B

Got character and some fruitiness to it. Great value.

Soave Classico Sanroseda 1996 14 C

Lovely lemony fulsomeness. Terrific shell-fish wine.

Soave NV, Asda 14 B

Fresh and friendly and astounding value. A thoroughly decent glug.

MALTESE WINE RED

Maltese Red 1997, Asda 13 C

MALTESE WINE WHITE

Maltese White 1997, Asda 11 C

St Paul's Bay White 1997 13.5 C

Some good rich fruit for squid stew (in it and with it).

MONTENEGRAN WINE RED

Monte Cheval Vranac, Montenegro 1996 13 C

Very sweet and boot polishy.

MOROCCAN WINE RED

Domaine Mellil Moroccan Red Wine 15 B

NEW ZEALAND WINE WHITE

Timara Sauvignon Blanc/Semillon, Marlborough 1997 

Good grassy richness here. Great fish wine.

PORTUGUESE WINE RED

Bright Douro Red 1996 

Real energy and richness here, modern and full yet also very dry and characterful.

PORTUGUESE WINE WHITE

Vinho Verde, Asda 11 B

SOUTH AFRICAN WINE RED

Cape Cabernet Sauvignon/Merlot Reserve 1997, Asda 13 D

Tobaccoey edge fails to live up to its exciting nicotine naughtiness on the finish.

Cape Cinsault/Cabernet Franc 1997, Asda 15.5 C

Loads of personality here. Juicy and ripe yet the hint of tannin saves it from soppiness.

Cape Cinsault/Ruby Cabernet 1997, Asda 14 C

Touch of gooey fruit here.

Cape Merlot 1997, Asda 14.5 C

Touch of new leather to the ripeness and modernity of the fruit.

Cape Pinot Noir Reserve 1997, Asda 13.5 D

Seriously farmyard pong of long-dead crows and cow dung but this classic first sentence of a classic novel fails to finish convincingly.

Cape Red NV, Asda 13.5 B

Fruity and very ripe. Terrific party wine.

Kumala Cabernet Sauvignon/Shiraz 1997 14 C

Dry and juicy. Has personality and versatility.

Landskroon Cabernet Franc 1997 15.5 C

Has loads of new world warmth and savoury fruitiness on one level and on another level it offers glimpses of the grape's old world twiggy vegetality and dry richness. A terrific glug with or without food.

South African Cabernet Sauvignon 1997, Asda 14 C

Another juicy Asda red with a touch of tannicity to give it character.

South African Pinotage 1997, Asda 14 C

Very juicy and ripe.

Stellenzicht Block Zinfandel 1996 13 D

Too juicy.

SOUTH AFRICAN WINE WHITE

Benguela Chardonnay 1997 13 C

Cape Chardonnay 1997, Asda 13 C

Cape Reserve Chardonnay 1997, Asda 13 D

Touch expensive.

Cape Sauvignon Blanc 1997, Asda 14 C

Crisp and nutty. Quietly impressive.

Cape White 1997, Asda 12 B

Kumala Chenin/Chardonnay 1997 13 C

Muscat de Frontignan Danie de Wet 1997 16.5 C

Waxy and rich. And the plastic corks means it'll never be tainted.

South African Chardonnay 1997, Asda 15.5 C

Has richness and depth, flavour and fullness, but none of it is overstated or OTT. Modern, stylish, gently rampant.

SPANISH WINE — RED

Baron de Ley Rioja Reserva 1991 15 D

Bodegas Campillo, Rioja Crianza 1993 14 C

Don Darias Tinto NV 13 B

Getting rather juicy and jammy. Where's its character gone?

El Meson Rioja CVC 13.5 C

Rioja NV, Asda 14.5 C

Solid plonking here. Good value.

Valencia Red NV, Asda 14 B

Fruity and plump. A lovely little glug.

SPANISH WINE WHITE

La Mancha, Asda 12 A

Moscatel de Valencia, Asda 14 B

Raimat Chardonnay 1997 15 D

Classy, ripe, rich, incisive. A stylish chardonnay of depth but rather than muscularity it has litheness.

Valencia Dry NV, Asda 12 B

Bit dull.

Valencia Medium Dry NV, Asda 11 B

USA WINE RED

Arius Barbera/Cabernet Sauvignon 1997, Asda 15 C

Good richness, nuttiness, and great acidic balance. Superb food wine.

Arius Carignane 1997, Asda 15.5 C

Astonishing plumpness of texture: creamy, ripe, rich and utterly riveting.

Arius Syrah 1997, Asda 14.5 C

Real California sun juice here with a hint of hedgerow character.

Arius Zinfandel 1997, Asda 16.5 C

Magnificent softness and zippy impudence of fruit. Just lovely glugging. Serious fun for the throat.

California Red 1997, Asda 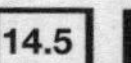

B

Light but pleasantly savoury and burnt-plummily flavoured with a hint of cherry on the finish. Immensely gluggable.

USA WINE — WHITE

Arius Californian Chenin Blanc 1997, Asda 

C

Touch sweet on the finish.

Arius Californian Oaked Colombard 1997, Asda 14.5 C

Creamy and rich. Very satisfying.

Arius Colombard/Chardonnay 1997, Asda 14.5 C

Nice richness of texture overtoning some lovely citric hints.

Arius White Zinfandel 1997, Asda 9 C

A rose. I loathe it. Nothing personal, Alistair, just don't like pink on you.

Californian White 1997, Asda 13 B

FORTIFIED WINE

Amontillado Sherry Medium Dry, Asda 14 C

Fine Ruby Port, Asda 13.5 D

Fino Sherry, Asda 14 C

LBV Port 1990, Asda 14 D

Tawny Port, Asda 14 D

Vintage Character Port, Asda 14 D

SPARKLING WINE/CHAMPAGNE

Asti Spumante, Asda 12 C

Barramundi Australian Brut 15.5 D

Blue Lake Ridge Brut NV (Australia) 14 C

Fun, fruity, fulfilling, dry. Take it seriously.

Blue Lake Ridge Rose NV (Australia) 13 C

Blue Lake Ridge Sparkling Grenache NV 10 D

Don't find it engaging enough to rate it higher.

Cava Brut, Asda 16 C

One of the best under a fiver Cavas on sale. Superb class in a glass here.

Cava Rosada, Asda 15 C

Justifies its colour.

Champagne Brut NV, Asda 14 F

Umm . . . Has some class.

Champagne Brut Rose NV, Asda 13 F

Not bad . . . But I'd rather pay less and get Asda's Cava Rose.

Codorniu Premier Brut Cava 15 D

Classy, rich, concentrated, better than a thousand Champagnes.

Cordoniu Premier Cuvee Brut (Spain) 14 D

Cranswick Pinot/Chardonnay Brut NV (Australia) 16.5 D

Superb class. Beats hundreds of champagnes on sheer texture alone.

Nicholas Feuillate Blanc de Blancs NV 14 G

Stylish and elegant . . . Pricey though.

Nicholas Feuillate Demi-sec Champagne 11 G

Nottage Hill Sparkling Chardonnay 1996 15 D

Classy, rich, very adventurous. An excellent Aussie bubbly.

Scharffenberger Brut (USA) 15 E

Seaview Rose Brut 15 D

Veuve Clicquot Yellow Label Brut NV 11 H

Vintage Champagne 1990, Asda 12 G

Too much money.

BOOTHS

CHRIS DEE CONTINUES TO ASTONISH – FROM £2.99 TO £225! AND THEN CHANGES HIS NAME TO SALLY!

As far as I know, this retailer is the only one in Britain to have been started by someone who left school at the age of ten. In 1838, however, when Edwin Henry Booth did this, it was no strange thing (Victoria had been on the throne barely one year); what was strange was that nine years later E. H. Booth had his first business on Market Street, Blackpool. Today, Booths is still the only retailer in this book to roast its own coffee and the only one to offer the travelling wine writer a spittoon of brass and copper which looks like the unexploded half of a once lethal flying munition.

To celebrate the firm's 150th anniversary last year, in a superb demonstration of how far the Booth family have taken their founder's dream, Bollinger were persuaded to deliver 300 magnums of Grand Annee champagne 1989 to go on sale in the stores at £75 a throw. Last time I saw any of these magnums they were being loaded into Edwin Booth's Jag. Customers, not unnaturally, steered clear of the things.

Or maybe some of these seductively large bottles were instrumental in persuading Sally Holloway to join this bijou chain of supermarkets (24 northern branches turning over between them £100 million a year) as wine buyer. The incumbent Mr Christopher Dee, who had been wine buyer at Booth's since 1995 after flogging his own Leeds off-licences, moved up to become the store's Marketing & IT Director. 'I'll leave her to get on with the job,' he said to me. 'Doesn't do to look over people's shoulders.' I got the distinct impression that Ms Holloway, who had been in the job barely a fortnight when I met her, was going to get into the job and make her mark in double quick time.

A worthy reward, board membership for Mr Dee; not only because he has assembled a decent range of wines from the lowliest priced to the most magnificently absurd, but because he took over as wine buyer from the guvnor, Mr Edwin Booth. Difficult act to follow, the boss's.

But Chris not only followed it but rewrote it and has carried it off the job with style and dedication. Indeed, this book formally congratulates him and happily confers on him the much coveted award of *Superplonk* IT Director of the Year. His prize is a pint of decent beer, Fullers London Pride, next time he is in town.

E.H. Booth & Co.Ltd
4–6 Fishergate
Preston
Lancs PR1 3LJ
Tel: 01772 261701
Fax: 01772 204316

ARGENTINIAN WINE RED

Barbera Valle de Vistalba, Mendoza 1996

Soft, almost bruised fruit, with a hint of herbs and savouriness.

Laranos Malbec, Mendoza 1997

Very full of itself and rich, savoury and textured. Loaded with flavour.

Libertad Sangiovese Malbec 1997

Dry but very bright.

Mission Peak Bonarda Tempranillo, Mendoza NV

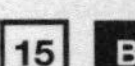

Real soupy wine, dry and richly textured, but finishing deliciously vegetal and arboreal.

Mission Peak Red 13 B

ARGENTINIAN WINE WHITE

Libertad Chenin Blanc 1997

Real dry, oyster-shell charm here.

AUSTRALIAN WINE RED

Australian Red, South Eastern Australia NV, Booths

Not very convincing to this palate. Seems an echo, and a faint one at that, of real Aussie wine.

Brown Brothers Tarrango 1997

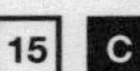

Quite offensively slurpable and richly soft and near-gooey, this is a wine to chill and serve to recent divorcees.

CV Shiraz, Western Australia 1996

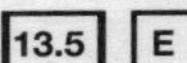

Bit soft on the fruit and hard on the pocket.

Metala Stonyfell Shiraz Cabernet, Saltram Estate 1995

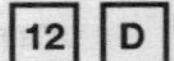

Soft, soppy and as daft as its label – like invalid juice.

Penfolds Bin 35 Cabernet Sauvignon/ Shiraz/Ruby Cabernet 1996 15.5 D

Rich, layered, clinging, ripe – a great steak and kidney pudding wine.

Penfolds Bin 407 Cabernet Sauvignon 1994

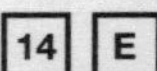

Riddoch Cabernet Shiraz, Coonawarra 1995

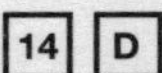

Rich, fleshy, ripe, and with a hint of mint. You may decide to pour it over your lamb chop as well as drinking it with it.

Rosemount Estate Shiraz/Cabernet 1996 15.5 C

Tim Knappstein Cabernet Franc 1995 16 E

An Australian red with guts and gorgeosity! Dry, rich, textured, classy and great with food.

Wakefield Estate Cabernet Sauvignon, Clare Valley 1996 16.5 D

A big soupy broth but it has backbone and character and a huge depth of smoky, almost hammy richness of fruit. Great price for such Aussie splendiferousness. It is something 'rich and strange' and mildly tempestuous.

Yaldara Grenache, Whitmore Old Vineyard 1997 14 D

Typical Aussie softie, caramel textured and savoury, but with a hint of whackiness.

AUSTRALIAN WINE — WHITE

Barramundi Semillon/Colombard/ Chardonnay NV 15 C

Cranswick Botrytis Semillon, Zirilli Vineyard, Riverina 1995 (half bottle) 15.5 F

Wonderful smoky, honeyed, waxy fruit with a huge larding of toffeenosed, textured sweetness and rich acidity. I'd keep it seven to eight years more. It could become a masterpiece.

CV Unwooded Chardonnay, Western Australia 1997 16.5 E

This is the year, '97, to wallow in the richness of the Aussie chardonnay, especially when no wood is aboard and the provenance is Western Australia. A gloriously uncluttered, elegant wine of potency, finesse and heavenly texture.

Deakin Estate Chardonnay, Victoria 1997

Unusual to find an under-a-fiver Aussie chardonnay so couth, civilised, classy and utterly delicious. Lovely texture and ripe, plump fruit.

Hardys Stamp Series Riesling/ Gewurztraminer 1996

Odd sort of fruit – isn't sure quite where it's going. Best served by pointing it in the direction of oriental food.

Kingston Chenin Verdelho 1995

Terrific oily texture and rich fruit – great for oriental food or exotic bookish mood.

Ninth Island Chardonnay, Tasmania 1996

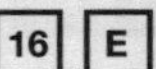

Lovely oily fruit which has a double whammy of ripe melon and fresh pineapple as it surges down the throat. Gorgeous!

Penfolds Clare Valley Organic Chardonnay/ Sauvignon Blanc 1997

Very calm, classy wine in complete command of its faculties: understated richness, firm acidity, delicate balance. Lovely tipple.

Penfolds Rawsons Retreat Bin 21 Semillon/Chardonnay/Colombard 1997

Superb fruit here, with loads of flavour yet that stylishness of tone and texture for which the '97 Aussie whites will become legendary.

Riddoch Chardonnay, Coonawarra 1996

Super mouth-filling plumpness of ripe fruit here, hint of caramel cream even, but the acidity surges alongside in support and the finish is regal. Very classy wine.

Shaw & Smith Sauvignon Blanc 1997

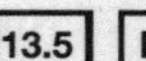

Yes, I like its cleanness. But I'm not sure I'd feel comfortable with parting with nine quid for a wash.

CHILEAN WINE RED

Carmen Grande Vidure Cabernet Sauvignon, Maipo 1996

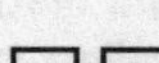

Very savoury with a hint of tobacco. Perhaps a touch expensive considering the paucity of tannins on offer.

Cono Sur Pinot Noir 1997

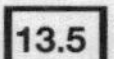

Errazuriz Cabernet Sauvignon, Aconcagua 1996

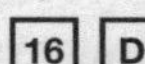

It unites the rich, charcoal tannins of Bordeaux with the soft ripeness of an Aussie construct and produces uniquely Chilean work.

Palmeras Estate Cabernet Sauvignon, Nancagua 1996 16 C

Approachable fruit seriously decked out in classic dress and keen to be of service to pleasure seekers. A dry, substantial wine of some vivacity and style.

Tierra del Rey Chilean Red 15 B

Vina Linderos Cabernet Sauvignon 1996 15.5 D

CHILEAN WINE WHITE

Cordillera Estate Chardonnay, Genesis Vineyard Casablanca 1996 16 C

Lovely controlled nutty richness and lingering flavour, a tad toasted. Has a positive sense of itself without posturing.

Isla Negra Chardonnay, Casablanca Valley 1997 15 C

Ripe, rich, raunchy – but beautifully rippling and rounded.

Via Vigna Chardonnay 1997 14.5 C

Touch glum on the finish and demure as a perfume, but solid overall.

Villard Reserve Chardonnay, Casablanca Valley 1996 16.5 E

Oozes class. Has litheness, muscularity, finesse and staying power.

Vina Tocornal, Rapel Valley 1997

FRENCH WINE RED

Bourgogne Pinot Noir, Jean Luc Joillot 1995

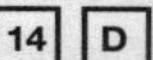

For a real burgundy to be under six quid and offer gutsy fruit is a revelation. Maybe it's the new world heresy of putting the grape variety on the label.

Chateau de Leyne Beaujolais Villages 1997

Chateau l'Euziere Pic St Loup, Coteaux du Languedoc 1994

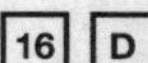

Gorgeous richness, earthiness, characterfulness and finally stylishness of finish. Lovely feel to this wine.

Claret NV, Booths

Tries but the juice covers even the tannins (such as they are).

Clos Ferdinand Rouge, VdP des Cotes de Thongue

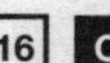

Real class here – it purrs like a well-tuned engine: rich, deep, throbbing smoothly. A terrific quaffing and food wine.

Cotes de Ventoux 'La Falaise' 1996

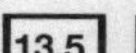

Cute little thing.

Cotes du Rhone Villages 'Epilogue', G. Darriaud 1995

Bit stern-visaged, but good with grilled meats.

Cuvee Aristide Yvon Mau, Haut Medoc 1995 14.5 D

So. This is what modern claret can sizzle the taste buds with. Kept the tannins in good order, I note. Impressive, well-cut fruit here.

Domaine Abbaye St Hilaire, Coteaux Varois 1996 14.5 B

Real quality earth here: rich, gripping, good value.

Domaine de l'Auris Syrah, Cotes de Roussillon Villages 1996 16 D

The ultimate communion wine label, in one sense, and the wine inside, far from sacerdotal, presents itself erect, very dry, earthy and most rudely rustic.

Domaine du Trillol Corbieres 1995 

Very dry and pebbly. Almost bristles.

Faugeres Gilbert Alquier 1996 16.5 D

Makes an impressive case for *not spending* seven quid on an Aussie shiraz. This wine is proud, rustic, tannic, rivetingly multi-textured and massively at home with food. It is the essence of a great French country red.

Fitou Cuvee Madame Claude Parmentier 1996 13 C

Gamay Jardin de la France 11 B

Julienas, Paul Boutinot 1996 12 D

La Reserve du Reverend Corbieres 1995

Earthiness and richness clog up the ripeness in the most perfect way so that the fruit coats both the taste buds and food.

Langi Shiraz, Mount Langi Ghiran 1996

Can't see what £12 buys you here except decent juice. Where are the thrills and sensuality we have a right to expect?

Oak-aged Claret Bordeaux Superieur 1996, Booths

Has some real claret touches – everywhere except the price tag.

Pernand Vergelesses, Rossignol-Cornu 1995

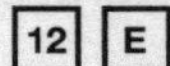

Has texture. But so does a wool sock.

Rasteau Cotes du Rhone Villages, Domaine des Coteaux Travers 1996

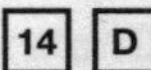

Has a cigar boxy edge to it, with some warm savouriness to the fruit, and a firm finish.

St Maurice Cuvee Reserve Cotes du Rhone Villages 1996

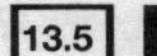

Juicy with a hint of earth.

Vin Rouge, Booths

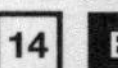

Vina Alarba Tinto, Catalayud 1997

Ripe, dry, gently baked cherries. Delicious chilled.

FRENCH WINE WHITE

Bergerac Blanc NV, Booths 14.5 B

Crisp, dry, incisive, great with fish, and thundering good value. A positive wine.

Bergerac Rouge, Booths 13 B

Berticot Semillon, Cotes de Duras 1997 15 B

Loads of creamy fruit held back from being OTT by the compensating acidity. Terrific value.

Bordeaux Blanc Sec NV, Booths 13.5 B

Some cleanness and freshness here.

Chablis Domaine de l'Eglantiere 1995 12 D

Chateau Lamothe-Vincent Bordeaux Rose 1997 14.5 C

A truly elegant rose of some class and substance.

Chateau Lamothe-Vincent Bordeaux Sec 1997 14 C

A terrific shell-fish wine. Almost grassy on the finish. The texture is well interwoven.

Cuvee Classique VdP des Cotes de Gascogne Plaimont 1997 14 B

Typical cheeky Gascogne. Zippy and fresh but with a good undertone of rich fruit.

Dom Casteillas Rose, Cotes de Roussillon 1996 14 D

A very classic rose with hints of strawberries and plums, but dry and very fresh to finish.

Domaine de la Touche Muscadet sur Lie 1996 13.5 C

Ooh . . . so close to being 14. It ought to be cheaper for a start and it ought to finish cleaner for another thing. Am I being hypercritical? It's your money I take into account.

Domaine Les Pradelles Sauvignon Blanc, VdP d'Oc 1996 13.5 D

Perhaps the most ambitious badging in the history of Oc. The wine, though worthy, is not so ambitious being dry, quiet and a touch sullen.

Domaine St Jean de Pinede Rose, VdP d'Oc 1997 13 B

Onion skin in colour rather than really rose, this is strictly a barbecue wine for prawns off the coals.

Gewurztraminer d'Alsace, Cave de Turckheim 1997 16 D

Now this has some excitement with its rich, gently spicy fruit, redolent of crushed rose petals and fresh lychee juice. It has a bold structure of texture yet crisp underflow and it finishes with complexity and even a touch of extravagance.

Honore de Berticot Cotes de Duras Sauvignon Blanc 1996 14 C

Comes in a useful half-priced half bottle (around £2.10) and has an impressive old-style label. The wine? Old Oxfam sweaters and bread knives. Good for fish.

James Herrick Chardonnay 1996 

Good age for a wine not designed to grow old with any great grace. Here it's perfectly mature, melony and lemony and strikes home with style.

Louis Chatel sur Lie, VdP d'Oc 1996 

Superb value for money here: freshness, cleanness, cheek and charm.

Petit Chablis Domaine de l'Eglantiere 1996 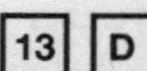

The ragged edge gives it character but I do feel class should out at this price and, coax it how you may, it stays backward.

Pinot Blanc d'Alsace, Cave de Turckheim 1997 

Terrific oriental food wine. Gently spicy, a touch sunny, but the fruit is always going forward. Delicious to sip after a tough day at the coal face.

Pouilly Fume 'Les Cornets', Cailbourdin 1996 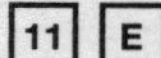

What can one say? Nothing. Eleven says it all.

Riesling d'Alsace, Aime Stentz 1996 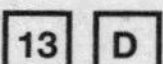

Touch disappointing at this price. I do ask for some real excitement at this price. This wine takes it too easy as it goes down the throat.

Riesling d'Alsace Sommerberg Grand Cru, Amie Stentz 1995 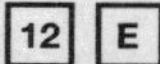

The bottle I tasted from was numb. Perhaps the shock of being in London?

Sancerre P & A Dezat, Domaine de P'tit Roy 1996 12 E

Eh, by gum (and by tongue), there's summat missing here.

Vin de Table Blanc NV, Booths

Somewhat muted on the finish.

GERMAN WINE WHITE

Liebfraumilch NV, Booths 13 B

Niersteiner Spiegelberg Riesling Spatlese 1996

More richness than dryness, less richness than sweetness – also at four quid it isn't cheap.

Piesporter Michelsberg NV, Booths

Has more precision that Booth's lieb but fits the same sort of bill (of fare) if not bill (of pocket).

HUNGARIAN WINE WHITE

Chapel Hill Oaked Chardonnay, Balaton Boglar NV

Thoroughly modern with piles of personality. Has richness and texture with a good multi-layered finish of soft fruit/hard fruit.

ITALIAN WINE RED

Amarone Classico, Brigaldara 1991 13.5 G

Chianti Classico Querciabella 1994 14 E

La Prendina Cabernet Sauvignon, Vigneto del Falcone 1994 14 F

Superb interwoven tannins and classic cabernet dryness and wry whimsicality. But as it finishes, it speaks volumes for how serious this wine is and takes itself.

Salice Salento, Vallone 1994 16.5 C

Big, brothy, savoury, coffee undertones swirling through a rich, soft-fruit centre of soft ripeness, this is a lovely glug.

ITALIAN WINE WHITE

Le Vaglie Verdicchio Classico 1996 14 E

A classy Verdicchio.

Muscate Sec Alasia Vino da Tavola 1995 15.5 C

Gorgeous spicy gooseberry and melon plus a sort of minty raspberry touch. Lovely idea for an appetite whetter.

NEW ZEALAND WINE — WHITE

Dashwood Sauvignon Blanc, Marlborough 1997 16 E

Very extruded sauvignon with lovely control of its rich, acidically perfect, herbaceousness. Very elegant.

Lincoln Chardonnay, Gisborne 1996 14 D

Richness and ripeness on one level, but a touch of young raw pineapple (a hint) as it finishes. I wish it were cheaper, though.

Vavasour Sauvignon Blanc 1996 13.5 E

Expensive, and doesn't quite clinch the promise of the initial attack as it presses its fruit home.

PORTUGUESE WINE — RED

Alta Mesa Estremadura 1996 13 B

Simple fruit juice – with a hint of cafe society.

Foral Douro Tinto 1996 14 B

A terrific roast meat wine. Real tannins here and fruity grip.

Jose Neiva Oak Aged Red, Estremadura 1996 13.5 B

Light and earthy.

Portada Estremadura Red 1996 12 C

Touch too light and juicy for me.

Quinta das Setencostas, Alenquer 1996 14 C

Very juicy initially then the lovely tannins start biting. A wine for roast chicken stuffed with something exotic.

Vinha Nova Vinho de Mesa 13.5 B

PORTUGUESE WINE WHITE

Portada Estremadura White 1997 14.5 C

Soft pear fruit with hard crisp apples undertoning it. Great little food wine.

SOUTH AFRICAN WINE RED

Leef Op Hoop Cabernet Sauvignon, Stellenbosch 1996 16 E

A most complex character, this. It takes some thinking about. It comes on as a fresh, cheeky, fruity fellow at first, then it develops some burnt multi-layered richness of compelling potency. A most individual wine.

SOUTH AFRICAN WINE — WHITE

Altus Sauvignon Blanc, Boland Wynkeller 1997

Perhaps too fleshy for the hardened sauvignon blanc buff but I find it engagingly soft and ripe and surging with flavour.

Jordan Chameleon Chardonnay Sauvignon 1997

Doesn't quite knit together as harmoniously as the figures on the price ticket.

Jordan Chardonnay, Stellenbosch 1996

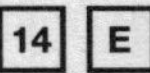

Creamy wood and hints of warm coconuts. If you like this sort of chew, this is your wine. Best, I suspect, with tarragon chicken.

SPANISH WINE — RED

Guelbenzu Jardin Garnacha, Navarra 1996

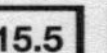

Has fresh cherries, ripe plum, some kind of nut, and it assembles itself in rich array from nose to throat.

Ochoa Tempranillo/Garnacha, Navarra 1996

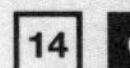

Bit smelly, but with food it comes into its own.

Scraping the Barrel Tempranillo, Utiel-Requena NV 14.5 B

Deliciously dry and personality-packed barrel it must have been . . .

Tapas Red 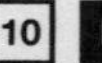

SPANISH WINE WHITE

Estrella Moscatel de Valencia 16 C

Either as a dessert wine or as a sweet, floral aperitif, this wine is brilliant. It is sunshine itself, packed into a bottle.

Santa Lucia Lightly Oaked Viura 1996 

Solid yet soft – wine is the only artefact capable of this delicious paradox.

Santara Chardonnay 1997 16 C

This wine wins on so many fronts: perfume, texture, richness, balance, wittiness of finish and price tag. Overall, it's very classy, modern, clean and complex. Amazing value.

USA WINE RED

Redwood Trail Pinot Noir 1996 14.5 D

Excellent, if slightly sulphurous, on first opening, but the texture and ripeness and sheer class of pinot are obvious.

USA WINE WHITE

Raymond Amberhill Chardonnay 1994 16 E

Extremely rich and creamy with a hint of nuttiness and a suggestion of vanilla and custard as it finishes. Very fleshy fruit here with perhaps untypical lack of Californian finesse, but as a brutal fruit lover, I like it. Great with dishes like spicy crab cakes or coronation chicken.

Redwood Trail Chardonnay 1996 15.5 D

Gorgeous texture here, ripe and softly Rubenesque.

FORTIFIED WINE

Amontillado, Booths 14 C

Churchill's White Port 13 E

Crusted Port Churchill, Bottled 1988, Booths 16 F

Lush, rich, utterly extravagant in its commitment to sheer pleasure.

Finest Reserve Port, Booths 14 E

Fino, Booths 14 C

The way to treat this fellow is to chill him and serve him with grilled prawns. It is a test of your friends' and neighbours' characters – if they gag or cannot stomach the wine's bone dry saline fruit with prawns, then you know them for what they are: softies.

Henriques & Henriques 5 year Old Madeira 15 F

Old classic, sweet and raisiny, to drink with a slice of Christmas cake.

Lustau Old East India Sherry 13.5 E

Manzanilla, Booths 14.5 C

Lovely nutty fruit. Great aperitif, chilled. Very dry, very tongue-puckering.

Niepoort Ruby Port 13 E

Taylors Quinta de Vargellas Port 1986 15.5 G

A gorgeous port of huge depth of texture and richness. It scores because of its sublime depth but the price, compared with Booths Crusted, is a touch out of kilter. The extra is worth spending in five or six years when this wine will have aged and developed even more style.

SPARKLING WINE/CHAMPAGNE

Argyll Brut, Williamette Valley 1989 (USA) 13 F

Getting on a bit. Hairline beginning to show. I know how it feels.

Bollinger Grande Annee 1989 9.5 H

I simply don't find it a thrill to drink and surely at nigh on forty quid it should be. Poor value bubbly, of little appeal to this curmudgeon.

Champagne Brossault Rose 11.5 F

Champagne Paul Nivelle NV 14 E

An excellent under-a-tenner champagne – has style and vim.

Cremant d'Alsace Cuvee Prestige (France) 13 E

Touch austere.

Deutz Marlborough Cuvee (New Zealand) 15.5 E

Better than most champagnes because of its hauteur and sheer textural class.

Moscato d'Asti Alasia 1996 (Italy) 14.5 D

Delightful apple, pear and muscat grape rich tipple.

Palau Brut (Spain) 14 D

Petillant de Listel, Traditional 12 A

Splendid soda-pop seal (no cork) and the fruit, in what technically is not a wine (barely 2.5% alcohol) is yukky. A spritzer? For backward students?

Piper Heidsieck Brut Champagne 12 G

Seaview Rose Brut 15 D

BUDGENS

FINNERTY FINESSES SOME OUT-OF-THE-WAY WINES! ALL AT THE FIRST U.K. RETAILER TO HAVE A POLLING STATION ON ITS PREMISES!

It has been an eventful year for Budgens. The store feels more confident than at any time in a decade. A measure of this was the retailer's first TV advertising for 10 years.

It also rolled out the first phase of an own-label wine packaging re-vamp with more new products on the way in 1998. It was reported in May that the new wine and beer offers were to play a crucial role in enhancing Budgens city centre stores and planned petrol forecourt outlets. This latter initiative involving up to 45 forecourt stores planned to open on Q8 petrol station sites over the year. The retailer also moved to linkup with BP for the so-called Budgens Express stores.

Late last year, Budgens also entered the convenience store market, buying 57 stores from 7-Eleven, and announced plans for a nationwide chain of such outlets trading under the Budgens name. Budgens also planned to make five of its London outlets 24-hour stores, but all this seemed humdrum commercial news set beside the innovation of the company's Rye store being used as a polling station in the Rother District Council elections.

Quite what Mr Tony Finnerty, Budgens wine buyer, made of all this is not recorded. On the day I was due to meet him and talk about the future, he was indisposed due to an accident, of the sort which he might have picked up on a ski slope collision. In the event, his wines have to do his talking for him and he has some unpredictable bottles, as the entries which follow will confirm.

Budgens Stores Limited
P O Box 9
Stonefield Way
Ruislip
Middlesex HA4 OJR
Tel: 0181 422 9511
Fax: 0181 422 1596

SEE STOP PRESS SECTION AT END OF BOOK FOR LAST-MINUTE ADDITIONS OR UPDATES TO THIS RETAILER'S RANGE.

AUSTRALIAN WINE RED

Penfolds Bin 389 1994 14 F

Tarvin Ridge Mataro Grenache 1996 12 C

Wynns Coonawarra Shiraz 1996 15.5 D

Delicious no-nonsense briskness from the savoury fruit, the bouncy tannins and the whole lingering depth of the finish.

AUSTRALIAN WINE WHITE

Brown Brothers Dry Muscat 1996 15 C

The perfect dry aperitif. The fruity muscat, gently spicy quality is an undertone only – the crispness is the big thing.

Loxton Lunchtime Light (4%) 13 B

Good stab at a less-than-wine. But though aromatically and on first sip it seems solid, it turns bleak and wimpish on the finish. It might be improved mixed with a hard, sparkling mineral water.

Normans Lone Gum Chenin Blanc 1996 14 C

Rawsons Retreat Bin 202 Riesling 1997 15 C

Great vigour and bite here and some degree of cellaring is

possible. It's young and feisty, and will age for a couple of years with discretion. But it's great now, with its cool knife-edge freshness.

Rosemount Estate Hunter Valley Chardonnay 1997 16.5 D

It's the lushly controlled fruit, that hint of creamy, woody vanilla on the finish, that establishes its silky class.

Rosemount Estate Semillon/Chardonnay 1997 15 D

Richly endowed with hints of melon and pineapple, it's not as classy as the chardonnay (qv) but it has potential with exotic fish dishes.

Rymill Coonawarra Botrytis Gewurztraminer 1996 (half bottle) 15 D

Tarvin Ridge Trebbiano 1996 13.5 C

AUSTRIAN WINE WHITE

Samling Trockenbeerenauslese 1995 (half bottle) 16.5 E

Honeyed grapefruit, waxy, rich, hint of lime.

BULGARIAN WINE WHITE

Preslav Chardonnay/Sauvignon Blanc 1995  B

CHILEAN WINE RED

Millaman Cabernet Malbec 1997 13 C

Some juice and flavour but most unlike Chilean reds which this palate, at least, encounters at this price.

Millaman Merlot 1997 

Not as engaging or smooth as other Chileans. Indeed, it's atypical.

CHILEAN WINE WHITE

Casablanca Sauvignon Blanc 1997 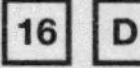

Coolly impressive sauvignon in the rich new world vein with a compelling texture (slightly oily) and a lovely balance of fruit and acidity as it descends.

Vina Tarapaca Chardonnay 1997  

A dry, wry wine of some substance and serious-minded demeanour – but the final fruity flourish is firm yet light-hearted. A classy wine.

CYPRIOT WINE RED

Keo Othello NV 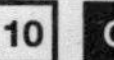

FRENCH WINE RED

Abbaye St Hilaire Coteaux Varois 1996 13.5 B

Dry, austere, but good with pink game or rare meats.

Bourgogne Rouge Vienot 1996 12 D

Cahors Marquis Rocadour 1995 14 C

Chateau Belvise Minervois 1995 11 C

Chateau de Malijay Cotes de Rhone 1995 13.5 C

Chateau Graulet Premieres Cotes de Blaye Bordeaux 1996 14 D

Smoky, rich, nicely fat on the finish, good peppery undertone. Great food claret.

Claret, Budgens 13 B

Corbieres Chateau Saint-Louis 1997 13 C

Good texture but a touch anodyne as it finishes. Rather less character than usual from a Corbieres.

Costieres de Nimes Fontanilles 1996 11 C

Cotes de Rhone Villages Cuvee Reserve 1996 12 C

Cotes Marmandais, Beaupuy 1996 13.5 C

Very dry and charcoal-edged, but with bangers and mash it would be most engaging.

Crozes Hermitage 1996 14 C

It seems to be impolite but its day-old growth of beard hides only soft-cheeked charm.

Domaine St Roch VdP de l'Aude 10 B

Faugeres Jean Jean 1996 10 C

Pretty dull on the whole (even in parts).

Gargantua Cotes du Rhone 1996 12 C

Gigondas Domaine de la Mourielle 1997 16.5 D

Gorgeous Rhone red of substance, wit, longevity and a lovely richness, developed tannicity, and the final dry finish is superb. A very classy wine indeed.

Le Haut Colombier VdP de la Drome 1995 11 B

Pontet Saint-Bris St Emilion 1996 13.5 D

Great introduction as one smells and sips but misses the spot, a little, as it flops over the adenoids.

Rouge de France Special Cuvee NV 10 B

Vin de Pays d'Agenais Rouge NV 10 B

Vin de Pays de l'Aude 10 B

FRENCH WINE WHITE

Blanc de Blancs Special Cuvee 13.5 B

Bordeaux Blanc Sec 1997 13.5 B

Austere, but not entirely bereft of charm. At this price, snap it up for large gatherings of fish stew-eaters (or fish and chips suppers).

Chardonnay VdP de l'Isle de Beaute 1997, Budgens 13.5 B

Good value here: plump fruit with some ripeness if simplicity of attack.

Chateau Lacroix Bordeaux 1997 13 C

Touch under-fruited and austere (and this is not necessarily to do with cleanness or freshness, it just seems tardy).

Chenet VdP Colombard Demi-sec 1997 13.5 C

Charming move-up for Lieb lovers looking to diversify. The blue bottle doesn't sting – nor does the price tag.

Cotes du Marmandais Beaupuy NV 13 C

Touch coarse but very good hearted and fresh-faced. Good with shellfish.

Domaine Barroque VdP des Cotes de Gascogne 1996 15 B

Domaine de Villeroy-Castellas Sauvignon Blanc 1996 11 C

Domaine l'Argentier Terret VdP des Cotes de Thau NV 13.5 B

Domaine Pascaly VdP de l'Aude 12 B

James Herrick Chardonnay VdP d'Oc 1996

Good age for a wine not designed to grow old with any great grace. Here it's perfectly mature, melony and lemony and strikes home with style.

Laroche Grande Cuvee Chardonnay VdP d'Oc 1997

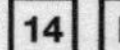

Has a posh woody feel and good clean fruit. Great with poached fish, chicken, salads.

Macon Ige 1996

Rosaline Cotes du Marmandais Rose 1997

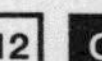

Rather uncertain as to what it is. It needs to lie on a couch and work out whether it's a red on holiday or a rose only half out of bed.

Rully Blanc Raoul Clercet 1992

Sancerre les Chasseignes 1996

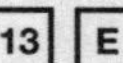

Very drinkable – up to the point where you swallow the price tag. Eight quid is on the outrageous side of chutzpah.

Valblanc VdP du Gers Colombard 1996

Very definitely for fish and chips – even throw in a welly.

GERMAN WINE — WHITE

Bereich Bernkastel Mosel Saar Ruwer 1996

The sweetness crowds the acidity so even a chilled glass on a humid day might seem less than perfect.

Flonheimer Adelberg Auslese 1994  

GREEK WINE RED

Kourtaki Vin de Crete 1996 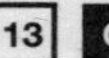

Dry, some texture and tannin to the fruit, but fearfully old-fashioned. The fruit is a bit bare-knuckle.

GREEK WINE WHITE

Kourtaki Vin de Crete 1996 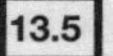 

Home of Europe's greatest vinous tragedy, oxidised red retsina, this wine is a far cry from such abominations. With a Greek octopus stew or squid with chili this wine is a stout performer.

Orino Spiropoulos Greek Dry White 1996 (organic)  

Unusually delicious crisp Greek white with hints of raspberry and melon and with a clean mineral-edged finish. Nicely textured, too.

Samos Vin Doux NV (half bottle)  

Brilliant value here. A rich, oily, waxy, almost biscuity, honey drenched pudding wine for the solo hedonist (in the useful half bottle) to get stuck into – and stuck is the carefully chosen word

– as he or she attacks a block of foie gras, a creme brulee with fresh blueberries, or simply a goat's cheese with a bunch of fresh grapes.

ITALIAN WINE — RED

Avignonesi Vino Nobile de Montepulciano 1993 12 E

Barolo Villademonte 1992 10 E

Merlot del Veneto, Ricordi 1995 12 C

Nexus Grave del Friuli San Simeone 1996 14 E

The sheer opulence of texture, finely polished and svelte, is what makes it so effective on the palate.

ITALIAN WINE — WHITE

Colombara Soave Classico, Zenato 1997  

Superb Soave of great class. Has flavour, texture, tenacity and a flourish on the finish.

Frascati Superiore Casale dei Grillo 1996, Budgens  

MEXICAN WINE RED

L A Cetto Petite Syrah 1996

Terrific value here, perhaps Budgens most attractive and subtly exotic red. Has rich plum and blackcurrant fruit, lovely mature tannins and a good gentle wallop on the finish. Great stuff!

NEW ZEALAND WINE RED

Montana Cabernet Sauvignon/Merlot 1996

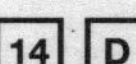

Very classy in its final flourish and this a fond farewell to the old herbaceous Kiwis of yesteryear. Merlot is a good NZ grape, its best red.

Waimanu Premium Dry 1995

Can't quite make up its mind whether to be or not to be. A classic drama? Not really.

NEW ZEALAND WINE WHITE

Nobilo Full Harvest Sauvignon Blanc 1996

Waimanu Muller Thurgau/Sauvignon Blanc 1996

Not convincing as a wine or as a Kiwi. Unless, I suppose, you take into account the absurdity of a flightless bird. This wine, then, is a perfect Kiwi. It doesn't quite get off the ground.

PORTUGUESE WINE — RED

Alta Mesa 1996 13.5 B

Simple fruity red best, to my mind, chilled.

Dao Reserve Dom Ferraz 1995 13 C

Good old-sockish fruit. Has some character, you have to say.

PORTUGUESE WINE — WHITE

Alta Mesa 1996 

Terrific value here – fruit of a gentle toffee texture and waxy finish. Excellent with chicken.

ROMANIAN WINE — RED

Pietroasa Vineyards Young Vatted Cabernet Sauvignon 1996 15 C

Cabernet in its dry yet juicy mould with a hugely approachable, perfumed fruitiness and lingering good humour.

SOUTH AFRICAN WINE — RED

Clear Mountain Cape Red 11 B

Helderberg Cinsaut Shiraz 1996 13 C

At £2.99 I think it's a decent glug. At a fiver, I must have more weight.

SOUTH AFRICAN WINE WHITE

Clear Mountain Chenin Blanc 13.5 B

Helderberg Sauvignon Blanc 1996 14 C

SPANISH WINE RED

Diego de Almagro Valdepenas 1993 13.5 B

Marques de Caro Garnacha Reserva 1991 12 B

Marques de Caro Merlot 1995 11 C

Marques del Puerto Gran Reserva Rioja 1989 13 E

Bit dry and dusty, but old-fashioned Rioja it is and it's proud of begging for food.

Palacio de la Vega Crianza 1994 16.5 C

Rich, dark, textured, soft yet vivid and muscular, this is a terrific food wine as well as offering very high class but not expensive tippling.

Rioja Don Marino NV 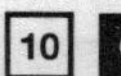 C

SPANISH WINE — WHITE

Moscatel de Valencia Vittore 14.5 B

SWISS WINE — WHITE

Chasselas Romand 1996 10 C

UKRAINIAN WINE — RED

Potemkin Bay Odessa Black NV 3 B

Oxidised and revolting. Might make an ingredient in a vinaigrette – or a prop for Russian roulette. Budgens' buyer says I had a rogue sampling. But . . .

URUGUAYAN WINE — RED

Irurtia Nebbiolo 1997 12 C

How brave! But the wine is not as exciting as the promise of its provenance.

URUGUAYAN WINE WHITE

Irurtia Pinot Blanc 1997 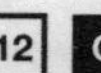

More bravery here! Uruguayan pinot blanc! It's crazy! Will it float? Will it hit the iceberg? Alas, it doesn't sink but it does scrape by.

USA WINE RED

Angelo d'Angelo Rustica Sangiovese 1995 

Rather too juicy for a wine at this price. It's like paying for a First Class rail seat and getting bare boards. True, you get to sit down but you feel bruised by the experience. A £3.50 wine.

Glen Ellen Cabernet Sauvignon 1996 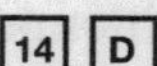

Good weight of fruit and tannin, depth of flavour and finish. Has some lingering presence to it.

Stonegate Merlot 1995 

£13? Come on, Tony, this is just grape juice with a hint of brickdust tannin. Might be okay at £2.49.

Sutter Home Zinfandel 1995 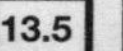

Juicy and ripe and soft as a baby's bum (but not quite so aromatic).

USA WINE — WHITE

Stonegate Chardonnay 1996 14 E

Very posh and plumply textured. Has lovely creamy vanilla hints to the fresh, firm fruit.

FORTIFIED WINE

Amontillado Sherry, Budgens 14 C

Blandy's Dry Special Madeira NV 13 E

Overpriced sweet thing, not really dry in any meaningful sense of the word, which is as a reasonable cold-weather blood warmer. But I find a tenner for this sort of thing, which I normally reserve to beef up gravies and game sauces, far too pricey.

Manzanilla La Guita 13 C

Marsala Cremovo Vino Aromatizzato all'Uovo, Filipetti NV 15 C

Excellent price for such richness, such multi-layered depth and warmth, and lovely taste-bud-curdling custardy finish. A lovely wine – most individual.

Rozes LBV Port 1992 13.5 E

Rich but not oversweet, rather heady on the finish.

Rozes Ruby Port NV 13 D

Sweet, rich, ripe and good for the honey-dentured.

Rozes Special Reserve Port NV 14 D

Bit more bite here than the Rozes Ruby and more evident class. Nicely textured, rich and full, and good with a slice of fruit cake.

Warre's Warrior Port NV 13 E

Rich and warm, comfortingly sweet.

SPARKLING WINE/CHAMPAGNE

Blanquette de Limoux Blanc de Blancs Divinaude 14 E

Brossault Rose Champagne 11.5 F

Champagne Husson NV 11 G

Rather an oddly soapy finish. The £15 price tag seems to take you to the cleaners as well.

Champagne Pierre Callot Blanc de Blancs Grand Cru Avize 12 G

Cremant de Bordeaux NV 13 D

Dry and classy. Good as many a Champagne.

Germain Brut Reserve Champagne 13 G

Lindauer Sparkling (New Zealand) 13 E

Seppelt Great Western Brut (Australia) 13.5 D

Still a bargain. Elegant and dry.

Seppelt Salinger 1992 (Australia) 13 E

Touch expensive, now it's approaching nine quid where certain supermarket Champagnes lurk. Is this any better? About as good (or bad, depending on your cynicism quotient).

CO-OP (CWS & CRS)

THE CWS'S WOODROW & BASTARD CONTINUE TO DOMINATE THE TONGUE-IN-CHEEK LABEL TABLE WHILST THE QUESTION FOR THE CRS'S BOYS AND GIRLS IS *CAN THEY MAKE IT IN THE BIG LEAGUE*?

There are two separate entries for the wines of these two co-operative movements because they are, where my own remit of wine is concerned, two distinct entities. The CWS has two enormously experienced and amusing wine buyers, Arabella Woodrow (marathon runner) and Paul Bastard (linguist and hispanophile). Between them they regularly stuff their shelves with wonderfully cheap and wonderfully fruity wines, many of which demonstrate that, though from outside the co-op movement seems somewhat humourless and dour, where wine labels are concerned wit is the order of the day.

It was Woodrow and Bastard who cooked up Fair Martina (a pun on vermentino) and Bad Tempered Cyril (pun on syrah) and since the fun here is disciplined and apposite, it comes across not as redundant and childish but unstuffy and entertaining.

The position at the CRS is not so free-flowing or so incisively marketing orientated, as the ratings given to many of their wines demonstrates. But the CRS is making great efforts, through Christine Sandys the wine buying manager and buyer Angus Clark (plus assistant buyer Karen Tranter), to compete more successfully against the major supermarkets and we will, I reckon, see greater and greater things emerging over the next few years.

The co-op movement's efforts to market itself in more modern ways was overshadowed by the extraordinary events caused by last year's attempted takeover for the business. A certain Mr Andrew Regan mounted a £1.15 billion bid for the CWS, causing huge controversy and allegations over dirty tricks in which Regan was described, at the kinder level of criticism, as merely an 'asset stripper'. Later, the CRS itself rejected the offer of a £6 billion merger with CWS. CWS said that its offer was not connected with the Regan affair, but that it was in the best interests of both groups to merge. This merger has been much discussed since the mid-1980s and many consider that it will eventually happen (some, like myself, believe it is the only dynamic way for the co-op movement to regenerate itself in the long term). The CRS and CWS were at least united in defence against Regan. As a shareholder in CWS, CRS said that it fully backed CWS's attempts to resist this gentleman's claws.

Then sensational developments: CWS suspended Allan Green (controller of retailing) and David Chambers (chief general manager for buying, marketing and the supply chain) over alleged collusion with Andrew Regan in his bid to buy the retailer. This resulted in the bid being aborted. As a result, Andrew Regan was reported in *The Times* to be around £40 million less well off after his failure to succeed and within a short while the CWS agreed 'substantial damages' in a civil settlement with Regan.The judge described Regan's unsuccessful bid as 'clearly dishonest' and a 'gross and wilful breach of confidence'.

In a bullish and celebratory mood, the Co-op lopped a fiver off the price of a bottle of Moet & Chandon. This move reduced the price of this outrageous bubbly to £14.99 from £19.99. The *FT* noted in a report that the original Rochdale pioneers back in 1844 would not have considered such a move because one of their original aims was to set up a 'temperance hotel'. Personally, I'd rather spend a fiver on the same retailer's terrific Cava rather than anything with Moet on the label.

The row over alcopops would hardly have endeared the modern Co-op to its founders. This argument split the co-operative movement, with the CWS and other societies banning them while the CRS refused to do any such thing. Reviewing these substances for the *Guardian*, especially one brand in particular whose name has passed out of my mind as swiftly as its taste left my palate, I felt distinctly ancient and old fogey-ish.

Had the Regan affair spurred the movement on? The CRS announced plans to create a single retail fascia across all its 500 food stores, replacing the Co-op Pioneer and Co-op Local trading identities and the CWS introduced a pilot wines and spirits department at its South-East Co-op outlet at Longfield in Kent. The new off-licence section was separately branded as Grape and Grains. The company was also reported to be very pleased with the success of the trial, reporting 'dramatically increased' sales.

Last year the Co-op took the plunge in to uncharted waters. It became the first undertaker to advertise on national TV. The Co-operative Funeral Service, in partnership with CWS's funeral division, underwrote the commercials and also re-designed its shops, reportedly using 'brighter colours'. I wait eagerly for the next step in the Co-op's belated move into the twentieth century: the introduction of wine shelves in to its funeral parlours. Bad Tempered Cyril should go down a storm.

In the autumn of last year the CRS cannily recruited Karen Carlyle from Asda as marketing director. All part of a £147 million re-launch. I held my breath. Three months later she left 'to pursue other interests'. Oh . . .

More innovatively, just as last year's *Superplonk* was published, the Co-op was reported to be on a marketing crusade against misleading labelling on food and drew up a code of practice which (as the so-called 'consumer-owned retailer') it hoped will be adopted by the government. The guidelines also included measures against own labels mimicking prominent brands. Its 3,000 own-labels, apparently, already met the standards. Since wine is a food, and the only one which does not have to state its contents on the label, I hope these measures are adopted and taken up by the wine label authorities. Apart from wanting to know any pesticide residues or sulphur levels in a wine, I would also like to see clearly stated the fining agent used. Many vegetarian readers ask me about this aspect of wine because certain agents, used to remove the minute particles which prevent perfect clarity in a wine, are animal based (milk, fish bladders, blood even). Mostly bentonite clay is employed, but why shouldn't we know the full story on every wine?

Overall, things this year have quietened down at the Co-op after the Regan debacle. This giant retailer is, one hopes, concentrating on becoming a true competitor to the major supermarkets where it matters most. And this surely means that wine departments of both the CWS and the CRS will get stronger and more diversified; with more own-labels perhaps. The fact that it is more secretive than its competitors, due in the main to an innate modesty and dislike of hype, is all to its credit.

However, as the entries which follow demonstrate, the Co-op is the place for a bargain.

Co-operative Wholesale Society Limited
P O Box 53
New Century House
Manchester M60 4ES
Tel: 0161 834 1212
Fax: 0161 834 4507

Co-operative Retail Services
Sandbrook Park
Sandbrook Way
Rochdale
Lancashire OL11 1SA
Tel: 01706 713000

ARGENTINIAN WINE RED

Argentine Malbec/Bonarda 1997, Co-op 15.5 B

Has a curious dryness melded with a rich, burnt rubber richness of texture. Terrific pasta plonk.

Elsa Barbera 1996 13 C

Libertad Sangiovese Malbec 1997 14.5 B

Black cherry meets rough velveteen. Delicious little glug. Available at Co-op Superstores.

Lost Pampas Oak Aged Cabernet/Malbec 1997, Co-op 14 C

Finishes with a briskness which belies the perfume and the supple fruit of the initial texture.

Marques de Grinon Dominio de Agrelo Malbec 1996 16 D

A very stylish malbec. Has perfume, presence, persistence, loads of flavour, dryness and depth, and a finish of considerable finesse yet weight. Superstores only.

Marques de Grinon Tempranillo 1997 16.5 C

Superbly well-grilled fruit, dry, dark, rich, subtly cherryish and blackberryish and the texture, with its well-knitted tannins, is unusually couth for a wine at this price.

Martins Merlot 1996 12 C

Mission Peak Argentine Red NV 13 B

Mission Peak Red 13 B

Valentin Bianchi Cabernet Sauvignon 1993 16.5 E

Cassis to smell, chocolate and cassis to finish plus dry tannins in fine fettle giving the overall polish of the fruit some deep character and serious style. A powerful bottle. Available at Co-op Superstores.

ARGENTINIAN WINE WHITE

Andino Chenin/Sauvignon Blanc 1997 15 B

Delicate, delicious, decisive, calm, gently classy but fruity. Serious fun here.

Argentine Sauvignon/Torrontes 1997, Co-op 14 B

Good shellfish wine.

Elsa Chardonnay/Semillon 1996 14 C

Has softness and hints of richness to the fruit but it finishes crisply and cleanly.

Etchart Rio de Plata Torrontes 1997 13 C

A muscat-like aperitif wine of dry fruitiness. Available at Co-op Superstores.

La Rural Chardonnay 1997 15 C

Has softness with a gentle pineapple and melon edge. Available at Co-op Superstores.

---

la Rural Merlot 1997 15.5 C

Delicate but decisive, demure but determined, this is a very calm, gently rich, softly finished and most agreeably well-mannered merlot. Available at Co-op Superstores.

Lost Pampas Oak-aged Chardonnay 1997, Co-op 13.5 C

Martins Chardonnay 1997 14.5 C

Rich, plump, ripe and delightfully fruitily textured and highly drinkable. Superstores only.

Mission Peak Argentine White NV 14.5 B

AUSTRALIAN WINE RED

Australian Cabernet Sauvignon 1995, Co-op 12.5 C

Juicy fruit.

Australian Red, Co-op 12 B

Baileys Shiraz 1995 15 D

Improving nicely in bottle. The maker understands tannin and the character it can bequeath to wine. Superstores only.

Barramundi Shiraz/Merlot 14 C

Hardys Cabernet Shiraz Merlot 1995 14.5 D

Rich and ripe and the tannins have not been allowed to escape the fruit, as in the Aussie habit, and some bite is present. Available at Co-op Superstores.

Hunter Cellars Night Harvest Red 1996 12 C

So juicy, they ought to maybe try picking during the day – they might, then, pick the less overripe grapes. Superstores only.

Jacaranda Hill Grenache 1996, Co-op 14.5 C

Jacaranda Hill Shiraz 1997, Co-op 13 C

Juice in the bottle, juice on the palate. Where is the character?

Kasbah Shiraz/Malbec/Mourvedre 1993 13 C

Kingston Shiraz/Mataro 1996 13 C

Leasingham Domaine Cabernet Malbec 1993 15 E

Lindemans Bin 45 Cabernet Sauvignon 1994 14.5 D

Night Harvest Hunters Cellars Bin 31 1996 13.5 C

Fruity, juicy and very ripe. For the nervous sipper of wine rather than full throated gluggers. Available at Co-op Superstores.

Oxford Landing Cabernet Shiraz 1996 13 C

Thomas Mitchell Shiraz 1996 14 C

Juice but at least it's juice with attitude – even if it's an old softie at heart.

Woodstock Grenache 1995 13 D

AUSTRALIAN WINE WHITE

Australian Chardonnay 1997, Co-op 15.5 C

One of the best own-label Aussie chardonnays around. The playfulness of the label belies the seriously beautiful and stylish texture of the rich, complex fruit.

Australian White, Co-op 14 B

Best's Late Harvest Muscat 1995 14.5 D

Butterfly Ridge Sauvignon Blanc/Chenin Blanc 1996 14 C

Hardys Chardonnay Sauvignon Blanc 1997 15.5 D

Great texture and controlled ripeness here. Terrific marriage of wit and muscle. Available at Co-op Superstores.

Houghton Wildflower Ridge Chardonnay 1996 14 D

Touch of the exotic on the edge is controlled beneath the surge of melony fruit. Superstores only.

Jacaranda Hill Chenin Verdelho 1996, Co-op 14 C

Leasingham Domaine Semillon 1993 16 D

Lindemans Bin 65 Chardonnay 1997 16.5 C

Brilliant value: rich, gently spicy (an echo really) to ripe fruit, and a great balance. The '97 is back to being the best under £5 Aussie white around – or one of them, certainly.

Oxford Landing Sauvignon Blanc 1997 14 C

Hints of clean classiness. Superstores only.

BULGARIAN WINE RED

Domaine Boyar Pomorie Cabernet Merlot NV 15 B

Lovico Suhindol Merlot Reserve 1991 13.5 C

Plovdiv Cabernet Sauvignon Rubin 1996 15.5 B

Light fruit a touch at odds with the brisk tannins but the overall warmth of the wine is very winning. Available at Co-op Superstores.

Rousse Cabernet Sauvignon/Cinsault Country Wine 15 B

The Bulgarian Vintners Sliven Merlot/Pinot Noir 14.5 B

BULGARIAN WINE — WHITE

Preslav Barrel-fermented Chardonnay 1995 13 B

Preslav Chardonnay/Sauvignon Blanc 1996 13.5 B

Perfectly respectable. Not exciting or unexpected, but drinkable.

CHILEAN WINE — RED

Alma Terra Mater Zinfandel Shiraz 1997 14 C

Frolicsome fruit here.

Casa Lapostolle Cabernet Sauvignon 1995 14.5 D

Rich and rampant but hugely well controlled, dry and classy. Superstores only.

Chilean Cabernet Sauvignon, Curico Valley, Co-op 15.5 C

Four Rivers Cabernet Sauvignon 1997 15.5 C

The serious left-banker's everyday glugging cabernet and three star Michelin restaurant house cabernet.

La Fortuna Malbec 1996 15 C

La Palma Cabernet Sauvignon, Rapel 1996 15.5 C

Quiet but deadly effective: dry, rich, stylish.

La Palma Merlot Reserve 1996

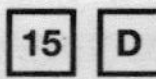

Good leathery overtones, soft and mature, with a rich texture. Very classy and poised. Available at Co-op Superstores.

La Palma Reserve Cabernet Sauvignon/ Merlot, Rapel 1996

A real Chilean food wine: rich, dry, fully formed and throaty.

Long Slim Cabernet Merlot 1997

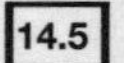 

Has charm and delicate richness with a hint of leather.

Tierra del Rey Chilean Red NV

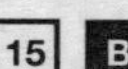 

Valdivieso Cabernet Franc Reserve 1996

A beautifully composed wine, rather Debussy-like in its seeming surreal edge but in fact gorgeously coloured, tonal, rich, multi-faceted and intensely lingering. A fine wine. Available at Co-op Superstores.

CHILEAN WINE — WHITE

Carmen Chardonnay Semillon 1995

It's the lilt on the finish which makes the biggest, lingering impact. The fruit is a triumph of warmth, generosity and charm. Available at Co-op Superstores.

Four Rivers Chardonnay 1997

Brilliance of tone, fingering, power and musicality. Great.

Tierra del Rey Chilean White NV 15.5 B

Tocornal Chardonnay 1997 13.5 C

Begins rather wanly, then picks up pace – but will it develop over the next six months?

Vina Casablanca Chardonnay Sauvignon Blanc 1997 16.5 D

Has zip and vigour, serious depth, rich lingering fruit, a beautiful turn of litheness as it slides down the throat, and its overall confidence is world class. Available at Co-op Superstores.

Vina Casablanca Sauvignon Blanc 1996 15.5 C

CYPRIOT WINE RED

Island Vines Red Wine 1997, Co-op 13 B

Soft, a touch flabby, but not entirely bereft of charm. But it is of the precocious rather than the properly developed kind.

CYPRIOT WINE WHITE

Island Vines White Wine 1997, Co-op 13.5 B

Fruity fun for fish and chips.

ENGLISH WINE — WHITE

Dart Valley Madeleine Angevin, Oak Aged, 1996, Co-op 11 C

Superstores only.

Summerhill Dry White NV 11 C

Superstores only.

FRENCH WINE — RED

Bad Tempered Cyril Tempranillo/Syrah NV 14 C

Beaujolais Villages, Domaine Granjean 1996 12 C

Available at Co-op Superstores.

Bergerac Rouge, Co-op 12 B

Cabernet Sauvignon VdP d'Oc, Co-op 13 B

Cahors, Co-op 12 C

Chateau Cissac 1988 12 F

Dull for the money. Available at Co-op Superstores.

Chateau Laurencon, Bordeaux Superior 1996 13.5 C

Mild mannered claret. Almost servile. Available at Co-op Superstores.

Chevaliere Vieilles Vignes Grenache 1996 13.5 C

Soft and juicy. Superstores only.

Claret Bordeaux, Co-op 15 C

The sere leaf colour of the label doesn't help the image of this delicious little claret which is mature, yes, but far from detached and sapless. The fruit and tannins are in perfect control.

Cotes de Beaune Villages Jules Vignon 1995 10 D

Cotes du Luberon, Co-op 11 B

Cotes du Rhone, Co-op 13 B

Cotes du Ventoux, Co-op 14 B

Domaine de Hauterive, Cotes du Rhone Villages 1996 14 C

A soft, lushly agreeable Rhone, not especially typical, but extremely difficult to dislike. Available at Co-op Superstores.

Domaine des Salices Merlot VdP d'Oc 1996 14 C

Delicious *fruit-brulee* aroma, toasty and rich, but the fruit isn't so fiery, being soft and gentle.

Fitou, Co-op 13.5 C

Some rough-edged charm here.

La Baume Cabernet Sauvignon 1995 14 C

Soft, only gently tannic, and fruity without feeling full.

La Ferme d'Angludet, Margaux 1994 13.5 E

A curious muted finish, which though it has tannin, seems anodyne rather than gently charming. Available at Co-op Superstores.

Les Celliers des Princes, Chateauneuf-du-Pape 1996 16 E

A beautifully aromatic, ripe C-de-P with a twinkle in its eye – an unusually warm, avuncular and humorous wine of great charm.

Merlot VdP d'Oc, Co-op 14 B

Minervois, Co-op 13 B

Moulin a Vent Pierre Leduc 1995 13 D

Oak-Aged Claret, Co-op 13.5 C

Pommard, Pierre Leduc 1994 10 F

Rivers Meet Cabernet Merlot, Bordeaux 1996 13.5 C

Eminently drinkable if not vastly thrilling. Superstores only.

St Chinian Berloup Royale 1996 13.5 C

Some ripeness and near-opulence here.

Vacqueyras, Cuvee du Marquis de Fonseguille 1996 15.5 D

Warm and rich, soft and full of textured fruit, with a nice layer of undertonal tannin. A soft, lushly agreeable Rhone, not especially typical, but extremely difficult to dislike. Available at Co-op Superstores.

Vin de Pays d'Oc Cabernet Merlot 14 C

Vin de Pays d'Oc Syrah/Malbec, Co-op (vegetarian) 13.5 C

Odd charred finish, but very chewy and well-fleshed-out. Not heavy in alcohol.

Vin de Pays de l'Aude, Co-op 10 B

Vin de Pays de l'Herault Rouge, Co-op 14 B

Vin de Table Red, Co-op (1-litre) 13 C

Price bracket has been adjusted to show bottle equivalent.

FRENCH WINE WHITE

Alsace Gewurztraminer 1996 16 D

Brilliant richness, like crushed rose petals and some kind of plant oil, with a plumpness and ripeness tempered by freshness. Lovely.

Bergerac Blanc, Co-op 11 B

Blanc de Blancs Dry White, Co-op 8 B

Indescribably naff.

Bordeaux Sauvignon Blanc, Co-op 13 B

Worthy rather than wonderful but fun with fish and chips.

Chardonnay VdP du Jardin de la France 1996 14 B

Almost an oily texture here and the fruit is warm and well balanced. Finished with some aplomb. Available at Co-op Superstores.

Fair Martina Vermentino NV 14.5 C

Fleur du Moulin Chardonnay VdP d'Oc 1996 12.5 C

La Baume Chardonnay 1996 13.5 C

Disappoints a bit on the finish, for a fiver bottle.

Macon Villages, Cave de Vire 1996 12 C

Superstores only.

Meursault, Jules Vignon 1994 10 G

Superstores only.

Monbazillac Domaine du Haut-Rauly 1995 (half bottle) 14.5 C

A delightful pudding wine, waxy and honeyed, but with a fresher touch than is normal. Good with fresh fruit at the end of a meal. Available at Co-op Superstores.

Premieres Cotes de Bordeaux, Co-op 13 C

Printemps Touraine Sauvignon 1996 13 B

Hints of grass – rather ragged edge.

Rose d'Anjou, Co-op 13.5 B

VdP d'Oc Sauvignon Blanc NV, Co-op 14 C

Real charm here, crisp and clean.

Vin de Pays d'Oc Chardonnay NV, Co-op 13.5 C

Finishes lemony. Some charm here (wish it were a quid cheaper, though).

Vin de Pays de l'Herault Blush 10 C

Vin de Pays de Vaucluse Chardonnay Viognier NV 14 C

Good value fish-food glugging.

Vin de Pays des Cotes de Gascogne, Co-op 13.5 B

Vin de Pays des Cotes des Pyrenees Orientales, Co-op 14 B

Vin de Pays Sauvignon Blanc, Co-op 12 C

Far too expensive for the style.

GERMAN WINE WHITE

4 Rs 1996, Co-op 12 B

Bad Bergzaberner Kloster Liebfrauenberg Auslese 1994 15 C

Forster Schnepfenflug Riesling Kabinett 1995 12 C

Hock Deutscher Tafelwein, Co-op 8 B

So thin it would blow away in a mild breeze.

Liebfraumilch, Co-op 10 B

Sweet nothing.

Lone Wolf Vineyards, Wolfenweiler, Baden 1996 11 C

Morio Muskat, Co-op 12.5 B

Mosel Deutscher Tafelwein, Co-op 10 B

Hell would be to have to taste a line-up of 100 wines (soi-disant) like this one.

Muller Thurgau, Co-op 10 B

Ockfener Bockstein Riesling Kabinett von Kesselstatt 1995 15.5 D

Classic Moselle richness of fruit plus crisp, mineral acidity.

Ockfener Bockstein Riesling von Kesselstatt 1996 14 D

Needs a few more years to add two or three points. But even so, its class is evident if not all its complex minerality.

Oppenheimer Krotenbrunnen 1996, Co-op 10 B

I refuse to believe it benefits anyone to spend hard earned money on wines which taste like Evian with sugar dissolved in it.

HUNGARIAN WINE — RED

Chapel Hill Cabernet Sauvignon NV 13.5 B

Charming cheapie. Cherry and cheery fruit, good chilled. Available at Co-op Superstores.

Hungarian Red, Co-op 13 B

HUNGARIAN WINE — WHITE

Chapel Hill Irsai Oliver NV 13.5 B

Good aperitif. Available at Co-op Superstores.

Hungarian White, Co-op 14.5 B

Excellent citric qualities for fish suppers.

Hungaroo Pinot Gris 1996 13.5 C

An aperitif of charm and citricity.

Hungaroo Sauvignon Blanc 1995 14 C

ITALIAN WINE RED

Bardolino Le Canne, Boscaini 1995 13.5 C

Barolo Terre del Barolo 1993 13.5 E

Barolo with bounce and flounce and light tannins – but a high price. Available at Co-op Superstores.

Merlot del Veneto, Co-op 12.5 C

Principato Rosso, Co-op 12 B

Sicilian Red, Co-op 12 B

Torresolada Sicilian Red 1995 13 B

Valpolicella, Co-op 13 B

Valpolicella Marano, Boscaini 1995 12 C

Villa Mantinera, Montepulciano de Molise NV 14 C

Vino da Tavola Rosso NV, Co-op 10 B

ITALIAN WINE — WHITE

Alasia Chardonnay del Piemonte 1995 14 C

Bianco di Custoza Vignagrande 1997 13.5 C

Prickly fruit. Available at Co-op Superstores.

Chardonnay Atesino, Co-op 11.5 C

Le Terracce Tuscan White, Cecchi 1996 12 C

Superstores only.

Monferrato Araldica 1996 14 C

Good fish wine with its crisp, clean fruit. Available at Co-op Superstores.

Orvieto Secco, Co-op 11 C

Principato Valdadige 1995 12 B

Puglian White NV 12 C

Superstores only.

Sicilian White, Co-op 13 B

Good with fish and chips (and heavy on the mushy peas).

Soave, Co-op 12 B

Soave Monteleone, Boscaini 1996 14 C

Terre dei Foschi Chardonnay & Garganega, Arcadia 1996 13 C

Superstores only.

Torresolada Bianco di Sicilia 1995 14.5 B

Vino da Tavola Bianco NV, Co-op 11 B

MEXICAN WINE RED

L A Cetto Petite Syrah 1993 14 C

MEXICAN WINE WHITE

Casa Madero 400 Chardonnay 1996 

Very rich and creamy with a hint of smoke to the woody, melony fruit. Impressive perfume and texture. Rather rampant in its own way.

MOROCCAN WINE RED

Moroccan Cabernet Sauvignon/Syrah 1995 15 B

NEW ZEALAND WINE — RED

Terrace View Cabernet Merlot 1995 13 C

NEW ZEALAND WINE — WHITE

Explorer's Vineyard Sauvignon Blanc 1996, Co-op 12 D

Grove Mill Chardonnay 1995 12 E

Terrace View Sauvignon Blanc 1996 12 C

Somewhat ragged but good with food.

PORTUGUESE WINE — RED

Portada Tinto 1995 16 C

Great value here. An aromatic, gorgeously soft, rich, ripe wine with a walloping fruity finish.

Portuguese Dao 1996, Co-op 13.5 C

Has some brightly fruity charm.

Star Mountain Oak Aged 1994 12 C

Vila Santa 1996 15.5 D

Delicious dry characterfulness and wry richness. Seriously good with food. Superstores only.

PORTUGUESE WINE WHITE

Campos dos Frades Chardonnay 1995 14 C

Portuguese Rose, Co-op 10 B

Bland and blossomless.

Vinho Verde, Co-op 12 B

ROMANIAN WINE RED

River Route Merlot 1995 16 B

Romanian Prairie Merlot 1997, Co-op 14 B

Dry and very cheerful and, as the monster on the label implies, it quickly reaches the pit of the stomach and suffuses warmly.

Sahateni Barrel Matured Merlot 1995 14 C

Plummy dryness and food compatibility.

SOUTH AFRICAN WINE RED

Cape Indaba Merlot 1996 14 C

Cape Red, Co-op 14.5 B

Elephant Trail Cinsault/Merlot 1997, Co-op 13.5 C

Rich, adolescent, plumpish.

Jacana Cabernet Sauvignon 1996 16 C

Rich, perfumed, gorgeously textured, rampant but not wild, elegant yet not simpering or reluctant. A terrific, forward wine of great class.

Jacana Merlot 1995 16.5 D

Oak Village Cabernet Sauvignon 1996 15.5 C

A deliciously herbal, vegetal (peppers and peas with a hint of cauliflower) and rich, baked, fruity edginess here. A warm, giving cabernet of some class.

SOUTH AFRICAN WINE WHITE

Cape Afrika Rhine Riesling 1996 14 C

Cape Indaba Chardonnay 1996 12 C

Superstores only.

Cape White, Co-op 12.5 B

Elephant River Colombard Chardonnay 1997, Co-op 12 B

Fairview Chardonnay 1996 15 D

Always one of the Cape's most quality driven producers, here turning chardonnay into a warm, full, richly textured, gently vanillary, melony wine of great charm. Available at Co-op Superstores.

Goudini Chardonnay 1996 15 C

Long Mountain Semillon Chardonnay 1997 12.5 C

Longridge Chardonnay 1996 10 E

Neethlingshof Gewurztraminer 1996 12 D

Superstores only.

SPANISH WINE RED

Berberana Tempranillo Rioja 1996 15.5 C

Delicious polish to the fruit here which has a gorgeous, dry coating. A lovely glug for the book worm. A witty companion for food.

Campo Rojo, Carinena 14 B

Marino Tinto NV 14 B

Palacio de la Vega Cabernet Sauvignon Reserva 1993 14 E

Rioja Tinto NV, Co-op 16 C

Spanish Pyrenees Tempranillo Cabernet 1996, Co-op 14 C

Juicy, but it has character to it as well. A warm, welcoming wine.

Spanish Red NV, Co-op 10 B

Dullsville. Will only give screw-capped wines a bad reputation.

Tempranillo Oak-Aged, Co-op 13.5 B

SPANISH WINE WHITE

Albacora Verdejo/Chardonnay 1996 14 C

Superstores only.

Berberana Carta de Oro 1995 13 C

Castillo de Monjardin Chardonnay 1995 14.5 C

Santara Chardonnay 1996 16 C

Plumply textured, rich, and firm on the palate, this has huge class and charming manners.

Spanish Dry NV, Co-op 10 B

Oh my God! Reminds me of 1975!

Spanish Pyrenees Chardonnay 1996, Co-op 11 C

USA WINE RED

California Red, Co-op 13.5 B

Gallo Ruby Cabernet 1996 14 C

Not at all bad considering the address of the grape. A soft, ripe wine with some character and likeability.

Gallo Sonoma Cabernet Sauvignon 1992 15 E

Redwood Trail Pinot Noir 1996 14.5 D

Excellent, if slightly sulphurous, on first opening, but the texture and ripeness and sheer class of pinot are obvious. Available at Co-op Superstores.

USA WINE WHITE

Arbor Crest Chardonnay 1995 14 E

California Colombard, Co-op 13 B

Glen Ellen Proprietor's Reserve Chardonnay 1995 16 C

Stowells of Chelsea California Blush (3-litre box) 12.5 B

Price bracket has been adjusted to show bottle equivalent.

SPARKLING WINE/CHAMPAGNE

Freixenet Cordon Negro NV (Spain) 13 D

This is packaged like some over-tanned monstrosity from the Marbella beaches with a dark hairy chest bestrewn with gold medallia. The wine inside is overrich and fleshy too, but rather better with smoked salmon than on its own.

Barramundi Sparkling (Australia) 15.5 D

Brown Bros Pinot Noir/Chardonnay NV 14.5 E

Marino Cava del Mediterraneo 16.5 C

Moscato Spumante, Co-op 14.5 C

Silver Ridge Sparkling Chardonnay Riesling NV 13.5 D

Touch of fruit on the finish gives it some immature attractiveness. Available at Co-op Superstores.

ARGENTINIAN WINE RED

Bright Bros Cabernet/Malbec NV 14 C

Real tannins and richness here. Hangs together well.

Etchart Rio de Plata Malbec 1995 11 C

Picaflor Malbec/Tempranillo 1997 15 C

Valle de Vistalba Cabernet Sauvignon 1994 14 C

ARGENTINIAN WINE WHITE

Bright Bros Sauvignon Blanc NV 13 C

Etchart Rio de Plata Torrontes 1997 13 C

A muscat-like aperitif wine of dry fruitiness.

AUSTRALIAN WINE RED

Australian Dry Red Wine (3-litre box) 14 B

Price bracket has been adjusted to reflect the cost for a single bottle.

Duck's Flat Dry Red Wine 5 C

Hardys Nottage Hill Cabernet Sauvignon/ Shiraz 1996 15 C

Elegant, rich, aromatic, balanced, most compellingly well priced, and more stylish than other vintages of the same brand.

Kingston Murray Valley Grenache 1997 12 C

Lindemans Cawarra Dry Red 12.5 C

McWilliams Hanwood Cabernet 1996 10 D

Come on, you can do better than this for a fiver and more.

Rosemount Estate Shiraz/Cabernet 1997 14.5 C

Got a bit of oomph and style to the finish – which is soft, rich, savoury.

AUSTRALIAN WINE WHITE

Best's Victoria Colombard 1997 15.5 D

Duck's Flat Dry White 10 C

Hardys Nottage Hill Chardonnay 1997 16.5 C

Fantastic oily/buttery texture, ripe fruit, just terrific.

Jacobs Creek Dry Riesling 1997 14 C

A genuinely dryly rich riesling for oriental food.

Jacobs Creek Semillon/Chardonnay 1997 14 C

Old Aussie warhorse, still soldiering on.

Lindemans Bin 65 Chardonnay 1997 

C

Brilliant value: rich, gently spicy (an echo really) to ripe fruit, and a great balance. The '97 is back to being the best under £5 Aussie white around – or one of them, certainly. Still, by the time this book comes out the '98 may be replacing this vintage on shelf (I haven't had a chance to try the '98 yet).

Lindemans Botrytis Riesling 1996 (half bottle) 16.5 D

Gorgeous richness of honeydew melon saturated with waxy honey and pineapple. A hugely sweet, tart white wine of style and great longevity. It will develop in bottle for twenty years.

Lindemans Semillon Chardonnay 1997 

Lovely ripe texture, touch of exoticism about the fruit (hint of mango), and a terrific, gushingly fresh finish. A wine to savour and to enjoy with food.

Lindemans Unoaked Cawarra Chardonnay 1997 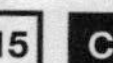

Shows the impressive richness and balance of Aussie's fruit unadulterated by wood. Delicious flavours here.

Normans Unwooded Chardonnay 1997 14.5 D

Rather austere but friendly with food.

Oxford Landing Sauvignon Blanc 1997 14 C

Hints of clean classiness.

Penfolds Bin 202 Riesling 1997 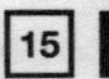

A crisp, clean, rather elegant wine for fish dishes which the cook has taken some trouble to prepare.

Penfolds Rawsons Retreat Bin 21 Semillon/Chardonnay/Colombard 1997 15 C

The gorgeously rich '97 vintage strikes the palate with polish, purpose and plumpness.

Rosemount Estate Semillon/Chardonnay 1997 15 D

Elegant and worldly. Serve it with grilled white fish.

BULGARIAN WINE RED

Hidden Valley Cabernet 1994 13 C

Sheer juice, dry but still juice.

Merlot/Pinot Noir Country Wine, Sliven 12 B

Oriachovitza Cabernet Sauvignon Reserve 1994 14.5 C

Good value tippling with a hint of cherry/blackcurrant ripeness peeking through the dryness. Has character and style.

BULGARIAN WINE WHITE

Aligote & Muskat Rousse Country White 10 B

CHILEAN WINE RED

Casa Porta Cabernet Sauvignon 1996 16 C

The rich fruit has a black, mysterious, almost charcoal edge to it (tannins). It's lovely.

Chilean Red NV, Co-operative 12 B

Cono Sur Cabernet Sauvignon Reserve 1995 14.5 D

Cono Sur Pinot Noir 1997 13 C

Valdezaro Cabernet Sauvignon 1996 12 C

Vistasur Merlot 1997 13.5 C

Some substance to the fruit and texture here. If only more under-a-fiver reds at this retailer exhibited such pizzazz!

CHILEAN WINE WHITE

Casa Porta Chardonnay 1997 15.5 C

Real elegance, style, richness, multi-layered fruitiness and sheer gusto. A joyous wine of vivacity yet finesse.

Chilean White NV, Co-operative 11 B

Santa Rita Cabernet Rose 1997 15 C

Super rose. Has balance, fruit, richness, freshness and sheer style. Great stuff. Puts rose on a new level of serious depth.

Valdezaro Sauvignon Blanc 1996 15 C

Vistasur Sauvignon Blanc 1997 14.5 C

Very dry and rich, with a tastebud-enveloping texture.

ENGLISH WINE WHITE

Chapel Down Summerhill Oaked White 12 C

Summerhill Dry White 11 C

FRENCH WINE RED

Beaujolais, Caves de la Reine Blanche 1997 11 C

Beaujolais Villages 1997 12 D

Bourgogne Rouge 1996 10 C

Cabernet Sauvignon VdP d'Oc, Co-operative 13 B

Chateau Cissac 1986 11 F

Chateau Gallion Bordeaux Rouge 1997 13.5 C

Chateau Mon Plaisir, Bordeaux 1996 13 C

Claret NV, Co-operative 14 B

Seriously dry and characterful and needs a lamb chop.

Corbieres NV, Co-operative 14.5 B

Character, dryness, earthiness, and some hint of hedgerow fruit. What more does the average plate of sausages call for?

Coteaux du Languedoc Les Caves St Romain 1995 13 B

Cotes du Rhone Louis Yerard 1996 12 B

Cotes du Rhone Villages du Peloux 1996 13 C

Domaine de Sarran-Fabre Faugeres 1996 15.5 C

A secret bargain here uncovered! This is a deep, rich, tobacco-y, dry wine. Sodden with herbs and Midi warmth, and wonderful with food. Has character without cost.

Domaine Sette Piana, VdP de l'Ile de Beaute 10 B

Gigondas Domaine de Mourielle 1995 14 D

Merlot VdP d'Oc, Co-operative 11 B

Minervois 1995, Co-operative 12 B

Rhone Valley VdP de Vaucluse Red NV 11 B

Scaramouche Cabernet 1996 13.5 C

A minor claret (in style).

Scaramouche Merlot 1996 15 C

New World in its chewy-fruit raunchiness and in its candiness of fruit. Great texture and ripeness.

Scaramouche Syrah 1996 12 C

VdP de l'Aude Rouge, Co-operative 10 B

Vin de Table de France Rouge 13.5 B

FRENCH WINE WHITE

Bourgogne Chardonnay 1997 14 D

A decent enough white burgundy with a very engaging, gently creamy texture.

Chateau Gallion Bordeaux White 1997 15.5 C

Classy hints of elegant melon ripeness with a hard edge of attendant acidity. Impressive style here for the money.

Chenin Blanc 'Les Fleurs', VdP du Jardin de la France 10 B

Cuckoo Hill Barrel Fermented Chardonnay 1996 11 C

Ludicrous price for such straightforward fruit.

Cuckoo Hill Cabernet Sauvignon Rose 1996 13 C

Pleasant little warm-weather tipple.

James Herrick Chardonnay 1996 15 C

Good age for a wine not designed to grow old with any great grace. Here it's perfectly mature, melony and lemony and strikes home with style.

Rhone Valley VdP de Vaucluse White NV 

Has a lovely plump texture, a ripe edge, and a crisp finish. Fantastic value for money.

Rougir VdP Syrah Rose 1996 

Sauvignon Saint Vincent Baron 1997 

Excellent whiplash clean fruit. Really fresh and cheeky. Yet, with food, a serious companion.

Scaramouche Chardonnay d'Oc 1997 

Curious lettuce-crisp and nettle-fresh wine with a hint of vegetality. Very crisp and clean, as implied by the lettuce, but the floral hints are nicely engaging and provoking.

VdP de l'Aude Les Gisconds NV, Co-operative 

A fantastic bargain. Not complex or big, but thoroughly decent and cleanly fruity.

Vin de Table de France Sec 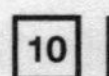

GERMAN WINE WHITE

Wine	Rating	Price
Binger St Rochuskapelle Kabinett, Langenbach 1995	13.5	B
Carl Reh Bereich Bernkastel	11	B
Kenderman Riesling 1997	12	C
Weinberg Hock	9	B

GREEK WINE RED

Mavrodaphne of Patras NV 14 C

Brilliant with a slice of rich fruit cake.

HUNGARIAN WINE WHITE

Eagle Mountain Pinot Grigio NV 13 B

ITALIAN WINE RED

Wine	Rating	Price
Barbera Oltrepo Pavese NV	11	C
Chianti Tenuta del Poggio 1995	10	B

Colli Perugini Rosso NV 12 C

Donelli Merlot del Veneto NV 10 B

La Sorte Bardolino 1997 10 C

Notarpanaro Rosso del Salento 1993 13 D

Oaked Valpolicella 1997 10 C

Rialto Lambrusco Rosso dell'Emilia 13.5 B

Sicilian Rosso 13 B

ITALIAN WINE WHITE

Oaked Soave 1997 12 C

Somewhat dull for four quid.

MALTESE WINE RED

Paradise Bay Maltese Red 1996 15 C

MALTESE WINE WHITE

Anchor Bay Maltese Rose 1996 13.5 C

Some decency here: soft fruit relieved by brisk acidity.

St Paul's Bay Maltese White 1996 14 C

MEXICAN WINE RED

Cortesa Cabernet/Malbec 1995 13 C

MOROCCAN WINE RED

Moroccan Cabernet/Syrah 15 B

Moroccan Red 14 B

NEW ZEALAND WINE RED

Delegat's Hawkes Bay Cabernet Merlot 1996 13 D

Unusually juicy with a hint of earth.

Timara Cabernet/Merlot 1995 13.5 C

Waimanu Dry Red 1996 10 C

Sheer juice.

NEW ZEALAND WINE WHITE

Cooks Gisborne Chardonnay 1997 13 D

Marlborough Gold Sauvignon Blanc 1997 15 C

Hints of rich grass with a full-throated texture of taste-bud-coating tenacity.

Montana Reserve Chardonnay 1997 14.5 E

Classy, grassy, rich, confident, voluptuous.

Montana Reserve Sauvignon 1997 15 E

Very elegant and relaxed wine, with touches of arboreally scented and flavoured fruit. A wine to serve with a chicken that's really special (i.e. farmyardy – a bit like the wine).

Villa Maria Private Bin Chardonnay, Marlborough 1997 14 D

Young (and it will improve) but very rich and ready to provide lingering fruity pleasures.

Villa Maria Private Bin Sauvignon Blanc, Marlborough 1997 16.5 D

Classic Marlborough concentration here: gooseberries, grass, melon, lime. Beautiful fruit, lithe, balanced, incisive.

Waimanu Muller Thurgau/Sauvignon 1996 12 C

Not convincing as a wine or as a Kiwi. Unless, I suppose you take into account the absurdity of a flightless bird. This wine, then, is a perfect Kiwi. It doesn't quite get off the ground.

PORTUGUESE WINE — RED

Bright Brothers 'Old Vines' Estramadura 1995 13.5 C

Portico Dao NV 12 C

Vila Regia Douro NV 13.5 C

Dry, very dry. Cleans out the molars like mouthwash.

PORTUGUESE WINE — WHITE

Fiuza Sauvignon Blanc 1996 16 C

ROMANIAN WINE — RED

Classic Cabernet Sauvignon, Dealul Mare 1991 13.5 B

Classic Romanian Pinot Noir 1994 14 B

Good pinot colour and even a sticky texture, but aromatically reluctant and rather uninspired to finish.

River Route Cabernet/Merlot 1997 13.5 B

Dry yet juicy.

River Route Merlot 1996 (3-litre box) 13.5 B

Price bracket has been adjusted to reflect the cost for a single bottle.

ROMANIAN WINE WHITE

Classic Sauvignon Blanc 1996 11 B

River Route Pinot Grigio 1997 13 B

Bit murky and stickily fruity.

Romanian Classic Gewurztraminer 1996 15.5 B

Terrific richness and oily textured fruit. Fantastic value for Peking duck and plum sauce. What a takeaway-feast opportunity this wine offers!

SLOVENIAN WINE RED

Dragonja Merlot 1994 11 B

SOUTH AFRICAN WINE RED

Bovlei Merlot 1995 12.5 C

Bovlei Shiraz 1995 12 C

Cape Cinsault/Ruby Cabernet (3-litre box) 13.5 B

Price bracket has been adjusted to reflect the cost for a single bottle.

Cape Red NV, Co-operative 9 B

Landskroon Pinotage 1996 13.5 C

Long Mountain Cabernet Sauvignon 1996 12 C

Sandbrook Cinsaut/Merlot 1998 10 C

SOUTH AFRICAN WINE WHITE

Cape Chenin Blanc NV, Co-operative 12 B

Kumala Chenin Blanc/Chardonnay 1997 13 C

Namaqua Classic Dry White (3-litre box) 13.5 B

Price bracket has been adjusted to reflect the cost for a single bottle.

Sandbrook Sauvignon Blanc 1998 11 C

Dull – a touch.

Van Loveren Spes Bona Chardonnay 1998 12 C

Bit overripe for me.

SOUTH AMERICAN WINE — RED

Two Tribes Red NV (Chile/Argentina) 13.5 C

SOUTH AMERICAN WINE — WHITE

Two Tribes White NV (Chile/Argentina) 13.5 C

Two tribes which can't quite agree. Should be a quid cheaper.

SPANISH WINE — RED

40.40.20 Navarra 1996 12 B

Alta Oaked Tempranillo 13.5 B

Bright Bros Old Vines Garnacha 1995 12 C

Campillo Rioja Crianza 1995 14 D

Elegant, rich, ripe, plump and a touch self-satisfied. Good with Christmas turkey and stuffing though. Like gravy for it, in truth.

Campo Rojo, Carinena 14 B

Castillo de Liria Valencia, Gandia 13.5 B

Gandia Hoya de Cadenas Reserva, Utiel-Requena 1989 15 C

Gandia Hoya Valley Cabernet Sauvignon, Utiel Requena 1994 13.5 B

Gandia Hoya Valley Merlot NV 13.5 B

Gandia Hoya Valley Tempranillo 1992 12.5 B

La Mancha, Co-operative 13.5 B

Vina Albali Cabernet 1993 14 C

Strictly for chicken and chorizo casserole. The wine is ripe, very dry, vanillary and opinionated. It needs the counter-argument of rich, ripe food.

Vina Albali Reserva 1989 15 C

Vina Azabache Garnacha 1997 11 B

SPANISH WINE WHITE

Alta Oaked White 14 B

Castillo de Liria Moscatel de Valencia 16 C

Vinas del Vero Barrel Fermented Chardonnay, Somontano 1995 16 D

URUGUAYAN WINE RED

Castel Pujol Tannat 1995 13.5 C

Bit sulphurous as it tickles the nose but the flavour of the fruit is full and ripe.

URUGUAYAN WINE WHITE

Castel Pujol Chardonnay 1996 13.5 C

USA WINE RED

Blossom Hill Californian Red 13 C

E & J Gallo Ruby Cabernet 1996 14 C

Not at all bad considering the address of the grape. A soft, ripe wine with some character and likeability.

E & J Gallo Turning Leaf Merlot 1996 12 D

Gallo Sonoma Cabernet Sauvignon 1992 15 E

Sterling Redwood Trail Pinot Noir 1996 14.5 D

Serious pinot aroma and depth with the added bomb of tannin and characterfulness.

Talus Zinfandel 1995 14 D

USA WINE WHITE

Blossom Hill White Zinfandel 1996 10 C

E & J Gallo Colombard 1996 9 C

Sutter Home Chenin Blanc 1995 8 C

Talus Chardonnay 1995 16 D

Gorgeous rich, ripe fruit combining dry, sticky-toffee texture with huge dollops of melon and pear.

FORTIFIED WINE

Delaforce Special White Port 13 E

A rich aperitif for the strong stomached, or to sip after a meal with Brazil nuts.

No 1 Ruby Port, Co-operative 13 D

Rich, hinting at sweetness.

No 1 Tawny Port, Co-operative 12 D

Seems to have lost what tawny represents.

No 1 Vintage Character Port, Co-operative 13 D

SPARKLING WINE/CHAMPAGNE

Blossom Hill Sparkling Brut NV (USA) 11 D

Good for geriatrics whose teeth are not all sweet.

Bouvet Ladubay Saumur NV (France) 14.5 E

Cava Brut NV, Co-operative 15 C

Classic dry bubbly.

Cava Rose NV, Co-operative 14 C

Fun, sheer fun.

Cavalier Blanc de Blancs Brut Vin Mousseux (France) 12 C

Cavalier Demi-sec Vin Mousseux (France) 10 C

Gallo Brut 10 D

Hardys Nottage Hill Bottle-fermented Sparkling Chardonnay 1996 14 D

Elegant yet with hints of ripe fruit.

Saumur Brut, Verdier NV 12 D

Seaview Brut Rose 15 D

KWIK SAVE STORES LIMITED

ANGELA SWALLOWS ANGELA AND DOESN'T GET INDIGESTION!

The past year and a half at this curious retailer (the very name reeks of rationing and the fifties) have been extremely eventful. In June 1997 – and we are talking here of a retailer where £3.99 is a lot of money for a bottle of wine – it introduced bottles retailing at up to eight quid in 70 of its stores following trials at its Northwich, Cheshire store. Previous attempts to break the £5 barrier had not been successful for a retailer which still sells wines at under two quid a bottle (including some 250,000 cases a year of the Les Oliviers French Red and White range). The new more expensive range includes the Gallo Sonoma Country Zinfandel at £7.89, Southcorp's Koonunga Hill Shiraz Cabernet at £6.39, and Penfolds Bin 128 Shiraz at £7.89.

In sultry August last year, Kwik Save's staff got uppity too. The union USDAW criticised the retailer over staff working conditions which it described as 'inhuman'. Stores were, apparently, too hot and staff had to wear nylon overalls and aprons in 91-degree heat. It was also reported that Kwik Save had acted to reduce high staff turnover (employee turnover at the retailer was running at 65% compared with the retail industry norm of 40%). A so-called 'Buddy' scheme was introduced, whereby every employee was allocated another employee as a mentor and there was also an explicit commitment to NVQ training. It was also reported that 'Exit interviews' were to be given to all employees so as to determine the reasons for jacking it in. I have absolutely no evidence to support the notion that Kwik Save employees leave because they can't stand their mentor. What on earth happened to the idea of management? If you can't bring your problems to a superior, no wonder people feel disgruntled and leave. I was pleased to read, in a copy of *Marriage Guidance Fortnightly*, that after this Buddy scheme had been running several months it had resulted in over two hundred engagements and marriages between employees who previously had not known one another.*

Kwik Save customers also feel attached to the retailer. The retailer introduced a special price guarantee telephone hotline which people can ring if they find products at cheaper prices than Kwik Save's elsewhere on the High Street. They also introduced own label wines and spirits (some thirty years after Tesco first did it with a sherry). The products began making their way into stores late last year, including French wine, beer, Scotch and white rum. At Christmas 1997, Kwik Save's Louis Raymond brand was selling for £7.99. Personally, I think KS's own-label Cava has more charm (especially at several quid less).

But is there to be a Kwik Save any more? Will the Angela (Mount) of Somerfield get to swallow the Angela (Muir) of Kwik Save or will there be a parting of the ways?

The latter wine buyer was never a KS employee anyway, being a wine consultant (of great experience and wide repute).

It is unlikely that this particular Angelic clash weighed in the balance when Margaret Beckett, President of the Board of Trade, cleared the £1.4 billion merger of KS and Somerfield. M. Beckett has gained something of a reputation in the City for not being as free and easy with corporate mergers as her predecessors and I believe she enjoys the leaden-witted nickname of Margaret Blockit.

The future, then, of this retailer is not entirely clear at time of going to press and I am unsure whether it will be still be a

* this is a complete lie. I made it up. Nice thought, though.

separate entry in the 2000 edition of *Superplonk.* Following the merger of KS and Somerfield, the latter's 28 Food Giant stores were re-badged as Kwik Save outlets so it may be things will carry on as before but with Somerfield's wine buying department calling the shots.

Kwik Save Stores Limited
Warren Drive
Prestatyn
Denbighshire LL19 7HU
Tel: 01745 887111
Fax: 01745 882504

ARGENTINIAN WINE RED

Maranon Malbec NV 13 B

Very juicy and ripe.

Maranon Syrah NV 13.5 B

Jammy with a hint of stale stogie.

AUSTRALIAN WINE RED

Barramundi Shiraz Merlot NV 14 C

A richly endowed duo, this blend, combining savouriness with wryness.

Pelican Bay Red NV 14 B

What aplomb here – what soft, dry, rich fruit of charm and character.

Pelican Bay Shiraz Cabernet NV 12.5 C

AUSTRALIAN WINE WHITE

Barramundi Semillon Chardonnay NV 14.5 C

Exuberant fruit, rich and gently toasted. Terrific with poultry.

Lindemans Bin 65 Chardonnay 1997 16.5 C

The most elegant of Aussie chardonnays. Gorgeous, rich, knock-out.

Pelican Bay Dry White NV 13.5 B

Fat little thing. Sits on the tongue and barks.

Pelican Bay Medium Dry White 14 B

Vigour and richness, dryness yet soft fruit – a conundrum it is pleasant to unravel.

BULGARIAN WINE RED

Domaine Boyar Lovico Suhindol Cabernet Sauvignon/Merlot 14.5 B

Domaine Boyar Reserve Gamza 1993 12 B

BULGARIAN WINE WHITE

Domaine Boyar Preslav Chardonnay/ Sauvignon Blanc 1996 16 B

Khan Krum Riesling-Dimiat NV 12 B

CHILEAN WINE RED

35 Sur Cabernet Sauvignon, Lontue 1996 15.5 C

Gorgeous rocky fruit, the patent product of deliciously disembowelled earthy grapes.

Deep Pacific Cabernet/Merlot 1997 15.5 B

Suggests richness and flavour, texture and gently spicy fruit. Fantastic value for money. Utterly compelling value.

CHILEAN WINE WHITE

Sur 35 Chardonnay, Lontue Valley 1997 15 C

Warm, richly inviting fruit with a plump, pillow-down luxuriousness.

White Pacific Sauvignon Blanc/Chardonnay 1997 14.5 B

Engaging softness with a nutty undertone.

ENGLISH WINE WHITE

Denbies 95 13.5 B

FRENCH WINE RED

Cabernet Malbec VdP d'Oc 1997

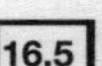

16.5 B

Difficult to believe this isn't the best of Bordeaux of a magical vintage. Stunning richness, warmth, character, food friendliness and sheer textured excellence. One of the UK's best reds for the money.

Cabernet Sauvignon VdP d'Oc 1997

14 B

Real cabernet fruit, hint of vegetal pepper, and something lingering on the finish.

Claret Cuvee V E 1997

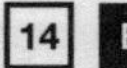

14 B

A classy little claret of typicity and real style. Good food wine.

Corbieres Reserve Gravade 1996

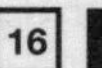

16 B

It is the savouriness, the dryness, the sheer texture of the humid fruit. It's gripping and very stylish indeed.

Cotes du Rhone 1997

13 B

Has some soft charm.

Les Oliviers VdT Francais NV

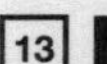

13 A

Very light, dry, basic fruit of rough-house brew. Good-ish chilled.

March Hare VdP d'Oc 1996

16 C

Lovely, the baked richness of the fruit which keeps its ripe elegance and doesn't go soppy, soft or blowsy. Limited distribution.

Minervois Chateau la Reze 1996 15 C

A ripe, rather saucy red of charm and wit. Nicely soft.

Morgon 1997 13.5 C

Not bad. Beaujolais will discover some real cru values in it.

Rivers Meet Merlot/Cabernet, Bordeaux 1997 13.5 C

Good with food if not with mood.

Rouge de France, Selection Cuvee V E 13 B

Skylark Hill Merlot, VdP d'Oc 1997 14.5 B

Bite and backbone, richness and dry plumminess. Terrific vigour and style here.

Skylark Hill Syrah VdP d'Oc 1997 15 B

Plump, dry, handsomely textured and well worth the detour to snap up.

Skylark Hill Very Special Red VdP d'Oc 1997 14 B

Dry, earthy hints of the Midi scrub. Good with food.

St Didier VdP du Tarn 1997 15.5 B

Brilliant value. A brightly plummy, gently earth red of charm and substance. Light but very likeable.

FRENCH WINE WHITE

Blanc de France Vin de Table NV 13.5 B

Soft with a hint of crisp. I wish it were more certain of itself but it does not lack charm.

Bordeaux Sauvignon Cuvee V E 1997 13.5 B

Good grassy touch. Fair fish wine here.

Chablis Domaine de Bouchots Cuvee Boissonneuse 1997 16 D

Beautifully structured fruit. A fatter style of this wine than normal but very incisive and rich. Limited distribution.

Chardonnay en sol Oxfordien, Bourgogne 1997 14.5 C

Terrific little burgundy: modern, fresh, rich, vegetal, complex and ripe. Won't last – so drink it quick (while sipping it slowly). Limited distribution.

Chenin Blanc, VdP du Jardin de la France 1997 13 B

Solid, rather than exciting.

Domaine La Fontaine Marsanne, VdP d'Oc 1997 15 D

Lovely richness and individuality here. Thick and oily (a touch) and very vigorously flavoursome. Limited distribution.

James Herrick Chardonnay VdP d'Oc 1996 15 C

Calm and classy. Perhaps more lemony than previous vintages. Limited distribution.

Les Oliviers VdT Francais NV 12 A

Basic lemon edged fruit.

Muscadet de Sevre et Maine, Les Vergers 1997 13.5 B

Good lemony fruit with a hint of earth.

Rivers Meet Sauvignon/Semillon, Bordeaux 1997 14 C

Crisply turned and well tuned in to modern fish dishes.

Rose de France Selection Cuvee V E 12 B

Skylark Hill Chardonnay VdP d'Oc 1997 13.5 B

Soft and gentle, almost caressing.

Skylark Hill Very Special White, VdP d'Oc 1997 14 B

Good oily texture, subtle, but good news for food and the balance is OK.

St Didier VdP du Tarn 1997 15 B

Gentle but lip smackingly tasty and fruity. New Worldish in feel if not in finish.

Stowells of Chelsea Vin de Pays du Tarn (3-litre box) 14 B

Price bracket has been adjusted to show bottle equivalent.

Wild Trout VdP d'Oc 1997 15 C

Lovely ripe complexity of fruit with some crisp acidic hints. Old world fruit – new world bravura. Limited distribution.

GERMAN WINE — WHITE

Mosel 1997 12 B

Niersteiner Spiegelberg Kabinett, Rheinhessen, 1997 14 B

Chilled in an armchair, the silence of the opened book in one hand, a glass in the other . . .

Palatine Springs Riesling 1997 13.5 B

Reasonable fish wine. Will show some character with fish.

Piesporter Michelsberg, K Linden 1997 12 B

GREEK WINE — RED

Mavrodaphne of Patras NV 14 C

Brilliant with a slice of fruit cake.

GREEK WINE — WHITE

Kourtakis Retsina NV 14 B

HUNGARIAN WINE RED

Chapel Hill Merlot 1997 14 B

Soft, juicy, warm – only vaguely leathery.

HUNGARIAN WINE WHITE

Hungarian Chardonnay, Buda Region 1997 14 B

Not yer big gob of fruit and loud mouth Aussie chardie but your discreet mittel-European lemon fruitiness.

Hungarian Pinot Grigio, Tolna Region 1997 14.5 B

Delicious: has a lingering dry peachiness yet freshness of great charm.

Hungarian Rhine Riesling 1997 13.5 B

Curious, nervous, textured riesling, untypical, strident, ripe – and very amusing.

ITALIAN WINE RED

Gabbia d'Oro VdT Rosso 11 B

Merlot Venezie 1997 14 B

Light cherry/plum fruit best enjoyed chilled.

Montepulciano d'Abruzzo, Venier NV 14 B

It has the uniquely Italian freshness and pizzazz with a juiciness yet dry finishing edge.

Solicella, VdT Umbria NV 15 B

Brilliant earthy fruit with great tannins and a dishy exotic-edged, ripe, dry fruit.

Terra Rossa Sangiovese 1997 16 B

Fantastic ripeness, clammy plums sweating richly all over the tannins, and the result is a gorgeous dry wine of great class.

Valpolicella Venier NV 13 B

Cheerful!

ITALIAN WINE WHITE

Gabbia d'Oro VdT Bianco 13 B

Pinot Grigio/Chardonnay Venezie 1997 15 B

Lots of vanilla and nut flavours with a hint of cream. Terrific fish wine.

Soave Venier NV 13 B

Touch of untypical and friendly warmth here.

Terra Bianca Trebbiano 1997 14 B

Here the texture is good and the plumpness of fruit nicely counterpointed by the acidic minerality.

Villa Pani Frascati Superiore 1997 13 B

Hint of sugar on the edge of the fruit. Oddly untypical.

PORTUGUESE WINE RED

Alta Mesa Estremadura 1996 13 B

Simple fruit juice – with a hint of cafe society.

Falua, Ribatejo 1997 15 B

Gorgeous ripe coating to the brisk, herby fruit. Great texture here.

Vila Regia 1995 15 B

Echoes of woody richness and dryness to the warm fruit. Delicious.

PORTUGUESE WINE WHITE

Falua Ribatejo 1997 13 B

Good food wine and indeed needs the lift of a pork and clam stew.

Rose de Cambriz 13.5 A

SOUTH AFRICAN WINE RED

Harewood Hills Ruby Cabernet/Cinsault 1997 13.5 B

Very light, very drinkable, most un-South African.

Jade Peaks Red NV 12 B

The price band has been adjusted to show the equivalent for a bottle, but in fact I tasted this wine from the bag-in-a-box only and have rated it down. I suspect it's better in bottle. KwikSave need to box cleverer, I reckon.

SOUTH AFRICAN WINE WHITE

Harewood Hills Colombard/Chardonnay 1997 13 B

No better or worse than when I first tasted it.

Jade Peaks White NV 14 B

Still good.

SPANISH WINE RED

d'Avalos Tempranillo 1997 15 B

A most classy wine with its rich earthiness and lingering tannins.

Flamenco Red NV 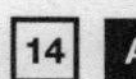

Dances with style on the taste buds.

Los Molinos Tempranillo, Valdepenas 1993 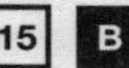

Warmth and texture here of the new world variety, i.e. plumpness and ripeness, cosiness and riproaring fruital (not brutal) attack.

Modernista Tempranillo 1997 

Dark cherry and earthy plum cruising alongside rich, vibrant tannins. Terrific stuff.

Teja Tempranillo Cabernet 1997 

Dry blackberry and a hint of raspberry but mostly twiggy and dry and very good with food.

SPANISH WINE — WHITE

Castillo de Liria Moscatel, Valencia 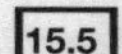

This is just as good as ever – and brilliant with Christmas cake or pudding. Great value here.

Flamenco Medium Dry White NV  

Good rich off-dry fruit of some charm.

Flamenco Sweet White NV 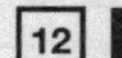

'Tis sweet, but not repulsively so.

USA WINE RED

California Cellars Red 11 B

E & J Gallo Cabernet Sauvignon 1996 10 C

Not a very typical cabernet. Indeed, it defies classification in many ways.

E & J Gallo Ruby Cabernet 1996 14 C

Like its cheekiness and rubber plant fruit. Good chilled.

Paul Masson Carafes 10 B

USA WINE WHITE

California Cellars White 11 B

E & J Gallo Chardonnay 1996 13.5 C

Not a bad stab at chardonnay here, but if only it were £1.50 cheaper . . .

Paul Masson Carafes 10 B

Sutter Home White Zinfandel 1996 10 C

SPARKLING WINE/CHAMPAGNE

Bonnet Brut Hermitage Champagne 13 F

Champagne Brut, Louis Raymond 14 E

Not bad value here. Touch raw, perhaps, but good with smoked fish.

Cristalino Cava Brut 15 C

Nutty, well-flavoured, never coarse but not elegant, this is, *au fond*, terrific tippling for the money.

Lambrusco Bianco '4' 8 A

Lambrusco Rose '4' 6 A

Lambrusco Rosso '4' 8 A

MARKS & SPENCER

CHRIS & JANE – WHICH ONE IS THE MASTER NOW?

M & S has a range of wines which is clichéd in one important respect: it is small but perfectly formed. This applies to the wine buying department as well. Jane Kay (recently passing her Master of Wine exams) and Chris Murphy (who regularly passes the far harder test of being an even-tempered Leeds F.C. supporter) are its sole members.

Expansion is not on the cards. M & S likes its wine department petite, dynamic, well-travelled and very friendly. (It was Mr Murphy who insisted on despatching to me one of the few useful bribes I have received from a retailer this year: two packets of Endekay chewing gum which he insisted was better for my teeth after a wine tasting than my normal habit of brushing my teeth; when I mentioned this to my dentist he was full of praise for this idea, only being surprised to learn that M & S had a wine department anyway).

Perhaps to help remedy this ignorance on the part of highly paid male professionals as to the existence of its wines, and indeed to give the wine department even more to worry about, M & S bought 19 stores from Littlewoods and announced a £2 billion expansion programme. Following the opening of its first store in Cologne, M & S is to open further stores in Germany. The retailer is also looking for a site for its first Australian store. It has also been revealed that the retailer wishes to open airport stores in collaboration with BAA (it already has one store at Jersey Airport). Other plans include the opening of neighbourhood food stores and smaller stores of the sort of size which go up to 800sq ft.

More unusually, and involving metre rather than square feet, M & S hired a poet, Peter Sansom, to give readings and workshops for its employees as part of a scheme being run by the Poetry Society. M & S participated in order to 'bring out employees' creative side'. Mr Sansom is being paid a fee by the retailer, but said all he really wanted was a discount on his favourite lambswool cardigans. I have yet to be invited to a reading of this poet's work but relish the opportunity when it comes (but only if one of M & S's Chilean red wines is also being served up).

M & S deservedly trounced Granada TV in a libel case about allegations made in a *World in Action* programme that the retailer knew of child exploitation at the factory of a supplier in Morocco and had sold clothes made outside the UK where the label said Made in the UK. Having by accident seen this programme (I cannot stand so-called factual 'sensationalist' news programmes), I felt my aversion to this sort of television fully vindicated.

M & S is a highly honourable retailer who, though never cheap, is wedded to the idea of value for money. What is true of the wines is also true of the clothes.

Earlier this year, three opera singers from the Royal Opera House went to M & S at Marble Arch for costumes for the production of *Cosi fan tutte* after Giorgio Armani had been reluctant to alter existing costumes which he had designed for the production. The cost differential was £120 versus £18,000.

It is not reported if the operatic trio also patronised the wine department of this branch. If they had I can assure them they would have found a tastier and cheaper red than the glass of expensive filth I encountered at ROH's bar last time I was persuaded to drink there.

Marks & Spencer
Michael House
57 Baker Street
London W1A 1DN
Tel: 0171 935 4422
Fax: 0171 487 2679

SEE STOP PRESS SECTION AT END OF BOOK FOR LAST-MINUTE ADDITIONS OR UPDATES TO THIS RETAILER'S RANGE.

ARGENTINIAN WINE RED

Merlot Mendoza 1996 16 C

Terrific developed tannins and warm, giving fruit give the wine immense charm. A quiet blockbuster: smooth deep, rich, never overbaked.

Tupungato Merlot/Malbec 1997 15.5 C

ARGENTINIAN WINE WHITE

Chardonnay Mendoza 1997 13.5 C

Mild and a touch reluctant to ooze charm or much fruit. Expensive for the style.

AUSTRALIAN WINE RED

Bin 201 Shiraz/Cabernet 1996 15.5 C

Has spice and all things nice: charm, character, texture, richness and depth. Not a big-muscled wine but nicely lithe and lissom.

Bin 201 Shiraz/Cabernet 1996 16 C

Has the polite cheek of the modern Aussie but with something of the cosmopolitan European. So it is well rounded and characterful.

Cellarmasters Cabernet Sauvignon 1996 15 D

Coonawarra Winegrowers Shiraz 1995 12 E

Honey Tree Shiraz Cabernet, Rosemount Estates 1996 14 D

Soft and soppy, yes, but it's not all doggy with no teeth and claws. Not so much a poodle and not cadaverous as a greyhound – more like a dachshund.

McLean's Farm Shiraz, Barossa 1994 14 E

Ridge Coonawarra Cabernet Sauvignon 1995 13 E

Rose Label Orange Vineyard Cabernet Sauvignon 1993 13.5 F

Impulsive until the last gasp – gets sweet and youthful when I want, for thirteen quid, real richness and complexity.

Rosemount Shiraz 1996 15.5 D

Not as soupy or as soppy as previous vintages. Here we have tannins and tenacity.

South East Australian Shiraz 1997 13 C

Has hints of quality but it's so well-polished it's tepid.

Vasarelli McLaren Vale Cabernet Sauvignon 1995 14 E

Ought to be a treat, wine at a tenner. This only scrapes home. The fruit is nicely aromatic and textured. The characterfulness is reserved for the last few seconds.

Vine Vale Cabernet Shiraz 1995 13.5 E

A health tonic of a wine with an ambiguous finish.

AUSTRALIAN WINE WHITE

Australian Medium Dry 1997 11 C

Australian Unoaked Chardonnay 1997 15.5 C

Superb quality of fruitiness which puts to shame many a Chablis at three times the dosh. Class, style and simplicity.

Bin 266 Semillon Chardonnay 1997 15 C

Delicious blend of grapes and mannerisms: pertness with affability, fruit without sweetness, dryness with real controlled vigour.

Haan Barossa Valley Semillon 1997 13.5 E

What a pity I can't rate it higher! I love the cockerel on the label, but he's not crowing loudly enough to wake up the fruit. Maybe in another twelve months this wine will be quite something. But now, and at eight quid, I want more chutzpah.

Honey Tree Semillon Chardonnay, Rosemount Estate 1997 16 D

Oh what a perky little beast we have here! It purrs, it gleams, it meows, it makes you sigh with pleasure.

Lindemans Bin 65 Chardonnay 1996 15.5 C

Pheasant Gully Semillon Chardonnay 1997 

Charming, smokey fruit, ripely melonic and melodic.

Rose Label Orange Vineyard Chardonnay, Rosemount 1996 

A superbly rich and creamy-edged masterpiece of structure, weight, finesse, lingering depth and great craftsmanship.

Rosemount Estate Hunter Valley Chardonnay 1996 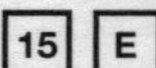

The usual class act from Rosemount, in this manifestation perhaps nuttier on the finish than other examples of the artist's work.

Vasarelli McLaren Vale Chardonnay 1997 

Somewhat hoity-toity and dainty-footed, but it does trip well with a plain grilled white fish. I'd really like to see more freshness in the wine. It's a touch sullen on the finish.

Vine Vale Chardonnay, Barossa Valley 1996 14.5 E

CHILEAN WINE — RED

Alta Mira Cabernet Sauvignon 1996 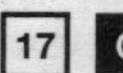

Quite brilliantly priced and poised. The fruit is aromatic, rich and deep but has good tannins. There is an echo of cassis to it but mostly it's rich plums deliciously textured and well finished. Superb wine.

Alta Mira Merlot 1997 

Like chewing an old leather Chesterfield strewn with soft, plump cushions heavily embroidered with images of sun and herbs.

Casa Leona Cabernet Sauvignon 1996 

What goes for the merlot, stands for the cabernet, too, except there are more tannins and texture and food is allowed to enter the picture.

Casa Leona Cabernet Sauvignon Reserve 1995 

What a silly price for such a seriously fruity cabernet. It's dry and coal-edged, deep, rich, very full and well structured.

Casa Leona Merlot 1997 

This is utter gluggability at the heights of soft, leathery richness. Not a food wine, much, and not massively complex but it is so demurely charming and companionable.

Casa Leona Merlot Reserve 1996 15.5 C

Sheer oaked pleasure here of a softness of fruit which defies description: taffeta? velvet? silk? None quite fits. But it does fit the blue mood hour and lifts it – instantly.

CHILEAN WINE — WHITE

Alta Mira Chardonnay 1997 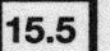

Lovely combination of apple acidity and ripe melon fruit. Elegant yet with a hint of wildness.

Carmen Reserve Chardonnay 1996 16.5 E

Toasted sesame seeds and ripe pineapple, pear and ogen melon form the heart of the attack, which is lengthy and lingering, hugely classy and delightfully devout to the principles of hedonism.

Casa Leona Chardonnay 1997

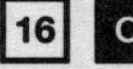

Such nerve-tingling, richly textured fruit for the money, you look at the price tag twice.

Lontue Sauvignon Blanc 1997

Superb wine for the money. It offers rich lushness and ripeness of melon plus compensating pineapple and lemon acidity.

ENGLISH WINE — WHITE

Leeford's Vineyard Lightly Oaked English White 1996

Certainly England's wittiest wine label. Pity the wine behind it isn't as witty or as forward.

FRENCH WINE — RED

Beaujolais 1997

Dull.

Bin 80 Cotes de Malepere 1996 16 C

French country wine dragged deliriously into the late nineteenth century! Fabulous quaffing wine, characterful, dry, rich, sunny, gently herby, which is also a terrific food wine.

Bin 90 Minervois 1996 15.5 C

Touch friskier and more playful than its Malepere stablemate but much the same quaffing qualities.

Cabernet Merlot Vigne Antique Domaine Virginie 1995 14 D

Chateau St Esteve, Bois de Vigne 1996 13.5 C

Chateauneuf-du-Pape Les Closiers 1996 16 E

A lovely vintage of this wine. Hugely savoury, ripe, yet elegant, firmly textured and beautifully controlled and lingering as it finishes.

Classic Claret Chateau Cazeau 1996 14 C

A most approachable claret with classic hints of charcoal-edged dryness and richness.

Domaine de Belle Feuille Cotes du Rhone 1995 11 C

Domaine Jeune Counoise VdP du Gard 1997 14 C

Unusually quaint quaffer of richness, depth and tone.

Domaine St Pierre 1997 12.5 B

Well . . .

Fleurie 1997 13.5 D

A most drinkable Fleurie. But a seven quid wine? Not quite.

Full Red, Cotes du Roussillon Villages (1-litre) 13 C

Price bracket has been adjusted to show bottle equivalent.

Gold Label Cabernet Sauvignon VdP d'Oc 1996 16.5 C

Superb frontal attack on the molars as the tannins take hold, varnished with a hint of plum and blackcurrant and a touch of old leather. Fantastic value.

Gold Label Merlot VdP d'Oc 1996 14.5 C

Dark cherry with a hint of almond. Lovely character here – like something Thomas Hardy would have written about.

House Red VdP de Gers 1997 15 B

Delightful, dry richness and impactful structure. Works all of a piece and has real Southern warmth and style.

La Tour de Prevot, Cotes de Ventoux 1996 15.5 C

Country bumpkin in an old leather jerkin but with polished manners and a rich vein of amusingly fruity anecdotes.

Le Bois de la Vigne Cotes du Rhone 1996 14 C

Le Vallon des Oliviers, Cotes de Ventoux 1996 15.5 C

Margaux 1994 13 E

Some class here but not nine quid's worth.

Merlot Cabernet Vigne Antique VdP d'Oc 1996 15.5 C

Very very dry – but wonderfully witty with it. A sort of laconic sonorousness lingers within the herbiness of the fruit – like the centre of an eccentric chocolate waiting to be revealed once bitten through.

Summer Red VdP d'Oc 1997 15.5 C

Superbly Beaujolais-like – old fashioned Beaujolais, I do not refer to the modern abomination – and so we have freshness, wit, a distant earthiness, rounded fruitiness (supple and clean) and a gush of flavour on the finish. Delightful fresh wine, good chilled.

Syrah Vigne Antique Domaine Virginie 1995 16 D

The final flourish of complexity, earthy and rich, as the fruit descends like a major northern Rhone red of legendary longevity and depth. It's a superb riposte, this syrah, to some of Australia's pretentiously priced specimens of the same grape.

FRENCH WINE WHITE

Chablis 1996 13 E

Chablis Premier Cru, Grande Cuvee 1988 15 F

Worth the dosh. It's very woody, textured, rich yet controlled, classy, finely intentioned and has finesse and wit.

Chardonnay Bourgogne 1997

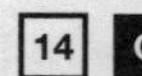

Charming rendezvous of old world hints of vegetality and new world fruit preservation. Astonishingly accomplished white burgundy.

Chardonnay Merlot Rose, VdP de l'Herault 1997

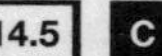

Has delicacy yet bite. A terrific food rose.

Cotes de Gascogne 1997

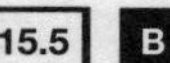

Lovely little pineapple-edged tipple, quite delicious.

Domaine de la Pouvraie Vouvray 1997

Rather raw and adolescent. Put it away somewhere chill and dark for a couple of years. It may emerge into the light a specimen of maturity and individuality.

Domaine Mandeville Chardonnay VdP d'Oc 1997

Superb texture: gobbets of fresh, plump, ripe fruit gripped by an acidic freshness giving the whole bite and real style.

Domaine Mandeville Viognier VdP d'Oc 1997

Superb plump apricot fruit, uniquely viognier in feel, and lushly ripe and fresh. A beautiful mouthful of fruit.

French Country White, VdP de l'Herault 1997

Has some aromatic charm and some fresh, apple-cheeked innocence but underneath it's modern, knowing, incisive.

French Dry White (1-litre) 14 C

Clean, nutty, fresh, charmingly simple and hugely gluggable.

French Rose, VdP de l'Herault 1997 12 B

Very cosmetic.

Gold Label Chardonnay VdP d'Oc 1997 14.5 C

Rich and warm, sunny and charmingly obesely fruity but with a hint of freshness on the finish under the ripe melon. A superb welcome-home-from-the-coalface quaffer.

Macon Villages, A. Rodet 1997 14.5 C

Gives us a deliciously close approximation to what fine white Burgundy is all about.

Montagny Premier Cru 1996 13 D

Not as impressive as its price tag suggests it ought to be, M&S has better chardonnays under a fiver than this.

Petit Chablis 1996 13.5 D

Pouilly Fume 1997 13.5 E

Clean, yes. But nine quid? Hum.

Rose de Syrah VdP d'Oc 1997 13 C

Rich.

Sancerre Les Ruettes 1996 13 D

Summer White VdP d'Oc 1997 15.5 C

Even the smell of a well-kept, crisply watered and neatly trimmed lawn here.

Vigne Antique Chardonnay d'Oc 1997

13.5 C

Almost sweet as it finishes, slightly vanillary and bitter-nutty.

Vin de Pays du Gers 1997

14.5 B

Plastic cork, mimicking the real thing in everything but 2-4-6-Trichloranisol (cork taint), this has some delightful acidic qualities of the mountain stream kind of poetic rubbish, and the fruit is crisp and clear. Direct. Drinkable.

GERMAN WINE — WHITE

Hock 1997 (1-litre)

Somewhat ordinary and a pound more than it should be. Much prefer M&S' Lieb. Price bracket has been adjusted to show the 75cl equivalent.

Liebfraumilch 1997

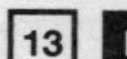

Good in a spritzer.

HUNGARIAN WINE — RED

Hungarian Merlot Kekfrankos 1997

Lovely glugging bottle of dry yet impishly rounded and softly caressing fruit.

HUNGARIAN WINE — WHITE

Hungarian Chardonnay 1997

13.5 C

Green-edged ripeness and crispness.

Hungarian Irsai Oliver 1997

Delightful aperitif: musky, rich, dry.

ITALIAN WINE — RED

Canfera VdT 1995

Superb Tuscan leatheriness and texture here, polished but finely grained, deep and very classy.

Castel del Monte 1997

Coffee and chocolate cake, crumbly and rich. Odd, but delicious.

Chianti Roberto Sorelli 1996

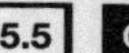

A remarkably modern, self-effacing Chianti of controlled baked earthy fruit which finishes, most uncharacteristically, sweet/dry dark cherry. Delicious Chianti of some wit and style.

Italian Red Table Wine (1-litre)

Price bracket has been adjusted to show bottle equivalent.

Montepulciano d'Abruzzo, Girelli 1996 13 C

Rosso di Puglia 1997 15.5 B

Brilliant value here. It has serious depth, rich tannins, a beguiling and gorgeously gripping texture and a weight well above its price tag. Terrific stuff.

Rosso Salento IGT 1997 15.5 B

Great flavour of baked plums and soft fruit with tannins richly and softly intertwined.

Sangiovese di Puglia 1997 15.5 C

Richer, darker, more mysterious, more elementally earthy and sangiovese-bright than many Classico Chiantis at twice the price.

Villa Cafaggio Chianti Classico 1996 13 

ITALIAN WINE — WHITE

Bianco di Puglia 1997 14 

In its wonderful, taint-free, cork-free, screw-cap way, this is a simple, dry white with some suggestion of its rustic Adriatic provenance in its nutty charm. Delicious, crisp, highly quaffable.

Chardonnay Verdeca di Puglia 1997 14.5 

A demure chardonnay of charm and understated richness. Very elegant, if a bit quiet.

Frascati Superiore DOC 1997 13.5 C

Italian White Table Wine (1-litre) 14 C

Price bracket has been adjusted to show bottle equivalent.

Orvieto Single Estate 1997 15.5 C

Delicious, nutty wine with a superbly crisp finish and hint of new worldliness but, in essence, this is northern Italian white wine making at its most Epicurean: as the baton to orchestrate a great fish meal.

Pinot Grigio 1997 15.5 C

Brilliant minerality of crispness, incisiveness and beautiful cleanness. Polished grapes, high class wine.

Rosato di Puglia 1997 13.5 B

Has some cherry fruit.

Soave Single Estate 1997 15 C

Terrific texture here, slightly plump, controlled, subtly rich. Great glug.

NEW ZEALAND WINE RED

Saints Cabernet Sauvignon/Merlot, Hawkes Bay 1995 14 E

Richness, forwardness, and ripeness in gentle array – the tannins only get carried away as the wine is deep down the throat.

NEW ZEALAND WINE — WHITE

Kaituna Hills Chardonnay 1997 13.5 D

Kaituna Hills Sauvignon Blanc 1997 15.5 D

Lovely gooseberry fruit with a delicious herbaceous border.

Saints Gisborne Chardonnay 1996 16.5 E

Real studied complexity yet utter unpretentiousness here, so it's a great wine to go with an author of similar mien like Barbara Pym, something, you know, dry yet quirkily relaxed, for the fruit is multi-layered, mature, and works on two levels: a perfumed, rich ripeness and a gentle, lingering vanillary, very very subtle floral quality.

SOUTH AFRICAN WINE — RED

Bellevue Estate 1996 14 D

So rich and invitingly deep it's more like soup.

Bin 121 1997 14 C

Boot polish and coal scuttles! Terrific with well grilled sausages.

Cabernet Sauvignon Coastal Region KWV 1993 13.5 C

Cape Reflections Cabernet Sauvignon/ Merlot 1995 16 E

Expensively polished pearl, fat and lustrous, with tannins, fruit and acidity in perfect balance. A seriously good wine.

Oaked Ruby Cabernet 1996 15.5 C

Lucky oak to have been cheek-by-jowl with such soft plump young flesh. Has a Balzacian sense of the luxurious sybarite, slightly corrupt, this sinfully gluggable wine.

Rock Ridge Cabernet Sauvignon 1996 13 C

SOUTH AFRICAN WINE WHITE

Cape Country Chenin Blanc 1997 13.5 C

Cape Country Colombard 1997 14 C

McGregor Chenin Blanc 1997 12.5 C

Perdeberg Sauvignon Blanc 1998 13.5 C

Rock Ridge Chardonnay 1997 13.5 C

Quiet but brash on the price tag.

SPANISH WINE RED

Las Falleras Red, Utiel-Requena 1997 15 B

Hugely drinkable with its plum dryness, richness, lightness yet, curiously, its impactful weight on the finish. Delicious stuff.

Marques del Romeral Rioja Reserva 1989 13 D

Soft,a touch sentimental and soppy, very mature and almost in its second childhood.

Rioja Bodegas AGE 14 C

Roseral Rioja Crianza, Bodegas AGE 1994 14 C

SPANISH WINE WHITE

House White, La Mancha 1997 14 B

Dry, clean, knife-edged, gently nutty.

Las Falleras Rose, Utiel-Requena 1997 13 B

Las Falleras White, Utiel-Requena 1997 14.5 B

Deliciously cheeky specimen of dry, charming fruit.

Moscatel de Valencia NV 16 C

A brilliant honeyed pre-prandial passion-arouser. Or drink it with fruit and blue cheese.

Rioja Roseral 1996 

URUGUAYAN WINE RED

Uruguayan Tannat 1996 14.5 C

USA WINE RED

Santa Monica Classic Red 1997 12 C

Fruit juice.

Santa Monica Reserve (Zinfandel) 1997 15.5 C

Lovely polish and depth here. Yes, it's overwhelmingly fruity and highly strung but it's also so well textured and deep.

USA WINE WHITE

Santa Monica Classic White 1997 14.5 C

Lush-edged, creamy fruit with a hint of lemon.

Santa Monica Reserve White (Chardonnay) 1997 15 C

Lots of flavour and richness here yet it's not overbaked or superficial.

FORTIFIED WINE

Cream Sherry 14 C

Medium Amontillado Sherry 13 C

Pale Dry Fino Sherry 16 C

One of the best finos around, blended specifically to M&S's instructions, in which the bone dry salinity of classic fino has a background echo of gentle fruit so the result is a lingering pleasure, still very dry, of residual richness. A fino of exceptional style – and still a great wine for grilled prawns.

Rich Cream Sherry 15.5 C

Vintage Character Port 15 D

Good rich style, not at all sweet or cloying, with the regulation figgy sweetness but this is well tempered by a hint of earthy dryness.

SPARKLING WINE/CHAMPAGNE

Australian Sparkling Shiraz 1994 16 E

One of Australia's brimfulest-of-personality contributors to civilised living: it's rich, ready, gushing with flavour and great with food!

Great Western Sparkling Shiraz 1993 16 E

Marlin Bay Australian Sparkling Brut NV 12 C

South African Pinot Noir/Chardonnay NV 14 E

Veuve Truffeau Colombard/Chardonnay Brut 13.5 C

A decent enough bubbly for kirs and spritzers.

Western Cape Pinot Noir/Chardonnay NV (South Africa) 14 D

Asti Spumante Consorzio 13 D

Bluff Hill Brut (New Zealand) 14 D

Light and fruity.

Bottle Fermented Blanc de Blancs 1994 (Australia) 13 E

Cava Brut (Spain) 16 C

I'd rather engage my taste buds with this soft yet finely finished Cava than any number of champagnes priced five times higher.

Champagne Chevalier de Melline, Premier Cru Blanc de Blancs 12 G

Champagne de St Gall, Premier Cru Blanc de Blancs NV 14.5 G

There is some hint of richness and playfulness to the fruit which sets it apart.

Champagne de St Gall, Premier Cru Brut NV 15 G

This is a seriously delicious tipple. Elegant, but not classically dry.

Champagne de St Gall, Premier Cru Vintage 1990 16 G

This is the exception which proves the rule.

Champagne Orpale 1988 13.5 H

Champagne Oudinot Grand Cru 1993 14 G

Very elegant, not at all austerely dry, and with a lifting fruitiness as it descends.

Medium Dry Cava (Spain) 14 C

Oudinot Brut Champagne 13.5 F

Lot of money. I'd rather drink the Cava.

Oudinot Rose Champagne 17 F

Delightful rose – it justified its soppy colour and steep price by being aromatically enticing, fruity in a most gentle way, with a finish of finesse.

Seppelt Chardonnay Blanc de Blanc Bottle Fermented Brut 1994 (Australia) 15 E

Veuve de Medts, Premier Cru Brut (France) 14.5 G

Vintage Cava 1994 16 D

Superbly crisp and insouciantly fruit-edged bubbly in the class of many Champagnes three times the price.

Yarden Blanc de Blancs Bottle Fermented Brut NV (Israel) 13.5 E

WM MORRISONS

FIONA GETS STUCK IN TO STUART AND DOESN'T COME UNHINGED.

My hope that my suggestion to this retailer that Wendy Cope opens the new Erith (Kent) branch proved fruitless. Ms Cope, a great poet, was born in the town but she did not open this great northern retailer's most southerly outpost (the other is in Banbury, Oxon).

Morrisons' expansion plans will create 2,400 jobs – with further moves on the cards. That insect-repellent-yellow and black symbol, behind which some superb supermarket bargains lurk, is expected to infiltrate such retail hot spots as Norwich and Letchworth. It plans to expand to take over from Asda as the no. 3 supermarket operator.

On many fronts, Morrisons has been busy. It announced a joint venture with Midland for in-store banking and opted to put the bank department just next to the wines and beer shelves. Shrewd move. Even shrewder, however, was turning Stuart Purdie, who had been Morrisons' sole wine buyer, into a department. Fiona Smith, the department, has proved she has a nose for the job and she makes up one of the great male/female duos in the world of supermarket wine buying (viz. M & S, CWS).

It is not often that a round peg finds a round hole. But Mr Purdie, getting rounder as the years pass, is a superbly comfortable fit in an increasingly well-rounded hole. I don't think I can name a better marriage than Purdie & Morrisons and the results of this harmony show in the bargains which follow.

Wm Morrison Supermarkets
Wakefield 41 Industrial Estate
Wakefield
W Yorks WF1 OXF
Tel: 01924 870000
Fax: 01934 875300

ALGERIAN WINE RED

Coteaux de Tlemcen 1994 14.5 B

A wonderfully rich, warm, soft wine of stunning sunny depth.

ARGENTINIAN WINE WHITE

Santa Cecilia Sauvignon Blanc NV 14 C

A roast chicken wine. Has the richness and depth for it.

AUSTRALIAN WINE RED

Barramundi Shiraz/Merlot NV 14 C

A richly endowed duo, this blend, combining savouriness with wryness.

Castle Ridge Bin CR1 Red 1996 13 C

Juice, Bruce, sheer juice.

Corinda Ridge Cabernet/Merlot 1997 13.5 D

Most drinkable. But its quirkiness, at this price, takes some swallowing.

Jamiesons Run Coonawarra Red 1994 13.5 E

Lindemans Bin 45 Cabernet Sauvignon 1996 14 D

Very fresh yet, curiously, dry. Possibly overpriced for its level of excitement.

Lindemans Bin 50 Shiraz 1996 13.5 D

A bit pricey for its total imprecision.

Penfolds Bin 35 Cabernet Sauvignon/ Shiraz/Ruby Cabernet 1996 15.5 D

Rich, layered, clinging, ripe – a great steak and kidney pudding wine.

AUSTRALIAN WINE WHITE

Castle Ridge Bin CR4 Colombard Chardonnay 1997 13.5 C

Bright and bonny, but too forward in the finish, perhaps.

Corinda Ridge Sauvignon/Semillon 1998 14 D

Rich and invitingly perfumed. Touch expensive but undeniably rewarding to glug.

Lindemans Bin 65 Chardonnay 1997 16.5 C

The tastiest under-a-fiver Aussie chardonnay on offer anywhere. This '97 vintage gives it its classiest, most impressive depth yet.

Penfolds Bin 21 Semillon-Chardonnay-Colombard 1997 15 C

Nice exotic edge, not overbaked, which mingles well with the minerally acidity. Good food wine.

Wyndham TR2 Classic White 1996 

So tarty you could wear it behind your ears. Strictly a wine for lovers of the obvious. Good with Chinese food, though.

BULGARIAN WINE RED

Bulgarian Reserve Merlot 1992 

Polished with a hint of vegetality to the ripeness. Delicate undertone.

Hidden Valley Reserve Cabernet Sauvignon 1993  

Earthy with tannin, bright with fruit. Most agreeable food wine.

BULGARIAN WINE WHITE

Bulgarian Reserve Chardonnay 1995 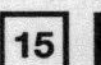 

Lovely clean depth of fruit here, superb richness and crisp, cos-lettuce freshness.

Bulgarian Sauvignon Blanc 1996 14.5 B

Delicious and crisp!

Bulgarian Snow Wine 14 B

This is a sweet white fresh-fruit wine.

CHILEAN WINE RED

35 Sur Cabernet Sauvignon 1996 15.5 C

Great texture and with a dry finish which only enhances the softness of the fruit.

Antu Mapu Cabernet Sauvignon 1997 15.5 C

Super polish yet cragginess. Great texture, ripeness, and with a compelling finish.

Chilean Cabernet Sauvignon 1997 15.5 B

Brilliant tannins and rich, velvet fruit – with a finish of brushed denim.

Montes Alpha Merlot 1995 16 E

This is developing beautifully in bottle. A real soupy treat. Simply lashings of savoury fruit.

Stowells of Chelsea Chilean Merlot Cabernet (3-litre box) 10 C

Price bracket has been adjusted to show the equivalent for a bottle.

CHILEAN WINE WHITE

Castillo de Molina Chardonnay 1996 15.5 C

Classy dryness yet fruity depth with a polished finish of underripe melon. Delicious.

Castillo de Molina Reserve Chardonnay 1997 16.5 D

Polish, plumpness, plushness of fruit, all in tone with texture, tightness, and sheer style. A terrific, balanced, extremely classy wine. Great price for such vivacity yet finesse.

Castillo de Molina Sauvignon Blanc 1996 13 C

Chilean Sauvignon Blanc 1997 14 B

A rich version of fresh sauvignon.

Montes Alpha Chardonnay 1996 17.5 E

Chile's greatest burgundian smell and taste alike? As if! This is better than any Montrachet I've tasted for twenty years. Except, of course, the great names (Comte Lafon etc). So – do you spend nine quid on this or £40 on a Lafon? True, the wines are different in mood. The Chilean has more verve.

Montes Alpha Sauvignon Blanc 1997 13.5 C

Curiously sticky-edged sauvignon, a pound too expensive but good with mussels.

Stowells of Chelsea Chilean Sauvignon Blanc (3-litre box) 15.5 B

Price bracket has been adjusted to show the equivalent for a bottle.

ENGLISH WINE WHITE

Three Choirs Estates Premium 1996 12 C

FRENCH WINE RED

Beaujolais NV 13 C

Bourgogne 1994 10 D

Cellier la Chouf, Minervois 14 B

Chais Cuxac Cabernet Sauvignon 1996 13 C

Very dry, very.

Chateau Cadillac Lesgourgues 1994 15.5 D

Finishes rich and soft and most untypically textured and polished. A terrific claret of real class, individuality and manner. Finesse runs all through it.

Chateau de Lauree Bordeaux Rouge 1995 14 C

Chateau Jougrand St Chinian 1996 15 C

Soft, gently earthy, raspberry edged, highly developed and drinkable.

Chateau Tour du Tertre 1996 14 C

A dry, charcoal-edged food wine.

Chateauneuf-du-Pape Domaine du Lazaret 1995 14 E

Big rich meaty wine now, heavier than the last batch, and some power on display here.

Claret, Morrisons 13 B

Corbieres Les Fenouillets 1995 15 B

Coteaux du Languedoc NV 14 B

Simple glugging country red – has some engaging fruit.

Cotes de Luberon 1997 14 B

Great value rustic glugging. No coarseness but some character.

Cotes du Rhone NV 13 B

Light and very friendly. Also available in a useful half bottle size.

Cotes du Roussillon, Morrisons 15 B

Domaine du Crouzel Corbieres 1995 13.5 C

Fitou NV 13 C

Juicy stuff.

Fox Mountain Syrah/Merlot VdP d'Oc 1996 15 B

Haut Poitou Gamay 1997 13 C

Odd little oxymoron: smells deeply shallow, tastes shallowly deep.

Julienas Galerie Aujoux 1996 14 C

Some texture and even tannin. Good age, weight of fruit and finish.

La Source Merlot VdP d'Oc 1995 14 B

La Source Syrah VdP d'Oc 1995 14 B

Le Pigeonnier Bergerac 1996 12 B

The label is ten times tastier than the fruit.

Oak Matured Bordeaux P. Sichel 1996 13 C

Dry, very clarety and old-fashioned. A bit like sucking the end of the Brigadier's toe-cap.

Oak Matured Claret 1996 (1-litre) 15 C

A brilliantly dry, classic claret of real character and bite. Great food wine (grilled meats especially).

St Emilion, Morrisons 13 C

Vin de Pays de l'Aude Red (half bottle) 13 A

Vin de Pays Marquis de l'Estouval 1997 13.5 A

To describe it as simple is to flatter it. But it is drinkable and the aroma excites.

Winter Hill Red VdP de l'Aude 1997 15.5 B

Lovely polished richness and ripeness. Gorgeous plump texture and svelteness of fruit.

FRENCH WINE WHITE

Bordeaux Blanc NV 14 B

It is crisp and dry as the label says. Good value fish wine.

Cascade Sauvignon Blanc Bordeaux 1996 13 B

Chablis La Lotte 1996 12 D

Touch tart.

Chais Cuxac Chardonnay 1996 15.5 C

A richly textured, opulently finished, highly polished, luxurious chardonnay of uncommon style at this price.

Chateau de Lauree Bordeaux 1995 12.5 B

Chateau Saint Galier 1996 16 C

Absolutely stunning bargain! Full of textured richness from its aroma to its melon and vegetal finish. A little classic.

Cotes de Luberon 1996 14.5 B

Entre Deux Mers 1996 13.5 B

Escoudou VdP de l'Herault Blanc 1997 13.5 A

So simple it thinks the moon is made of green cheese.

Fox Mountain Sauvignon/Chardonnay, VdP d'Oc 1996 13 B

Gewurztraminer Preisszimmer 1997 15.5 D

Brilliant youth and richness. Reeks of roses! Terrific oriental food wine.

Haut Poitou Sauvignon Blanc 1996 14 C

Delicious crisp, apple-skin fruit with a real surge of freshness on the finish.

La Source Sauvignon Blanc VdP d'Oc 1996 15 B

'M' Muscadet Sevre et Maine 12 B

Macon Villages Chatenay 1995 15 C

A real white burgundy of studied calm and style. Has real solid depth and weight.

Pinot Gris Preiss Zimmer 1996 14 D

Very rich, faintly apricoty, and great with Thai fish and poultry dishes. Few bottles left.

Pouilly Fume J.P. Bailly 1997 13 D

Very drinkable but I can't entirely see the logic of paying the price for it. Ah! You mean you have the word *Pouilly* on a label? I see . . .

Rameaux de France Chardonnay, VdP de l'Isle de Beaute 1997 14 B

Rich and full of itself – very good salad, pasta and rich fish dish wine.

Rose d'Anjou, Morrisons 14 B

Sancerre Andre Vatan 1996 13.5 D

One of the better Sancerres, very crisp and clean, but still an expensive purchase.

Sauvignon de St Bris, Marquis de Bieville 1996 15 C

Sirius Bordeaux White 1995 15.5 D

Goodness, what a surprise in store here. A very classy white Bordeaux but also a stride into the future with soft stealthy fruit of genuine old-world food compatibility. A wine of style and decisive drinkability. Top thirty stores only.

Vin de Pays de l'Aude White (half bottle) 

Vouvray Jean Michel 1996 13 C

Winter Hill White 1997 

Super class here: crisp, clean, rich, full, developed, engaging. Terrific value.

GERMAN WINE — WHITE

Bereich Bernkastel 1996 11 B

Bernkasteler Riesling Auslese 1994 13 D

Needs fresh fruit.

Erdener Treppchen Spatlese 1993 16.5 D

Remarkable price for a remarkable aperitif: subtly sticky, gently honeyed but not sweet, and perfumed like sherbet with a hint of decaying melon.

Fire Mountain Riesling 1996 14 C

Getting there, this new style riesling. Dry, classic edge, but still too austere for New World fruit lovers.

Flonheimer Adelberg Kabinett Johannes Egberts 1995 13 B

Franz Reh Kabinett 1996 12 B

Sweet.

Franz Reh Spatlese 1994 12 B

Sweet but good ingredient in a spritzer.

Klussterather St Michael Spatlese 1996 11.5 C

Sweet.

'M' Mosel Light & Flinty 11 B

Nusdorfer Bischofkreuz Auslese 1996 14 C

Few bottles left.

Seafish Dry Rheinhessen 1995 12 B

Urziger Wurzgarten Riesling Auslese, Ewald Pfeiffer 1993 15 D

Weinheimer Sybilenstein Beerenauslese (half bottle) 14 C

Zimmermann Riesling NV 13 C

GREEK WINE RED

Boutari Xinomavro 1995 14 E

Interesting change from cabernet sauvignon. Pricey but classy: very dry, wry, deep.

Mavrodaphne of Patras 14 C

A sweet red wine which is great with a slice of fruit cake (which its fruit resembles).

HUNGARIAN WINE RED

Chapel Hill Pinot Noir 10 B

Hungarian Country Red 12 B

HUNGARIAN WINE WHITE

Chapel Hill Irsai Oliver 13.5 B

Chapel Hill Pinot Noir Blanc 12 B

Hungarian Country Wine NV 13 B

A good fish stew wine.

ITALIAN WINE RED

Barbera d'Alba, Feyles 1993 13.5 D

Barbera Piemonte 1997 12 B

Juicy as a breakfast tipple.

Bardolino Classico Casona 1995 16 C

Amazing price for such a demurely classy Bardolino. Has typicity, richness yet lightness, and that lovely plum and cherry fruitiness.

Chianti Classico Uggiano 1995 13 C

Chianti Colli Fiorentini Uggiano 1994 12 C

Rampant fruit juice.

Chianti Reserva Uggiano 1993 15 D

Terrific edgy richness and dryness, baked and deep. A true Tuscan tearaway.

Chianti Uggiano 1996 14 C

Sweet but the hints of earthiness save it from suicidal soppiness.

Eclisse VdT di Puglia Rosso 14.5 B

Good Italian Red 12 B

Very juicy and ripe.

Merlot del Veneto, Vigneti del Sole 1996 13.5 B

Montepulciano d'Abruzzo 1997 15 B

Superb freshness, cherry-ripe, and richness here. Great personality and fun-packed fruit. Great price too.

Valpolicella NV 12 B

ITALIAN WINE — WHITE

Eclisse White 12 B

Frascati Superiore 1996, Morrisons 12.5 A

Good Italian White 14 B

And good is the word for it! A fresh-faced, nicely textured bargain. Well done, Stuart and Fiona.

Oaked Soave 1996 11 C

Somewhat dull and pricey.

Orvieto Classico, Uggiano 1996 12 B

Bit sharpish.

Pinot Grigio del Veneto 1996 13 C

Slight perfumed edge.

Soave NV 13 B

Good value fish wine.

MEXICAN WINE RED

Dona Elena Cabernet Sauvignon/Malbec 1995 13.5 B

If you get past the aroma, a fair level of old-sock fruit awaits you. Needs food.

MOROCCAN WINE RED

Cabernet Syrah 14 B

NEW ZEALAND WINE WHITE

Montana Reserve Barrique Fermented Chardonnay 1996 14 E

Whitecliff Sacred Hill Sauvignon Blanc 1997 10 C

I simply find it begging to be disliked with its thinness of fruit and hint of poorly cut grass.

PORTUGUESE WINE RED

Bairrada Reserva, Borges 1994 13.5 C

Touch light and sweet on the finish.

Dao Meia Encosta 1994 11 C

Dao Meia Encosta 1996 14 C

Brilliant value here. A dry food wine of real substance.

Val Longa Country Wine NV 14 B

PORTUGUESE WINE WHITE

Bright Brothers Fernao Pires/Chardonnay 1995  B

Brilliant soft yet nut-edged fruit of great charm, character and depth.

Val Longa Country Wine NV  B

Vinho Verde 10 B

ROMANIAN WINE — RED

Romanian Border Pinot Noir 1995 15 B

A grand little glug for sausages and mash.

Romanian Country Red 12 B

Romanian Merlot 1993 15 B

Very fruity and very ripe but deeply engaging too. Terrific value. Has great polish.

ROMANIAN WINE — WHITE

Romanian Classic Sauvignon Blanc 1996 14 B

Well, I don't know about classic but it's unusually drinkable, cheerful and cheap.

Romanian Late Harvest Chardonnay 1985 15 C

SOUTH AFRICAN WINE — RED

Mamreweg Cabernet Shiraz 1996 14 C

Warm, sunny, soupy, simply sip-uppable. Few bottles left.

Neil Joubert Pinotage 1996 15.5 C

Brilliant jazzy label – almost as complex, ripe, daft, odd, drinkable and smashing as the wine.

Riebeek Oak Aged Shiraz 1996 15.5 D

Superb shiraz, bouncy and ripe, dry and deep. It's huge fruity fun. Only very few bottles left, alas.

South African Red NV 13 B

Very juicy.

SOUTH AFRICAN WINE WHITE

Black Wood Chenin Blanc 1997 15.5 B

Brilliant value here: crisp, fresh, nutty, textured, classy.

Dukesfield Chardonnay 1997 15 C

Made by Danie de Wet, Cape chardonnay wizard, this is a great buy at this price.

Fair Cape Sauvignon Blanc 1997 14 B

Delicious crispness of fineness of finish.

Faircape Chenin Blanc 1996 14 B

Kleinbosch Early Release Chenin Blanc 1998 15.5 B

Brilliant zippiness and richness here. Lovely glugging!

'M' South African White Crisp and Fruity 13.5 

SPANISH WINE — RED

Chateldon Cabernet Sauvignon Reserva 1994 15 C

Superb sweet vanilla fruit. Tasted only weeks before going to press, yet already the new vintage is on its way (haven't seen it yet, though).

Clos d'en Ton Cabernet Sauvignon Costers del Segre 1996 14 D

Good Spanish Red 13.5 B

Navajas Reserve Rioja 1991 16.5 D

Brilliant fruit! The essence of vanilla-cured ham. Yes, it's meaty and baked and gluggable beyond belief. Only a few bottles left.

Pinard Clos de Torribas Crianza 1994 16 C

Gorgeous hints of wild raspberry, earth and vanilla. Texture, bite and character.

Rio Rojo Spanish Red 14 B

Light and friendly.

Rioja, Morrisons 15.5 C

A rich, comfortingly fruity wine with a hint of vanilla. Terrific value.

Stowells of Chelsea Tempranillo (3-litre box) 14 B

Price bracket has been adjusted to show the bottle equivalent.

Torres Sangre de Toro 1996 

Fantastic vintage for this old warhorse. No bull! This is classy, rich, dry, complex, polished, characterful and very very stylish. It has texture and ripeness. Rich and riveting.

SPANISH WINE — WHITE

Solana Torrontes Treixadura 1994 15 C

Torres Vina Sol 1997 

Good solid fruit of some depth which will develop more perfume and complexity over the next year.

URUGUAYAN WINE — RED

Castel Pujol Las Violetas Tannat 1994 

Castel Pujol Pinot Noir 1996 

Not remotely pinot noirish but hugely drinkable.

USA WINE RED

Blossom Hill, California 10 C

Californian Red NV 13 B

Murieta's Well, Livermore Valley 1995 14.5 F

Very lingering, meaty wine with a deal of finesse and delicacy. It has a faint air of exoticism which stretches, alas, to the price tag. But a very interesting wine.

Sutter Home Zinfandel 1995 13 C

Talus Cabernet Sauvignon 1994 14.5 D

Rich, soft and very fruity. Textured and ripe, it's good with food and mood.

Willamette Valley Pinot Noir 1996 13.5 D

Good initial attack (perfume and fruit) but falls away on the finish.

USA WINE WHITE

Blossom Hill, California 10 C

Californian White NV 13 B

Canyon Springs Barbera Rose 1996 14 C

Charming freshness and near tart-ness. Delicious knife-edge fruit.

Talus Chardonnay 1995 

Gorgeous rich, ripe fruit combining dry, sticky-toffee texture with huge dollops of melon and pear.

Willamette Valley Chardonnay 1996 13.5 E

Rather muted, touch pricey for the style.

FORTIFIED WINE

Rozes Special Reserve Port NV 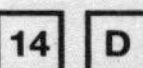

Bit more bite here than the Rozes Ruby and more evident class. Nicely textured, rich, and full and good with a slice of rich cake.

SPARKLING WINE/CHAMPAGNE

Asti Spumante Gianni (Italian) 14 C

Now here I like the sweetness of finish.

Nicole d'Aurigny Brut Champagne 14 E

One of the best under a tenner champagnes around.

Paul Herard Blanc de Noirs Brut Champagne (half bottle) 14 D

Paul Herard Demi Sec Champagne (half bottle) 13.5 D

Rondel Cava Brut 14 D

Has a nice hint of ripe fruit under the dryness. But it's still dry and classy.

Rondel Cava Rose 14 D

Expensive but haughty, dry and with a nice rosy lilt on the finish.

Santa Carolina Chardonnay 1996 (Chile) 15 D

Interesting fruit here. Elegant yet impudent.

Seaview Brut 14 D

Seaview Brut Rose (Australia) 15 D

Seppelt Great Western Brut (Australia) 13.5 D

Still a bargain. Elegant and dry.

Sparkling Zero (alcohol free) 15 A

The best non-alcoholic wine about. Real bubbles, real style, real freshness. Zippy from label to throat. Great for TT Christmases.

Vintage Cava Brut 1993 14.5 D

Delicious, dry, classy fruit.

SAFEWAY PLC

IS LIZ NOW LEADING THE BEST TEAM EVER?

Ms Elizabeth Robertson MW carries one of those job titles which simple scribblers like myself can never quite figure out. In effect she runs the wine department but she always says she never buys any wines; this disavowal must be considered on the same basis that Mr Arsene Wenger can claim never to kick a football yet at the same time be recognised as the smartest head on any set of shoulders in the Arsenal team set-up.

Whatever the niceties of job titles and the modesty of its wine leader, Safeway now has the most dynamic and focused wine buying department in its history. I note that Sir Alastair Grant was paid £669,000 in his last year as chairman of Safeway and will receive a pension of £427,000. In all justice, he ought to share some of this lucre with his wine buyers who have surely done more than any other department to entice customers in and keep them coming back. True, the store invested rather rashly in a design scheme and taxonomic system for its wine shelves which did not work, but the intention was clear: to make life easier for the customers.

In other areas of its business, there was much to admire in Safeway's attitude. In June 1997 it became the first retailer to supply its network by rail. The first consignment chosen to inaugurate this welcome breakthrough was a stack of wine which chugged up to Glasgow before being delivered to the retailer's 79 Scottish stores. As someone who passionately feels that we should do all we can to encourage rail travel and recognise its superiority to motor transport, I wonder if Safeway might consider a small label to be affixed to future such consignments? I have in mind something along the lines of 'Freshly delivered by Rail.'

This rail initiative was followed by news that Safeway planned to launch branch sub-brands along the lines of Tesco Express and Tesco Metro stores; and these smaller stores would carry limited ranges of wines. I have yet to see any evidence that this has happened during 1998. Perhaps the retailer was not pleased to announce an unexciting set of half-year results and to issue a profit warning. Then the rumours began that Asda was scheming a takeover bid for Safeway. Sainsbury was also reported to be planning a bid to thwart Asda's.

More amusingly, and more based on concrete fact, the news broke that Safeway's charming TV advertising campaign, featuring two infants, Harry and Molly, had to be put on hold because the actors who provided their voices joined an Equity strike involving commercial voice-overs. The voices of Jeremy Clarkson and Cilla Black are being used instead – on the basis that neither is a member of Equity.

What has this to do with wine? Absolutely nothing.

Safeway plc
Safeway House
6 Millington Road
Hayes
Middlesex UB3 4AY
Tel: 0181 848 8744
Fax: 0181 573 1865

SEE STOP PRESS SECTION AT END OF BOOK FOR LAST-MINUTE ADDITIONS OR UPDATES TO THIS RETAILER'S RANGE.

ARGENTINIAN WINE RED

Alamos Ridge Cabernet Sauvignon, Mendoza 1995 15.5 D

Has such mature tannins spiking the fruit. Lovely texture and finish.

Balbi Vineyard Malbec 1997 14 C

Juicy and rich, as all Balbi's wines seem to be. It bounces around the taste buds like a big bonny bowl of fruit (dryish).

Isla Negra Bonarda, Mendoza 1997 15 C

Rich and juicy and an alternative to overpriced Beaujolais.

Isla Negra Malbec Reserve, Mendoza 1997 15 D

Classic Argentine malbec, it seems to me: juicy and ripe yet dry.

Mendoza Merlot 1997, Safeway 13.5 C

Very forward, the hussy.

Mendoza Oak-aged Tempranillo 1997, Safeway 14 C

Bit ragged on the edge but wonderfully at home with food.

Rafael Estate Malbec, Mendoza 1997 16 D

Good heavens what nerve! It's the cheekiest amalgam of fruit and tannin I've tasted for years. Selected stores.

Santa Ana Cabernet/Malbec, Mendoza 1997 14.5 C

Great energy and pace to the fruit here. Really strides across the palate.

ARGENTINIAN WINE WHITE

Alamos Ridge Chardonnay, Mendoza 1996 15.5 C

Rafael Estate Chardonnay/Chenin, Mendoza 1997 14.5 C

Real quality of subtle fruitiness here.

Santa Ana Chardonnay/Semillon, Mendoza 1997 13.5 C

Needs another six months in bottle to meld the spiky relationship of acid and fruit.

Vino Blanco Chenin Blanc, San Rafael 1997 14 B

Terrific value: pace, balance, flavour, individuality.

AUSTRALIAN WINE RED

Australian Oaked Shiraz 1997, Safeway 13.5 C

Soft and plump – bit jammy on the finish.

Australian Shiraz 1997, Safeway 13 C

Curiously unAussie in feel, flavour and price.

Basedow Bush Vine Grenache, Barossa Valley 1996 13.5 D

Breakaway Grenache Shiraz 1996 14.5 C

Deliciously rich and dry and warm as if it's made in the Midi not Oz. Great value glugging here.

Chateau Reynella Basket-Pressed Shiraz 1995 15.5 F

Getting expensive but its fruit is getting more vivacious and more luxurious. Top thirty-three stores.

CV Shiraz 1996 13.5 E

Bit soft on the fruit and hard on the pocket. Top thirty-three stores.

Dawn Ridge Australian Red (3-litre box) 15 

New blend of one of the tastiest boxed wines around. Has more tannins this time. The price band has been adjusted to show the equivalent per bottle.

Hardys Barossa Valley Shiraz 1995 14 D

Very rich and warmly textured with a lovely ripe yet dry finish.

Hardys Coonawarra Cabernet Sauvignon 1994 16 E

A Christmas treat. So well turned out and smooth it seems

effortless. A surprising quality in an Aussie? Not when the finish strikes home. Plenty of character there.

Hardys Nottage Hill Cabernet Sauvignon/ Shiraz 1996 15 C

Elegant, rich, aromatic, balanced, most compellingly well priced, and more stylish than other vintages of the same brand.

Jamiesons Run, Coonawarra 1995 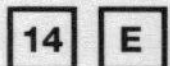

Jammy but has savoury undertones. Selected stores.

Knappstein Cabernet/Merlot 1995 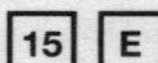

Knappstein understands tannin. It might be Sanskrit for all some Aussie winemakers are fluent in it. Top thirty-three stores.

Lindemans Pyrus, Coonawarra 1993 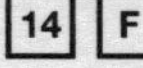

Look out for the '94 (not had a chance to taste it yet).

McPherson Shiraz, SE Australia 1997 

More like Aussie reds should be – soft, cheap, rich, dry, biting, food-friendly, characterful.

Metala Stonyfell Shiraz/Cabernet 1995 12 D

Juicy. Selected stores.

Oaked Cabernet Sauvignon 1997, Safeway 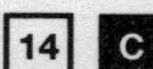

A warning. This wine is seriously delicious but very very ripe and rampant.

Penfolds Bin 389 Cabernet/Shiraz 1995 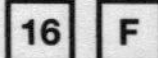

Expensive treat for Christmas: spicy, rich, deep, floods of layered fruit, tannins, complexity and great style. Selected stores.

Peter Lehmann Clancy's Chardonnay Semillon, Barossa Valley 1996 16 D

Rich and rampant yet never overdone. A lovely food wine.

Peter Lehmann The Barossa Cabernet Sauvignon 1996 16.5 E

Fabulously good value for an Aussie nowadays: dry, balanced, witty, rich, lengthy, deep and fully dimensional. Great stuff.

Tim Knappstein Cabernet Franc 1995 16 E

An Australian red with guts and gorgeousity! Dry, rich, textured, classy and great with food.

Woolshed Cabernet/Shiraz/Merlot, Coonawarra 1995 13 D

AUSTRALIAN WINE WHITE

Australian Marsanne 1997, Safeway 13.5 D

Good fish wine.

Australian Oaked Chardonnay 1997, Safeway 15.5 D

Basedow Semillon, Barossa Valley 1996 14 D

Brilliant fish wine.

Breakaway Grenache Rose 1996 11 C

Chardonnay/Colombard 1997, Safeway 15 C

Wonderful opulence and richness, full and deep, with a great crispness to the finish.

CV Unwooded Chardonnay 1997 16.5 E

This is the year, '97, to wallow in the richness of the Aussie chardonnay, especially when no wood is aboard and the provenance is Western Australia. A gloriously uncluttered, elegant wine of potency, finesse and heavenly texture. Top sixty-four stores.

Hardy's Bankside Chardonnay 1996 16 D

Ooh! What riproaring style! Love it!

Hardy's Barossa Valley Chardonnay 1996 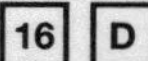

Why bother with Meursault?

Hardys Nottage Hill Chardonnay 1997  C

Fantastic oily/buttery texture, ripe fruit, just terrific.

Lindemans Bin 65 Chardonnay 1998  C

One of the chicest, most expressive chardonnays under a fiver out of Australia.

Lindemans Winemaker's Reserve Padthaway 1995 13 G

Impressively woody but it's the cardboard of the price tag which unbalances it. Top twenty-nine stores.

McPherson Chardonnay, SE Australia 1997 15.5 C

Mount Hurtle Chardonnay 1996 15 D

Good double act of zippy acidity and rich rolling soft fruit.

Penfolds Bin 202 Riesling, South Australia 1997 13.5 C

I think it needs a year to eighteen months to develop character.

Penfolds Rawsons Retreat Bin 21 Semillon/Chardonnay/Colombard 1997 15 C

The gorgeously rich '97 vintage strikes the palate with polish, purpose and plumpness.

Penfolds The Valleys Chardonnay 1997 14.5 E

Lush yet possessing finesse and real style, and will no doubt improve in bottle over the next few months. Top sixty-four stores.

Peter Lehmann Semillon, Barossa Valley 1997 16 D

Gorgeous display of two-faced insidiously delicious fruit. Has a soft, exotic ripe fruit on one hand and a rippling mineral acidity on the other.

Riddoch Chardonnay, Coonawarra 1996 16 D

Super mouth-filling plumpness of ripe fruit here, hint of caramel cream even, but the acidity surges alongside in support and the finish is regal. Very classy wine.

Rosemount Estate Chardonnay 1997 16 D

A classy beast of true pedigree feel from start to finish. Superbly chic and classy.

Rosemount Estate Semillon/Chardonnay 1997 15 D

Elegant and worldly. Serve it with grilled white fish.

Rosemount Estate Show Reserve Chardonnay 1996 15.5 E

Gently woody with incisive yet calm and very collected fruit. Sophisticated in feel.

Woolshed Chardonnay, Coonawarra 1996 15 D

Complex yet subtle. Real class here.

BULGARIAN WINE RED

Bulgarian Country Wine, Merlot/Pinot Noir 1997, Safeway 15.5 B

Marvellous little glug. Dry, bright, characterful, cheap.

Oaked Merlot, Rousse 1997, Safeway 13.5 C

Very jammy fruit here.

Vinenka Merlot/Gamza Reserve, Suhindol 1993, Safeway 14 B

A simple, jammy quaffing wine.

Young Vatted Cabernet Sauvignon, Sliven 1997, Safeway 14 B

Dry vegetality hemmed in by some ripe fruit.

Young Vatted Merlot, Rousse 1997, Safeway 14 B

A fruit bowl with wit.

BULGARIAN WINE — WHITE

Bulgarian Chardonnay, Rousse 1997, Safeway 14.5 B

Deliciously light-minded, more Gilbert & Sullivan than Wagner, but hugely enjoyable.

CHILEAN WINE — RED

35 Sur Cabernet Sauvignon, Lontue 1996 15.5 C

Gorgeous rocky fruit, the patent product of deliciously disembowelled earthy grapes.

Alpaca Plain Cabernet Sauvignon, Central Valley (3-litre box) 15 B

Price band has been adjusted to show the equivalent for a bottle.

Caballo Loco No 2, Valdivieso NV 15.5 F

Much better than the first release of this wine. The number two is more elegant and very impactful.

Casa Lapostolle Cuvee Alexandre Merlot, Rapel 1996 17 E

One of Chile's most stunning merlots: thick, plaited tannin and leathery fruit, and a richness of flavour which defies the price tag. Petrus? Forget it.

Castillo de Molina Cabernet Sauvignon Reserva, Lontue 1996 16 D

It lurks on the palate like a dark avenger. Then it strikes and simply floods down the throat. Selected stores.

Chilean Red, Lontue 1997, Safeway 15.5 C

Errazuriz Cabernet Sauvignon, El Ceibo Estate, Aconcagua Valley 1996 16.5 D

What magnificent texture and temperament! It's fully committed cabernet of huge class and depth.

Errazuriz Syrah Reserve, Aconcagua 1996 18 E

So seductive it makes the knees go weak. A huge attack of plum/raspberry/blackberry fruit with a hint of fig and twig. Massively characterful, dry, rich, positive, loads of tannins and piles of rich, textured fruit of world class wit and style.

Genesis Vineyards, Palmeras Estate Oak Aged Cabernet Sauvignon, Nancagua 1996, Safeway 16 C

Brilliance and bite here from the vigour of the fruit, dry and lingering, to the cigar-box finish. Very classy stuff. Astonishingly good value.

Soleca Cabernet/Merlot, Colchagua 1997 

Perfect ripeness, richness, tannic background, and finish.

Terra Mater Zinfandel/Shiraz, Maipo 1997 

Has some ripe sensuality and alertness. Selected stores.

Valdivieso Cabernet Franc Reserve, Lontue 1996 

Stunning texture and cultured fruit. Makes a mockery of overpriced Bordeaux.

Valdivieso Malbec Reserve, Lontue 1996 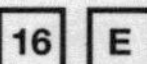

Deeply classy and committed to pleasure provision. Selected stores.

Valdivieso Merlot Reserve, Lontue 1996 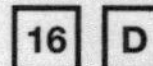

That crunchy velvet texture coating the rich fruit is beautifully tailored.

Villard Vineyards Cabernet Sauvignon, Maipo 1996 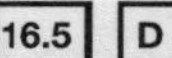

Why is this wine so good? Let me tell you. It has texture (soft) plus character (raunchy) and such well-knitted tannins to the ripe fruit. Selected stores.

CHILEAN WINE WHITE

35 Sur Chardonnay, Lontue 1997 

Warm, richly inviting fruit with a plump, pillow-down luxuriousness.

Casa Lapostolle Cuvee Alexandre Chardonnay, Casablanca 1996 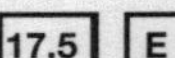

One of the best chardonnays in the world. Simply gorgeous texture, complex fruit and sheer charm. Top twenty-nine stores only.

Castillo de Molina Reserva Semillon, Lontue 1997 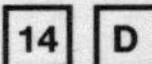

Very richly coated fruit. Has a lot of flavour on the finish, very molar crunching. Selected stores.

Cordillera Estate Oak Aged Chardonnay Reserva 1997, Safeway 

Superb value for such flavour and lingering vanilla overtones.

Errazuriz Chardonnay La Escultura Estate, Casablanca Valley 1996 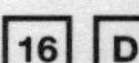

Gorgeous edge to the rich fruit of smoky melon and some kind of soft fruit but its delicious finish has lemon and nuts.

Soleca Semillon/Chardonnay, Colchagua 1997 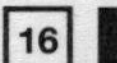

Clever winemaking here. Modern wizardry creating class, richness and style.

Vina Gracia Chardonnay 'Reposado', Cachapoal 1997 14 C

Curiously cosmetic in feel, but I like its cheek.

ENGLISH WINE WHITE

Stanlake, Thames Valley Vineyards 1996, Safeway 13.5 C

FRENCH WINE RED

Beaune 1996, Safeway 10 E

Lot of loot for glum fruit.

Bourgueil 'Les Chevaliers' 1996 13 C

Plumbaceous, raspberry fruit.

Cabernet Sauvignon VdP d'Oc 1996, Safeway 14 C

Nicely lingering, coal-edged fruit – good bangers 'n' mash wine.

Chateau du Grison, Bordeaux 1995 13 C

Chateau du Piras, Premieres Cotes de Bordeaux 1994 14 D

Good with food.

Chateau Soudars, Cru Bourgeois 1994 14 E

Expensive but classic.

Connetable Talbot, Saint-Julien 1994 14 F

Lovely texture.

Cotes du Rhone Oak Aged 1997, Safeway 12 C

Crozes-Hermitage, Domaine Barret 1996 12 D

Domaine de Boriettes Syrah, VdP d'Oc 1997 13.5 C

Almost terrific. I wonder if it doesn't just need time.

Domaine Vieux Manoir de Maransan Cuvee Speciale 1997, Safeway 15 C

Meaty, savoury, bold, dry but softly textured and tenacious, this is a striking wine.

Graves Cuvee Prestige 1994 13 D

Hautes Cotes de Nuits Cuvee Speciale 1995 12 D

J & F Lurton Syrah 'Les Bateaux', VdP d'Oc 1997 13.5 C

James Herrick Cuvee Simone, VdP d'Oc 1996 16 C

I love the insouciance of the delicious fruit.

La Reserve de Leoville-Barton, Saint-Julien 1992 13 E

'La Source de Mirail' Grenache/Syrah, VdP de Vaucluse 1997 15 B

Drives the tannins to the back of the throat with rich, plummy fruitiness.

Le Haut-Medoc de Giscours 1995 13.5 E

Thick but clueless – the initial creaminess wears too thin for an eight quid wine. (Is this the *real* scandal here?)

Les Hauts de Montauriol, Cotes du Frontonnais 1996 15.5 D

One of the most individual and attractive reds on any supermarket shelf: dry, vigorous, characterful, earthy, food-friendly. Coming on nicely in bottle, too.

Marquis de Beaulieu, Bordeaux 1995 13 D

Touch austere and bashful.

Mercurey Raoul Clerget 1996 12 E

Merlot VdP d'Oc 1996, Safeway 13.5 C

Oak-aged Medoc 1996, Safeway 13.5 D

Seems a touch pricey.

Organic French Red VdP du Gard NV, Safeway 14 C

Hugely gluggable yet characterful.

Pommard 1er Cru 'Les Clos des Boucherottes' 1996 10 G

Richemont Montbrun Old Vine Carignan VdP de l'Aude 1995 14 D

Very jammy and ripe, but saved from soppy soupiness by a dry herby tinge to the edge.

Saint-Joseph 'Cuvee Cote-Diane' 1995 14 E

Touches of ripe cherry, charcoal, plum, vegetality, and very dry in the finish (in spite of the ripe fruit). Selected stores.

Savigny du Domaine du Chateau de Meursault 1996 11 E

Very juicy for a tenner. Top thirty-three stores.

St Emilion 1996 13.5 D

Bit tight but then it's young. Might score much better in two or three years.

Syrah VdP d'Oc 1996, Safeway 13 C

Winter Hill Red VdP de l'Aude 1997 15.5 B

Lovely polished richness and ripeness. Gorgeous plump texture and svelteness of fruit.

FRENCH WINE — WHITE

Anjou 'Les Caudanettes' 1997 — 13.5 — B

Light, crisp, perfumed, touch sweet.

Bordeaux Blanc Sec Aged in Oak 1997, Safeway — 13 — C

Starts very well, finishes a touch wimpishly.

Bordeaux Sauvignon, Calvet 1997 — 12 — C

Chablis Cuvee Domaine Yvon Pautre 1996, Safeway — 11 — E

Chablis Grand Cru Grenouille 1993 — 13.5 — G

Classy feel – but not enough to make me feel happy at parting with fifteen quid.

Chablis Premier Cru Montmains 1997 — 10 — F

Goodness what a price!

Chardonnay VdP de l'Herault 1997, Safeway — 13.5 — C

Almost very good but a slight nagging edge mars it a bit.

Chateau du Plantier Entre Deux Mers 1997 — 13 — C

Cotes du Luberon Rose 1997, Safeway — 14 — C

Cheerful, dry, fruitily expressive and gluggable. Also good with food.

Dom Brial, Muscat de Rivesaltes 1997 (half bottle) 15 C

A brilliant little pud wine in the perfect size for a single hedonist.

Domaine du Rey, VdP des Cotes de Gascogne 1997 (vegetarian) 13.5 C

Bit dull on the finish for four quid.

Gewurztraminer d'Alsace 1997, Safeway 16 D

Utterly delicious and sybaritic fruit here: spicy, roseate, singing, scrumptious.

La Baume Sauvignon Blanc, VdP d'Oc 1997 14 C

Classic sauvignon minerality and crispness.

Laperouse White VdP d'Oc 1996 14 C

Very clean and fresh-faced.

Rochemartain Sauvignon Touraine 1997 14 C

Clean, flinty, integrated, mineral-tinged – an excellent fish wine.

Sancerre 'Les Bonnes Bouches' Domaine Henri Bourgeois 1997 12.5 E

Selected stores.

Winter Hill VdP de l'Aude 1997 15.5 B

Super class here: crisp, clean, rich, full, developed, engaging. Terrific value.

GERMAN WINE WHITE

Fire Mountain Riesling, Pfalz 1996 

Getting there, this new style riesling. Dry, classic edge, but still too austere for New World fruit lovers.

Gold Crest Liebfraumilch, Rheinhessen 1996 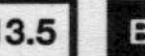

Try it! It's worth a glug to refresh the palate. It's not soppy and sweet but lime-edged and decently balanced.

Hattenheimer Heiligenberg Riesling Kabinett, Rheingau 1996 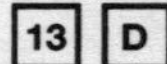

Needs another five years. Top sixty-four stores.

Oppenheimer Sacktrager Riesling Kabinett, Rheinhessen 1996 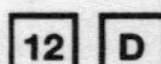

Selected stores.

Pudding Wine, Pfalz Auslese NV (half bottle)  

Gorgeous acidity here. Wonderful with fresh fruit.

Riesling Classic, Pfalz 1996  B

The best packaged and among the most incisively balanced of the new German rieslings. Quaffable, great with fish.

Scharzhofberger Riesling Spatlese, Mosel-Saar-Ruwer 1996

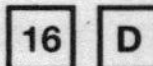

Gorgeous! And what a stylish aperitif it makes. Top sixty-four stores.

Weinheimer Sybillenstein Beerenauslese, Rheinhessen 1993 (half bottle)

Superb, honeyed, nutty, sweet wine with rampant fruitiness and compatibility with fresh fruit and desserts. Selected stores.

GREEK WINE RED

Mavrodaphne of Patras NV

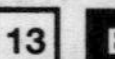

Brilliant with a slice of rich fruit cake.

HUNGARIAN WINE RED

Bull's Blood 1997 13 B

Well, it's better than it was but no bull ever had blood this juicy.

Cabernet Sauvignon, Villany 1996

Superb cabernet here with its freshness, modernity, dryness and great tannins.

River Duna Kekfrancos, Szekszard 1997 14.5 B

Great clods of deliciously earthy fruit here, plump and fulsome.

HUNGARIAN WINE WHITE

Chapel Hill Barrique-fermented Chardonnay 1996, Safeway 15 C

Delicious, calm, nicely textured (gentle voluptuousness without Rubenesque fatness), and charm of finish.

Hungarian Chardonnay, Buda 1997, Safeway 13.5 B

Well, it's clean.

Hungarian Dry Muscat Nagyrede 1997, Safeway 14 B

Delicious ripe edged spicy melon – yet dry.

Hungarian Irsai Oliver, Neszmely 1997, Safeway 12 B

Touch lacking in life.

Matra Mountain Oaked Chardonnay, Nagyrede 1997, Safeway 13 C

Matra Mountain Sauvignon Blanc, Tolna 1997, Safeway 15 C

Gorgeous classic dryness, hint of oil, touch of grass and a lovely mineral finish.

Pinot Blanc, Nagyrede 1996, Safeway 14.5 B

Riverview Chardonnay/Pinot Gris, Neszmely 1996 13.5 C

Tart, good with oysters.

Woodcutter's White 1997 14 B

Terrific, crisp fish 'n' chip wine.

ITALIAN WINE RED

Amarone delle Valpolicella Classico 1993 

Uniquely cherry/plum/blackberry dry, rich wine with a hint of marzipan. Wonderful fruit here.

Barrique Aged Cabernet Sauvignon di Toscana 1995, Safeway 14 D

Has the classic dry hints of green pepper and I suspect this quality, allied to the tannins will give the wine a few more years of developmental excitement. It needs food now. Will be tastier in twenty months.

Chianti 1997, Safeway 14 C

An excellent vintage for Chianti, on the basis of this brisk specimen.

Chianti Classico 1995, Safeway 13.5 D

Di Giorno Merlot/Corvina, Veneto 1997 13.5 B

Juiciness with subdued character.

Salice Salento Riserva 1994 14 D

Great clinging richness to the very ripe and figgy fruit which is very much in need of accompanying food.

Sicilian Red 1997, Safeway 12 B

Tenuta San Vito Chianti Putto 1996 (organic) 13 D

Valpolicella Valpatena 'Corte Alta' 1997 14 C

Very plump and polished. Could almost mount it on a lolly stick.

Young Vatted Teroldego, Atesino 1996, Safeway 14.5 C

ITALIAN WINE WHITE

Alasia Arneis, Langhe 1995 13 D

Chardonnay del Salento Barrique-aged, Caramia 1996 15 D

Gorgeous nutty fruit with the soft/crisp paradox.

Chardonnay delle Venezie 1997, Safeway 14 C

Elegance, bite, richness and charm.

Frascati Superiore 1997, Safeway 14 C

Just as you think 'oh not Frascati again' this specimen surprises you with a brisk nutty finish.

Le Monferrine Moscato d'Asti 1997 (5%) 14.5 C

I love the gentle petillance of this ripely fruity, muscat-edged aperitif. It is so deliciously civilised!!

Pinot Grigio delle Venezie 1997, Safeway 13.5 C

Sicilian White 1997, Safeway 14.5 B

Superb value here: has richness, texture and style.

Soave Classico 'Cortechiara', Zenato 1997 15 C

One of the deftest Soaves around. Delicious. Selected stores.

Verdicchio dei Castelli di Jesi Classico 1997 14 C

Real Italian fish wine. Terrific. Selected stores.

MONTENEGRAN WINE RED

Montecheval Vranac 1993 13.5 C

Pity it's not a quid cheaper.

MOROCCAN WINE RED

Domaine Sapt Inour NV, Safeway 14.5 B

Real bargain: earthy ripe, honest, fruity, great with food.

NEW ZEALAND WINE — WHITE

Kim Crawford Unoaked Chardonnay, Marlborough 1997 15 D

Classy, rich but controlled, fresh but mature. Impressive. Top sixty-four stores.

Kohi Point Sauvignon/Semillon, Marlborough 1997 12 C

Oyster Bay Chardonnay, Marlborough 1997 16 D

Raspberries, melons, lemons and hints of pineapple. It's all fruit – yet it's got finesse and elegance. Selected stores.

Timara Dry White 1997 13 C

Villa Maria Private Bin Sauvignon Blanc, Marlborough 1997 16.5 D

Superb and knows it! Better than any Sancerre, it delivers crispness and complexity.

PORTUGUESE WINE — RED

Miradouro Portuguese Red, Terras do Sado 1996 13 B

Vila Regia Douro 1995 14 C

Rather classy and ripe. Dry and food friendly.

ROMANIAN WINE RED

Pinot Noir Special Reserve 1995, Safeway 

Wild raspberry and black cherry – can't say fairer than that for a dirt cheap pinot.

SOUTH AFRICAN WINE RED

Bouwland Cabernet Sauvignon/Merlot, Stellenbosch 1997 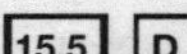

Very stylish fruit which is very loving, lush, lengthy and languorous. Great class on the finish.

Kanonkop Cabernet Sauvignon, Stellenbosch 1994 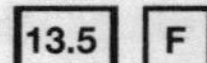

Kanonkop 'Kadette' Estate Wine, Stellenbosch 1996 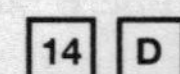

A thundering good wine for roast and lamb.

Kleindal Pinotage 1997, Safeway 

Ooh! This new vintage is sheer chutzpah in a glass. Destroys Beaujolais.

Moutainside Shiraz, Paarl 1997 

Oak-aged Pinotage Coastal Region 1996, Safeway 

Bit juicy for a fiver.

Plaisir de Merle Cabernet Sauvignon, Paarl 1995 15 F

One of the classiest Cape cabernets. Has lush fruit with active tannins. Selected stores.

Simonsvlei Shiraz, Paarl 1996 14 C

Dry yet vigorous on the finish. Has a tobaccoey edge of some charm.

South African Cinsaut, Stellenbosch 1997, Safeway 13.5 C

Light and fluffy – bit toy poodleish.

Stellenbosch Cabernet Sauvignon 1997 13 C

Good firm start but a touch tart on the finish.

Stellenbosch Merlot 1997 13.5 C

SOUTH AFRICAN WINE WHITE

Bouchard Finlayson Oak Valley Chardonnay, 1996 14.5 E

Very classy if not entirely uncluttered with wood as it finishes. Top twenty-nine stores.

Brampton Sauvignon Blanc 1997 14.5 D

Classic grassy sauvignon with New World freshness and concentration. Smashing to drink with smoked fish. Selected stores.

Chenin Blanc Stellenbosch, Safeway 1998 12 B

Very ripe on the finish.

Fairview Estate Semillon, Paarl 1997 16.5 D

Wonderfully concentrated and freshly turned out. Has great lingering dry peach, vanillary and icy mineral undertones all packed together stylishly and sagely. Utterly delicious wine of class and composure.

Kleinbosch Bush Vine Dry Muscat, Paarl 1997 13 B

Kleinezalze Sauvignon Blanc 1997 12.5 C

Robertson Barrel-fermented Chardonnay 1997 16 C

Chardonnay in the new-world, sub-citrus, gently woody style where the fruit is freshly picked, never cloying or taut, but just giving, clean and delicious.

Swartland Reserve Bush Vine Chenin Blanc 1997 15 D

Classic shellfish wine with dryness and stylish freshness with an engaging mineral edge to the acidity.

SPANISH WINE RED

Bach Merlot, Penedes 1996 16.5 D

Beware! Tannin attack! Oh what heaven! The squeamish are warned! Selected stores.

Berberana Tempranillo Rioja, 1996 14 C

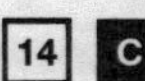

Needs rich food to combat the ripe, vanillary fruit which is bruised and aromatic.

Bright Brothers Old Vines Garnacha 1996 15.5 C

Ripe, rich, sunny and utterly, quaffably delicious.

Cosme Palacio y Hermanos Rioja 1996 14.5 D

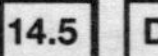

Blends an old-style sense of soul with a modern sense of full-frontal fruit.

Don Coyote Red, Valencia 1996 15 B

Superb little plonk: dry, not-quite-hearty, gleeful.

El Leon de Bierzo 1997 15.5 C

Not remotely as ferocious as the beast on the label. In fact, it's a soft-hearted purring pussycat.

Faustino Rivero Ulecia Rioja Reserva 1989 13 E

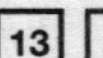

Rather fresh price for such simple fresh fruit (though middle-aged).

Leon Marzot Tempranillo, Navarra 1996 13 B

Marques de Murrieta, Rioja Reserva 1993 13.5 E

Marques de Riscal Rioja Gran Reserva 1989 16 G

A point for every pound it costs. The acme of old style, vanilla rich, tannic Rioja. Fabulous stuff. Top thirty-three stores.

Muruve Toro 1997 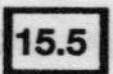 

One of Safeway's most triumphant value-for-money reds. Has lovely tannins and rich, deep fruit. Great fun with a serious edge.

Ribera del Duero Crianza, Conde de Siruela 1994  D

One of Spain's best kept secrets – a dry, rich, textured red of class, wit, style and finish. Has polish but it's the polish of a beautifully rough diamond. Selected stores.

Valdepenas Reserva Aged in Oak 1991, Safeway  

Young Vatted Tempranillo, La Mancha 1997, Safeway  

Has an interesting bruised fruit edge.

SPANISH WINE WHITE

Agramont Navarra Viura/Chardonnay 1996  

Aromatic. fruity, rich, deep, beautifully balanced and terrific value. A very classy wine indeed.

CVNE Monopole Barrel-fermented Rioja 1995 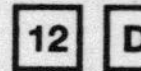

Rather a lot of soggy wood.

Torres Gran Vina Sol Chardonnay 1996 16 D

One of the best and cleanest vintages of this wine for some time. Very classy stuff. Selected stores.

USA WINE — RED

Californian Oak Aged Cabernet Sauvignon 1996, Safeway

Very juicy with a hint of vegetality to suggest it might be cabernet.

Dunnewood Zinfandel, Barrel Select 1994

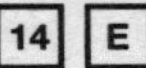

Juicy, bramble-fruited, soft, yummy, spreadable on toast, finishes a bit juicy (raspberries) for eight quid but immensely gluggable.

Fetzer Vineyards Pinot Noir 1996

Classic stuff – if a touch warmer than normal.

Kenwood Lodi Old Vine Zinfandel 1995

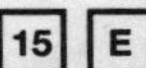

So plump you have to gape to drink it. Offers a cataract of flavours. Top thirty-three stores.

USA WINE — WHITE

Californian Oak-aged Chardonnay 1997, Safeway

Great stuff for under a fiver! Delivers great texture and positive pleasure.

Dunnewood California Chardonnay 1996 16.5 E

Gorgeous texture and great litheness with the balance of wood and fruit in perfect harmony. A hugely impressive Californian chardonnay without being attached to an obscene price tag.

Fetzer Barrel Select Chardonnay, Mendocino 1995 15.5 E

Not as woody as the nomenclature might suggest for the gentle toasty edge is well controlled by the lemon/pineapple subtleties of the fruit. A delicious wine.

Fetzer Chardonnay Reserve 1995 16 F

Did white burgundy, Montrachet say, ever taste this good in the good old days? Nope, never. This is a white wine of great class, richness, balance, and sheer world-class finish.

FORTIFIED WINE

10 Year Old Tawny Port, Safeway 14.5 F

Amontillado, Safeway 13 C

Cream and nuts, sweet.

Barbadillo Solear Manzanilla 14 D

Clean and bone dry with the acquired taste of saline, tea-leaf fruit. I love this sort of passionate eccentricity.

Dow's 20-year old Tawny 16 H

What a price! What a wine! To be drunk the night before the morning you get taken out and shot.

Fino, Safeway 14 C

A must for grilled prawns.

Fonseca Guimaraens 1982 13 G

Penfolds Magill Tawny (half bottle) 14 D

Warre's Traditional LBV 1984 14.5 G

Warre's Vintage Port, Quinta da Cavadinha 1986 17 G

The quintessence of great food. It finishes dry and complex yet it's hugely rich.

Warre's Warrior Finest Reserva 14 E

SPARKLING WINE/CHAMPAGNE

Albert Etienne Champagne Brut NV, Safeway 13.5 F

Barrel Fermented Sparkling Chardonnay (Italy) 15 D

Charles Heidsieck 'Mis en Cave 1994' Champagne 13 H

Classy but too pricey for the degree of it.

Chenin Brut, Val de Loire NV (France) 14 C

Clean and fresh and good with smoked salmon.

Chenin Brut, Vin Mousseux de Qualite (France) 14 C

Brilliant value and a terrific basis for a spritzer.

Edwards & Chaffey Pinot Noir/Chardonnay 1993 (Australia) 13 E

Graham Beck Brut (South Africa) 13 E

Hardys Nottage Sparkling Chardonnay 1996 15 D

Classy, rich, very adventurous. An excellent Aussie bubbly.

J. Bourgeois Pere et Fils Champagne Brut 13 E

Montana Lindauer Brut (New Zealand) 13.5 D

Nicholas Feuillate Champagne Blanc de Blancs NV 14 G

Stylish and elegant . . . Pricey though.

Pol Acker Chardonnay Brut (France) 14 C

Segura Viudas Cava Brut 1994 13 E

Not as convincing as some Cavas. Top sixty-four stores.

Veuve Clicquot Champagne Vintage Reserve 1990 10 H

Oh come on! Thirty-four quid! It's the price of a case of Bulgarian red. Top sixty-four stores.

Veuve Clicquot Champagne Yellow Label Brut NV

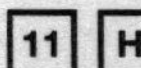

SAINSBURY'S

ALLAN & ROBIN PUT TOGETHER AN ALL-STAR TEAM BUT FAIL TO WIN THE WORLD CUP!

Sainsbury was the 'official England supermarket' for the World Cup and it spent some £15 million promoting itself as such. Assembling the wine team which makes up Sainsbury's wine department, however, has been a less expensive affair and yet considerably more successful. England did not win the World Cup but Sainsbury's wine department scored some great goals. The credit for this is to be laid at the door of Mr Allan Cheesman, director of off-licence buying, and Mr Robin Tapper, manager of the department

Allan Cheesman, even more than myself (this year's prize winning envelope to amuse my children was addressed to Malcolm Clunk), has a name it is deceptively easy for the scribbler to trip over. Note the subtleties: the unusual two l's in the first name and the peculiarity of the lack of a third e in the second. These are more than just drolleries of a birth certificate; they are symbols of an individuality and preciseness of vision which is totally reflected in the way Sainsbury retails wine. Robin Tapper, on the other hand, it is difficult to misspell (except by an illiterate) but, for some stuffy wine commentators, difficult to believe. How can he be a wine buying manager at all; did he not once run a delicatessen? Or was it fish? Hasn't he even had a spell in haberdashery?

Thus, in a somewhat complex nutshell, we discern Sainsbury's strength (and perhaps also its weakness) revealed. The wine department is fluid, strongly managed, promotes from within the organisation when it can, and though it only encourages the calculated risk it is nevertheless – to this watcher at least – in better shape than it has ever been. Mr Cheesman was quoted in *Supermarketing* magazine as saying 'that Sainsbury's partnerships with suppliers are now as important in wine as they are with other sectors of the market' and the wine entries which follow demonstrate that. These entries also provide ample evidence of the depth of the range from wine buyer Mr Gerard Barnes' clarets to wine buyer Miss Joanne Convert's South Africans and Australians. Mr Barnes, alas, has since quit.

Outside the world of wine, Sainsbury was involved in certain controversies over the past year or so. In its eagerness, it had to apologise after it placed job advertisements (for a new store set to open in Calne in Wiltshire) before planning permission had actually been given to build the supermarket. Planning permission came through some time afterwards. A little later I was personally delighted to hear Sainsbury's had decided to axe its own brand alcopops and had pledged itself to recruit 1,000 young unemployed people as part of the New Deal the Labour government is striving to achieve. These events were, of course, unconnected but I can't help feeling that the same group of people benefited from both.

In October last year, Sainsbury's also committed itself to moving more deliveries by rail freight. And this cyclist raised a silent cheer. A family walk-in surgery opened at Sainsbury's Sheffield store a little later, following a tie-up with Sinclair Montrose Healthcare. I'm told Sainsbury is planning further in-store surgeries; this is soon to be followed by in-store masseuses, acupuncturists, pedicurists, marriage guidance counsellors, and sports psychologists.*

In spite of this activity, there are still old farts out there unable to believe that supermarkets like Sainsbury are places to buy wine. Meeting a university teacher just before this book

* this is a partial fabrication. I made it all up except the bit about the surgeries.

went to press I was staggered to hear him remark that of course such stores might be all right for simple everyday plonk but for refined palates like his only rieslings from single great German estates and mature Bordeaux were appropriate.

I am pleased to report that I laughed, restrained my immediate instincts, and agreed with him. Well, such great rieslings as Sainsbury has (admittedly very very few) and terrific Bordeaux (much better selection here) I would prefer to keep out of the hands of the old farts on the grounds that there is more for deserving readers like yourself.

(Sorry to suck up to you like this, but an author has to make a living.)

Sainsbury's Supermarkets Limited
Stamford House
Stamford Street
London SE1 9LL
Tel: 0171 695 6000
Fax: 0171 695 7925
Customer Care Line: 0800 636262
e-mail www.sainsbury.co.uk.

SEE STOP PRESS SECTION AT END OF BOOK FOR LAST-MINUTE ADDITIONS OR UPDATES TO THIS RETAILER'S RANGE.

ARGENTINIAN WINE RED

Mendoza Cabernet Sauvignon/Malbec, Sainsbury's 14 C

Fruit juice with attitude! Hugely lap-uppable. Selected stores.

Mendoza Country Red, Sainsbury's 15 B

Mendoza Tempranillo, Sainsbury's 16 C

ARGENTINIAN WINE WHITE

Mendoza Country White, Sainsbury's 14 B

AUSTRALIAN WINE RED

Australian Cabernet Sauvignon, Sainsbury's 13 C

Australian Red Wine NV, Sainsbury's (3-litre box) 15 B

Brilliant aroma, plummy fruit, tannins, character, warmth and vegetality. Price bracket has been adjusted to show bottle equivalent.

Clancy's Shiraz/Cabernet Sauvignon/ Merlot/Cabernet Franc 1996 15 E

Here the initial rich jamminess strikes as under adult but the character of finishing tannins gives it poise and maturity. 170 selected stores.

Hardys Banrock Station Mataro/Grenache/ Shiraz 1997 

Very perky and apple-pie-ish – soft, fruity, all over the palate.

Hardys Stamp Series Shiraz Cabernet Sauvignon 1997 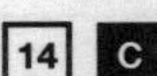

Touch soupy and puppyish but hugely drinkable.

Leasingham Cabernet Sauvignon Malbec 1996 

Juicy and rich. 150 selected stores.

Leasingham Shiraz 1996 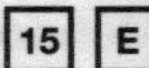

Again that delicious Aussie trick of ripe juiciness with dry, characterful tannins. 140 selected stores.

Lindemans Padthaway Pinot Noir 1997 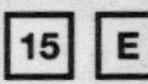

Wonderful cheek here. Takes on the Burgundian trick of truffles and long dead grouse and adds jam-laden fruit. 160 selected stores.

Lindemans Pyrus Coonawarra 1992 15 F

McPhersons Shiraz 1997 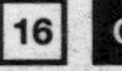

More like Aussie reds should be – soft, cheap, rich, dry, biting, food-friendly, characterful. Forty-four selected stores.

Mount Hurtle Cabernet Merlot 1996 14 D

Juicy and ripe yet plump and with good tannins interwoven. Lush yet sly. 200 selected stores.

Penfolds Bin 389 Cabernet/Shiraz 1995 16 F

Expensive treat for Christmas: spicy, rich, deep, floods of layered fruit, tannins, complexity and great style. Eighty selected stores.

Rosemount Diamond Label Shiraz 1997 15 D

Yes, it's jammy and ripe but it's also dry and serious. Not at all stores.

Rosemount Estate Shiraz Cabernet 1997 14.5 D

Got a bit of oomph and style to the finish – which is soft, rich, savoury.

Saltram Classic Shiraz 1996 13.5 C

Juicy and soupy.

Stowells Australian Red Mataro/Shiraz NV (3-litre box) 15.5 C

Real richness and rampancy of flavour here. Terrific fruit: warm, multi-layered, figgy and very deep. Price bracket has been adjusted to show bottle equivalent.

Tarrawingee Shiraz Mourvedre, Sainsbury's 12 C

AUSTRALIAN WINE WHITE

Australian Chardonnay, Sainsbury's 14.5 C

Australian Semillon Chardonnay NV, Sainsbury's (3-litre box) 15 B

It does pall a touch on the finish but this is of no interest to the frontal attack mounted by the rich fruit. Good ripe aroma. Price bracket has been adjusted to show bottle equivalent.

Australian Semillon Sauvignon Blanc, Sainsbury's 16 C

Delicious texture, gently oily and rich, lots of rich vegetal hints (unusual in an Aussie white), and a dry, hint-of-nut finish. Selected stores.

Australian White Wine NV, Sainsbury's (3-litre box) 14 B

Most unusually dry and demure for an Aussie – with a hint of minerals on the finish. Price bracket has been adjusted to show bottle equivalent.

Classic Selection Australian Chardonnay 1995, Sainsbury's 16 D

Like sticky toffee in texture but this extravagance is full of flavour, rich baked melon fruit, and it finishes with real style.

Hardys Banrock Station Unoaked Chardonnay 1997 15.5 

Aussie chardonnay as great-tasting, unmuckedaboutwith plonk of warmth, simplicity and compelling freshness.

Jacobs Creek Chardonnay 1997  

An excellent ripe, polished texture combined with smoky melon and lemon fruit.

Jacobs Creek Riesling 1997 15 C

A lovely wine for oriental cuisine: quirky, rich, dry, exotic, gently spicy.

Jacobs Creek Semillon Chardonnay 1997 

Old Aussie warhorse, still soldiering on.

Lindemans Bin 65 Chardonnay 1997 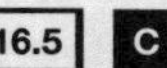

The tastiest under-a-fiver Aussie chardonnay on offer anywhere. This '97 vintage gives it its classiest, most impressive depth yet.

Lindemans Cawarra Colombard/ Chardonnay 1997 

An excellent, ripely textured fish stew wine.

Lindemans Cawarra Unoaked Chardonnay 1997 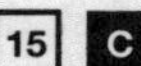

Shows the impressive richness and balance of Aussie's fruit unadulterated by wood. Delicious flavours here.

Lindemans Padthaway Chardonnay 1996 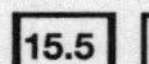

A Bordelais in whose company I tasted this wine, complained of its woodiness! What is the world coming to? It's luscious, gently woody (it's true) and deeply flavoured, but it's delicious and not OTT wood-wise. Selected stores.

Penfolds Rawsons Retreat Bin 21 Semillon/Chardonnay/Colombard 1997 

The gorgeously rich '97 vintage strikes the palate with polish, purpose and plumpness. Not at all stores.

Penfolds The Valleys Chardonnay 1997 14.5 E

Good double act of crispness and precision with soft ripeness and slightly off-centre richness. Selected stores.

Rosemount Estate Diamond Label Chardonnay 1997 16 D

One of the great island's classiest chardonnays – here showing the forwardness of the brilliant '97 vintage.

Rosemount Show Reserve Chardonnay 1997 16 E

Hugely elegant treat wine with classic richness, vegetality, finesse and masses of real depth of charm. Eighty-five selected stores.

Wynns Coonawarra Estate Chardonnay 1996 16.5 E

Most delightful chardonnay with a lingering depth of flavour like gently toffeed melon. Zippy fun. Ninety selected stores.

Wynns Coonawarra Riesling 1996 15 C

BULGARIAN WINE RED

Bulgarian Cabernet Sauvignon, Sainsbury's (3-litre box) 13.5 C

Touch coarse but good with food – very good. Price band has been adjusted to show bottle equivalent.

Bulgarian Country Dry Red, Russe, Sainsbury's (1.5-litre) 14.5 B

A magnum of dry, plummy wine of gently earthy manners. Price band has been adjusted to show the equivalent per bottle.

Bulgarian Reserve Merlot, Suhindol 1994 13.5 C

Juicy rather than leathery. Not at all stores.

Czar Simeon Bulgarian Cabernet Sauvignon 1990 13.5 D

Soft and ripe and has a touch of haughty class. But it's twice the price of many Bulgarian cabs which carry more character. Selected stores.

JS Bulgarian Merlot, Oak Aged, Russe 13.5 B

Vintage Blend Oriachovitza Merlot & Cabernet Sauvignon Reserve 1994 16 C

Very ripe and mature yet still in its prime fruitwise as it finishes: dry, plum and blackcurranty, with a hint of thick tannin. Lovely stuff. Not at all stores.

CHILEAN WINE RED

Carolina Merlot Reservado 1996, Sainsbury's 17 D

It is so devilishly fruity, seductive, angelically textured and ripe yet serene, you wonder if the grapes are alien produce. Wonderful wine. Not at all stores.

Chilean Cabernet Sauvignon/Merlot NV, Sainsbury's 16 C

Volatile on the nostrils and slightly overripe but the fruit is brilliant: dry, rich, flavourful and character packed. Real class runs through it. Wonderful rich, dry, textured stuff. Also available in a 3-litre box.

Chilean Merlot, Sainsbury's 16.5 C

Wonderful richness of tone, texture, and even a touch of soulfulness. A gorgeous, savoury, smooth wine of lingering depth.

Chilean Red, Sainsbury's 13 C

La Palma Reserva Cabernet/Merlot 1996 16 C

A real Chilean food wine: rich, dry, fully formed and throaty. Selected stores.

Santa Carolina Merlot, 1997 16.5 C

Wonderful richness and textured fruit here. Sticks to the molars like emulsion having delivered loads of multi-layered fruit. Forty selected stores.

Valdivieso Malbec 1997 16 C

So rich, beautifully textured and ripe yet, curiously, dry and elegant, it surprises. It's a delightfully warm expression of a tough grape. Selected stores.

Valdivieso Merlot, Lontue 1997 16.5 C

Gorgeous texture for such youth! Deep, rich, softly leathery, aromatic and bold.

Valdivieso Pinot Noir 1997 15 D

Fat, rich, cloying, chewy, not remotely pinot-like on the finish. Lovely texture. 115 selected stores.

Valdivieso Reserve Cabernet Sauvignon 1996 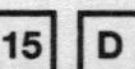

Vibrant richness, tonality and a good dry finish. 175 selected stores.

CHILEAN WINE — WHITE

Casablanca White Label Chardonnay 1997 

Are there any words I have left unsung when singing the praises of chardonnay from Chile? This beauty leaves me voiceless with its deliciousness. Not at all stores.

Chilean Chardonnay, Sainsbury's 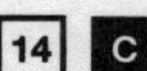

Chilean Sauvignon Blanc, Sainsbury's 

Chilean Semillon Sauvignon NV, Sainsbury's (3-litre box) 

Most unusual Chilean. Tastes dry and French. Price bracket has been adjusted to show bottle equivalent.

Santa Carolina Chardonnay 1997 

Calm but lush, ripe but controlled, this is the essence of smoky melon chardonnay in the new world mould. The finish is lemon silk, smooth, subtle, compelling. Selected stores.

Santa Rita Chardonnay, Estate Reserve 1996 16 D

Stowells Chilean Sauvignon Blanc NV (3-litre box) 12 C

Somewhat dull on the mid-palate. Price bracket has been adjusted to show bottle equivalent.

ENGLISH WINE — WHITE

Denbies Estate English Table Wine, 1992 10 C

Lamberhurst Sovereign Medium Dry 10 B

FRENCH WINE — RED

Barrel Aged Syrah VdP d'Oc, Maurel Vedeau 1995 16 C

Goodness! What a lovely syrah. It's softer and riper than many a Rhone and more exciting, at the price, than many a shiraz. A lovely bottle. Sixty selected stores.

Beaujolais, Sainsbury's 12 C

Beaujolais Villages, Les Roches Grillees 1997 13.5 C

Very pleasant grilled fruit edge, not typical and fresh, but somewhat serious.

Bordeaux Rouge, Sainsbury's 13 B

Gor, blimey! Real old trooper! Needs food!!

Bourgogne Pinot Noir, Boisset 1996 12.5 D

Selected stores.

Cabernet Sauvignon d'Oc NV, Sainsbury's 

C

Terrific cabernet fruit: dry, tense, peppery, rich and black-curranty, and finishes with tannin, style and a surge of flavour. Also available in 3-litre boxes.

Cabernet Sauvignon VdP d'Oc, Caroline Beaulieu 1996 15 C

Cahors, Sainsbury's 13.5 C

Dry, a touch arid on the finish.

Cave Kuhnel Moulin-a-Vent 1996 13.5 E

Nothing wrong with its drinkability. I merely resent paying £7.99 for it. Not at all stores.

Chartreuse de la Garde, Pessac-Leognan 1995 15 E

Gorgeous rich, earthy tannins. Wonderful wine for rare beef and lamb. 150 selected stores.

Chateau Agram, Corbieres 1996 

Selected stores.

Chateau Barreyres, Haut-Medoc 1996 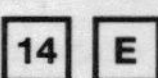

Claret lover's charcoal-edged fruit well to the fore. Selected stores.

Chateau Carsin, Premieres Cotes de Bordeaux 1996 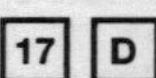

Magnificent texture, ripeness, with an initial perfume of great charm, an immediate lushness which then turns seriously oily and fat in the mouth buttressed by perfectly precise tannins. A fabulous modern claret of superb depth and elegance. 150 selected stores.

Chateau Clement-Pichon, Haut-Medoc 1995 

Rather smug and portly.

Chateau de la Tour Bordeaux Rouge 1996 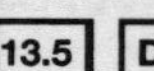

The dry attack turns soppy and soft on the finish.

Chateau de Lunes, Coteaux du Languedoc 1996  

A richly spicy specimen with hints of plum and blackberry plus a touch of twiggy dryness.

Chateau Gloria, St Julien 1993 

It rates a point for every pound it costs. This unique rating is deservedly attached to this glorious bottle of classic claret because of its meaty fruitiness, beautiful tannic structure, and gorgeous rich deep finish. Seventy-six selected stores only.

Chateau Haut Bergey, Pessac Leognan 1995 16 F

Staggeringly good texture, fronted by lush aroma and rich almost ripe blackcurrant concentration. A superb, classy Graves. Sixty selected stores.

Chateau la Vieille Cure, Fronsac 1994 16 F

A big, beautifully characterful, rich, complex wine with dryness yet wit – has a lovely fruity finish. Selected stores.

Chateau Tassin Bordeaux Rouge 1996 15 C

Deliciously classy, dry Bordeaux with charcoal-edged rich fruit. Selected stores.

Chorey Les Beaune, Paul Dugenais 1997 13.5 D

Ooh . . . so herby but the price tag's harder to swallow than the fruit. Not at all stores.

Claret Cuvee Prestige, Sainsbury's 13 C

Claret, Sainsbury's 12.5 C

Classic Selection Brouilly 1997, Sainsbury's 14 D

Very plump and full of itself. Not at all stores.

Clos Magne Figeac, St Emilion 1994 16 E

Gorgeous rich texture, high class fruit – rich and dry – and a broad, multi-faceted finish. Good now, very good, but will develop for five to seven years. Selected stores.

Cornas Les Serres Delas Freres 1992

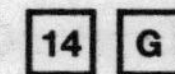

Expensive and still developing.

Cotes du Rhone, Sainsbury's 14.5 B

A deliciously simple, fruity yet dry, rounded yet characterful red of utter quaffability. Good with food, too.

Cotes du Rhone Villages Michel-Bernard 1996

Has a most exotic bottle and a pointed-ogive label – so the fruit isn't straightforward or too rounded either. It has spice, herbs and sun. Selected stores.

Crozes Hermitage, Cave de Tain l'Hermitage 1996

Has a lot of softness and juiciness which has the distinctive, though subtle, edge of charcoal. 255 selected stores.

Cuvee Prestige Cotes du Rhone 1996, Sainsbury's

A rich, layered red Rhone of simplicity yet direct, rich, rolling charm.

Gevrey Chambertin Vieilles Vignes 1992

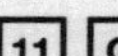

It's a bit rich asking nigh on twenty quid for it!

Grenache/Merlot VdP de l'Ardeche, Sainsbury's

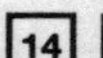

A glug-worthy dry, rustic bumpkin of rough-edged charm. Selected stores.

Hautes Cotes de Nuits Les Dames Huguettes, Domaine Bertagna 1997 15 D

Goodness . . . a real old burgundy under seven quid! It even dares to flaunt tannins to the tenacity of its rich, velvety fruit. It's better than many a Volnay. 150 selected stores.

La Baume Cabernet Sauvignon, VdP d'Oc 1996 15.5 C

Dry, rich, very accomplished red with hints of herb and sun. Has character and charm.

Les Hauts de Pontet, Pauillac 1995 13 G

Has some lip-smacking tannins, but the fruit gets a little left behind.

Merlot Bankside Gallery, VdP d'Oc 1996 17 C

A dry but chocolatey red of immensely warming texture of finely wrought tannins, rich fruit with real classy weight of flavour and complex tones. A stunning fiver's worth.

Merlot VdP de la Cite de Carcassonne, Caroline de Beaulieu 1997 15.5 C

Lovely warm hints of new leather and strawberries, a touch of herby plumminess and a hint of tannin. Great style here. Available at most stores.

Minervois, Sainsbury's 15 B

A sticky, plum-pudding-fruited wine which sticks to the teeth deliciously.

Pinot Noir Joseph de Bel-Air, VdP d'Oc 1996 12 D

Sixty-five selected stores.

Red Burgundy, Sainsbury's 13 D

Reserve du Chateau la Garde, Pessac Leognan 1992 14.5 E

If you want a degree of tannicity which would jettison the dentures then go for this hairy specimen. It's loaded with durable tannins which will keep it going for years. Seventy-five selected stores.

Reserve St Marc Shiraz VdP d'Oc 1997 15 C

Lively, fresh, fruity, with a hint of spice, this is a fulsome rebuke to the Aussies to whom the £3.99 shiraz is almost a museum piece. Available at most stores.

St Joseph Le Grand Pompee, Jaboulet Ainee 1994 13.5 E

Stowells Claret NV (3-litre box) 10 C

Acid fruit. Price bracket has been adjusted to show bottle equivalent.

Syrah Bankside Gallery, VdP d'Oc 1996 16 C

A gentle spiciness and dry hedge-row fruitiness give the wine some great quaffing qualities but it is also a food wine for many things, meaty or cheesy.

Syrah VdP d'Oc NV, Sainsbury's 13.5 B

Valreas Domaine de la Grande Bellane 1997 15.5 D

Wonderful posh feel to the usually earthy Valreas fruitiness. It's a polished wine, this, with loads of charm. 200 selected stores.

Vin de Pays de l'Aude Rouge, Sainsbury's 16 B

Vin de Pays des Bouches du Rhone, Sainsbury's 13 B

Vin Rouge de France Dry Red Wine, Sainsbury's (3-litre box) 12 B

Price bracket has been adjusted to show bottle equivalent.

Vougeot Domaine Bertagna 1995 13 G

Has some warmth and texture but the depth is left to the price tag. Available at seventy-five Fine Wine stores.

FRENCH WINE WHITE

Alsace Blanc de Blancs 1997 14 C

A simple keen-edged fish wine. Seventy selected stores.

Alsace Gewurztraminer 1997, Sainsbury's 16 D

Even better than the '96! And that was superb. This shows how a rich vintage bestows crispness and spiciness brilliantly in one. 260 selected stores.

Blanc Anjou, Medium Dry, Sainsbury's 12 B

Rather woolly in the mouth and coarse smelling.

Bordeaux Blanc, Sainsbury's 12 C

Bourgogne Chardonnay, Boisset 1997 13.5 D

125 selected stores.

Cabernet Rose d'Anjou 1997, Sainsbury's 15 C

Delicious little bargain. Too light for pungent food but has a rich edge to its finish.

Cabernet Rose de Loire 1997 13.5 C

Has some real richness. 115 selected stores.

Chablis Premier Cru Cotes de Jouan, Sainte Celine 1995 14 E

Expensive, too expensive for the style in actuality, but I'm feeling benevolent. It's a classy tipple. Eighty selected stores.

Chardonnay Bankside Gallery, VdP d'Oc 1996 16.5 C

This is a very rich, compelling chardonnay, very Australian in style but with a French elegance and insouciance to it.

Chardonnay VdP d'Oc, Sainsbury's (3-litre box) 15 C

Terrific richness and fruit with a touch of southern warmth and character. Price band has been adjusted to show equivalent per bottle.

Chateau Carsin, Cadillac 1996 (half bottle) 15 D

Terrific – softly textured and waxy. Very sweet and honeyed. 140 selected stores.

Chateau de Cerons 1990 16 E

Gorgeous honeyed texture and rich sweetness.

Classic Selection Chablis Domaine Sainte Celine 1997, Sainsbury's 13 E

Expensive and not quite as complex as it should be.

Classic Selection Muscadet de Sevre et Maine sur Lie 1997, Sainsbury's 13.5 C

Selected stores.

Classic Selection Pouilly Fuisse 1997, Sainsbury's 13.5 D

Expensive, though very attractive with shellfish.

Classic Selection Sancerre 1997, Sainsbury's 13.5 D

Good fish wine but lacks the classic mineral intensity of Sancerre of old.

Clos du Portail, Graves Superieures 1996 (half bottle) 13.5 C

Curious, cloth-edged finish to the sweet fruit.

Domaine de Grandchamp Sauvignon Blanc, Bergerac 1996 14 D

Grenache Rose VdP de l'Ardeche, Sainsbury's 12 B

Hugh Ryman Chardonnay, VdP d'Oc 1997 16 C

What class and understated fruitiness here. It's dry, pert, gently lemony and melony but finishes crisp as a cos. Has a purity of purpose. By the time this book appears it will probably have been replaced by the '98 vintage so keep your eyes peeled for any odd bottle which might be left. Not at all stores.

Hugh Ryman Rose VdP d'Oc 1997 13.5 C

Selected stores.

La Baume Chardonnay VdP d'Oc 1997 15.5 C

A mild-mannered chardonnay but delicious in its finesse and restraint. Lovely calm to it. 230 selected stores.

LPA Cotes de St Mont Blanc 1997 13 C

105 selected stores.

Moulin des Groyes, Cotes de Duras Blanc 1997 14 C

Hints of grass, earth, finely polished pebbles, and a hint of gooseberry. Fifty-five selected stores.

Muscadet de Sevre et Maine sur Lie NV, Sainsbury's (3-litre box) 13 B

Fruity with a hint of sour melon. Attractive with food. Not rich or complex. Price bracket has been adjusted to show bottle equivalent.

Muscadet Sevre et Maine sur Lie, La Goelette 1997 15 C

At last, Muscadet is reborn! This is the best I've tasted in a decade: crisp, fruity, clean, incisive, quaffable and food friendly. Not at all stores.

Pacherenc du Vic Bilh, Moelleux Automnal 1995 (half bottle) 15.5 D

I'm not sure it's rich and honeyed enough for pud but it'd be great with blue cheese and grapes for lunch. Has an interesting cinnamon, clove undertone. Thirty-five selected stores.

Pernand-Vergelesses Domaine Laleure Piot 1996 13.5 F

Crisp and clean now but needs to develop the vegetality of the breed. It might do this over three or four years. Seventy-five selected stores.

Quincy Clos des Victoires 1997 13.5 D

A dry fish wine. Touch expensive. Eighty-five selected stores.

Reserve St Marc Sauvignon Blanc, VdP d'Oc 1997 16 C

An impressively rich sauvignon of class, crispness, softness and great style.

Sancerre Domaine la Croix Canat 1997 14 E

Interesting Sancerre. Will develop well in bottle over the next six months and show more classic mineral bite. 155 selected stores.

Sauvignon Blanc, VdP du Jardin de la France, Lurton 1997 14 C

Not a classic sauvignon, the finish is too full for this, but it's dry and stylish and a good fish wine. 150 selected stores.

Touraine Sauvignon Blanc, Chapelle de Cray 1997 14 C

Dry, curiously earthy edge of some individuality and charm, and a hint of class.

Vin Blanc de France Dry White Wine, Sainsbury's (3-litre box) 13 B

Very basic, clean, touch of sweet fruit. Very simple fun. Price bracket has been adjusted to show bottle equivalent.

Vin de Pays de l'Aude Blanc, Sainsbury's 14 B

Vin de Pays des Cotes de Gascogne NV, Sainsbury's 15 B

One of my favourites: rich, cheeky, pert, quick to refresh and very clean. Also available in a 3-litre box.

Vouvray la Couronne des Plantagenets 1997 13.5 C

Not quite as concentrated as the '96, but it will improve in bottle for a couple of years.

White Burgundy, Sainsbury's 13.5 D

GERMAN WINE WHITE

Black Soil Rivaner Riesling 1997 15 C

Delicious combination of grapes. If only the Germans realised the huge potential of rivaner to make pure, fresh, crisp, clean wines at a seductive price like this example they'd revolutionise their moribund wine industry. 175 selected stores.

Blue Nun Liebfraumilch 13 C

Fire Mountain Riesling 1997 14 C

Interesting accompaniment to things fishy. An improvement on the '96, but still austere to New World fruit lovers.

Hock NV, Sainsbury's 11.5 B

Brilliant price for sweet-toothed tipplers. And it makes a great spritzer! Also available in a 3-litre box.

Liebfraumilch NV, Sainsbury's 11 B

Sweet and simple. Also available in a 3-litre box.

Mainzer St Alban Kabinett, Rheinhessen 1995 13 C

Mainzer St Alban Spatlese, Rheinhessen 1994 13.5 C

Mosel, Sainsbury's 14 B

A crisp glugging Mosel for hot lazy days.

Niersteiner Gutes Domtal, Sainsbury's 12 B

Oppenheimer Krotenbrunnen Kabinett, Sainsbury's 12.5 B

Piesporter Michelsberg, Sainsbury's 12 B

GREEK WINE RED

Kourtakis VdP de Crete Red 14 B

GREEK WINE — WHITE

Retsina, Sainsbury's  

HUNGARIAN WINE — WHITE

Family Reserve Gewurztraminer, Mor Region 1997 

Touch soapy rather than roseate. Selected stores.

Family Reserve Sauvignon Blanc, Sopron Region 1997 

Hugely grassy and ripe yet very crisp and finely knitted elements on the finish. A classy sauvignon of some wit. Selected stores.

Tokaji Aszu 5 Puttonyos 1990 (50cl) 

Give it ten years or drink it now with a slice of Christmas cake. Forty selected stores.

ITALIAN WINE — RED

Allora Primitivo, Puglia 1997 

Alive with earthy, herby fruit flavours with a lingering tannin aftertaste. Great food wine. 150 selected stores.

d'Istinto Sangiovese Merlot 1997 (Sicily) 15.5 C

Great gobbets of earthy rich tannins. Gorgeous bristly fruit here. Great for food. Selected stores.

Due Monti Nero di Troia Cabernet Sauvignon Puglia 1996 15.5 C

Lovely combination of vegetal earthiness and rich, soft, opulently textured edginess of a wine costing a lot more. The balance of tannins and fruit is excellent. Selected stores.

Lambrusco Rosso, Sainsbury's 10 B

Cosmetic wine of interest to candy lovers.

Lambrusco Secco Rosso 'Vecchia-Modena' 14 B

Merlot delle Venezie 1997, Sainsbury's 14 C

Sweet yet dry, characterful yet far from rustic, the fruit is a mite deceitful – deliciously so. Not at all stores.

Montepulciano d'Abruzzo 1996, Sainsbury's 15.5 C

A beautifully textured wine of character and class. Lovely, dusky, herby, gently savoury, dry, terrific.

Ripassa Valpolicella Classico, Zenato 1994 17 E

The smell of baked fruit, ginger, figs, and ripe raisins. A brilliant Valpolicella made in the old-fashioned Ripassa way, and it's rich and gorgeous. Brilliant with food. Seventy selected stores. The '95 may be as good. I said *may*.

Rosso di Puglia, Sainsbury's

Down-to-earth fruit, price, flavour and gluggability. Enjoy it with pastas.

Sangiovese dell'Umbria, Tenuta di Corbara 1997

Wonderful vigour here from the rich plums and fresh blackcurrants of the fruit to tannins on the finish. A fabulous sangiovese. 180 selected stores.

Sangiovese di Toscana, Cecchi 1997

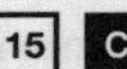

Rich, fresh, no sign of surliness or unrepentant earthiness – just oodles of lush fruit.

Selvapiana Vigneto Bucerchiale, Chianti Rufina Riserva 1993

Ripe, dry, earthy but very far from vegetal or rustic, this has class, aplomb and character. Seventy-five selected stores.

Sicilian Red, Sainsbury's

Stowells Montepulciano del Molise NV (3-litre box)

Fades dramatically on the finish but the fruit on the middle of the tongue is typical M del M. Price bracket has been adjusted to show bottle equivalent.

Teuzzo Chianti Classico, Cecchi 1995

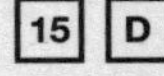

The typical baked earth fruit is harmonious and very dry. 150 selected stores.

Valpolicella Classico, Allegrini 1996 13 D

Ninety selected stores.

Valpolicella NV, Sainsbury's 13.5 B

Treat it like a white: chill it. It's like cherry pie but dry and light. Also available in a 3-litre box.

Vigna Farina Cantine Ascheri Giacomo Barolo 1993 15.5 G

Expensive but highly civilised and genuine. Probably needs three or four more years to be at its peak but elegantly fruity now with soft tannins, marzipan and licorice. Only for Barolo devotees.

ITALIAN WINE — WHITE

Allora Chardonnay 1997 13.5 C

150 selected stores.

Bianco di Custoza, Geoff Merrill 1997 14 C

What I like is the cheeky flash of fat fruit on the finish.

Bianco di Provincia di Verona, Sainsbury's 15.5 B

Delicious weight of fruit with a perfect weight of alcohol (10.5%) but no wait for the thrills. Immediately charming.

Chardonnay del Salento 1997 15.5 D

Superb lime-edged fruit with a plump middle of rich fruit. Deliciously assertive. 231 selected stores.

Chardonnay i Fossilli 1997 

Good crispness of attack with an underlying fruity nuttiness. 250 selected stores.

Cortese del Piemonte 1997 

Has a nice chewy edge to the fruit with a lilt to the fruit on the finish. Terrific quaffing wine. Selected stores.

---

d'Istinto Catarratto Chardonnay 1997 (Sicily) 

Combines some fleshiness of fruit with a taut acidity of finish. Selected stores.

Frascati Secco Superiore 1997, Sainsbury's 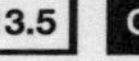

Garganega IGT delle Venezie 1997, Sainsbury's 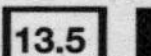

Lambrusco dell'Emilia Bianco. Sainsbury's 

Possibly has some merit for comforting the ill, hence its 12 points, but it is a beginner's tipple at best – or an ender's.

Lambrusco Rosato, Sainsbury's 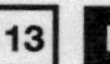

Lambrusco Secco, Sainsbury's 

Pinot Grigio Atesino, Sainsbury's 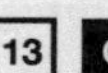

Pinot Grigio Collio 1996 

Rosso di Provincia di Verona, Sainsbury's 

Dry, black cherry-edged fruit of winsomeness and light with a most agreeable alcohol level (10.5%).

Soave, Sainsbury's 15.5 B

Superb clean, crisp fruit and a lovely echo of melon and lemon on the finish.

Tenuta di Corbara Orvieto Classico Superiore 1997 14 C

Nice one, Geoff. Yes, this is an Aussie's idea of Orvieto Bianco and, as you would expect, the fruit is energetic yet dry. 100 selected stores.

Trebbiano di Romagna, Sainsbury's 14.5 B

Tuscan White, Cecchi 13 B

Verdicchio dei Castelli di Jesi Classico 1997, Sainsbury's 15.5 C

Unusually flatly fruity Verdicchio but still that wonderful lazy nuttiness. Not at all stores.

LEBANESE WINE RED

Chateau Musar 1989 12 E

MACEDONIAN WINE RED

Macedonian Cabernet Sauvignon 1996 13 B

Macedonian Country Red 1996 13.5 B

NEW ZEALAND WINE — WHITE

Lone Tree Riesling 1997 13 C

I'd be inclined to stick it away for the Millennium. It'll be balmier by then. It's too prim and stiff at present.

Montana Sauvignon Blanc 1997 15 D

Classy cut of grass – smooth as the lawn on a croquet pitch. But it isn't grotesquely herbaceous whatsoever.

Villa Maria Private Bin Sauvignon Blanc, Marlborough 1997 16.5 D

Superbly greasy grassiness which thunders across the palate with silken hooves; such stealth and purpose here. Not at all stores.

PORTUGUESE WINE — RED

Cabernet Sauvignon Ribatejo 1996, Sainsbury's

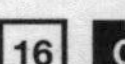

Loaded with flavour and textured ripeness with a hint of earth, cherries and blackberries, and a hint of vegetality. Selected stores.

Do Campo Tinto, Sainsbury's 14.5 B

PORTUGUESE WINE WHITE

Do Campo Branco, Sainsbury's 14 B

Gently earthy, touch of green peach, hint of apple. Good with fish.

Do Campo Rosado, Sainsbury's 12 B

Portuguese Rose, Sainsbury's 13.5 B

Vinho Verde, Sainsbury's 13.5 B

ROMANIAN WINE RED

Idle Rock Merlot Reserve 1997 14 C

Juicier than hitherto but has, curiously, more cheroot-edged fruitiness. Not at all stores.

Idle Rock Pinot Noir Reserve 1997 13 C

Fresh green bean fruit, uncooked, may not be to everyone's taste. Not at all stores.

SOUTH AFRICAN WINE RED

Bellingham Merlot 1996 15.5 D

Lovely tobacco-scented and fruited jamminess. Terrific fruit here. Not at all stores.

Bellingham Shiraz 1997 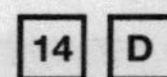

Very juicy and fresh. Forty-five selected stores.

Fairview Pinotage 1997 

Such brilliant fun on the tongue! It trips, it prances, it lies down and laughs, it caresses the taste buds like a ballet dancer's heel crossed with a racing driver's throttle foot. Thirty-two selected stores only.

Reserve Selection Merlot 1996, Sainsbury's 

Real juicy leather – quite remarkable. 150 selected stores.

South African Cabernet Sauvignon/Merlot Reserve Selection 1996, Sainsbury's 

Quite a layered, rich beast, this, with a lovely ripe thwack of soft, rich fruit on the finish. Has classic overtones but invigorating modern undertones.

South African Pinotage, Sainsbury's 

Hums along with some great rich, rolling fruit of depth, flavour and wit.

South African Red, Sainsbury's 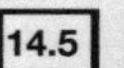

Has ripeness tempered by a gently burnt, savoury dryness. Yummy.

South African Reserve Selection Pinotage 1996, Sainsbury's 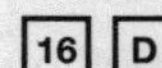

Rich, ripe, complex, textured, rousing, very sunny and savoury, and so drinkable it's sinful. Selected stores.

SOUTH AFRICAN WINE WHITE

Cape Dry White Wine, Sainsbury's 13.5 B

Good enough for a fish and chip supper in our house.

Mont Rochelle Sauvignon Blanc 1997 15 C

Demurely fruity, subtly rich, coolly collected: yes, it's a lovely paradox of a wine. Watch out for this vintage because the '98 will be starting to come in as this book is published (haven't had a chance to try the '98 yet). 105 selected stores.

South African Chardonnay, Sainsbury's 15 C

South African Chenin Blanc NV, Sainsbury's (3-litre box) 14.5 B

Dry with a good surge of nutty fruit on the finish. Terrific rich fish dish wine. Price bracket has been adjusted to show bottle equivalent.

South African Colombard, Sainsbury's 15.5 B

Delightful combination of crispness and soft-edged flavoursomeness. Lovely.

South African Medium Wine, Sainsbury's 11 B

Don't like the touch of sugar but your grandma might.

South African Sauvignon Blanc Reserve Selection 1998, Sainsbury's 15.5 C

Extraordinary ripeness and textured fruitiness here: pear drops, lemon sherbet, raspberry sorbet. It really socks it to the taste buds. 220 selected stores.

South African Sauvignon Blanc, Sainsbury's 15 B

Deliciously priced and fruited with a dry edge to the fresh-faced flavour.

Springfield Estate Special Cuvee Sauvignon Blanc 1998 15.5 D

Slightly nervous edge to the fruit which hits home like a freshly sharpened rapier. Not available at all stores.

Vergelegen Chardonnay Reserve 1997 16 E

Expensive but it's like a forward, rich, white burgundy of an unusually wonderful vintage. It's vegetal, textured, ripe, deep, lingering and very very classy. Fifty selected stores.

Vergelegen Sauvignon Blanc 1998 16 D

Real class here: fruity yet fresh, clean yet full and rich. Very ripe but also balanced and elegant. Seventy selected stores.

SPANISH WINE RED

Alicante Tinto, Sainsbury's 15 B

This is dry, fruity, and almost rude (by virtue of a suggestion of cheekiness) and it finishes with some aplomb. Good with mood and food.

El Conde Oak Aged Vinho de Mesa, Sainsbury's 16 B

A gorgeously flavoured, cherry-and-vanilla-undertoned wine of soupy warmth.

Jumilla, Sainsbury's 15.5 C

Laztana Tempranillo Rioja 1997 15.5 B

Old boot leather, plums, touch of spice – the perfect recipe for meat off the grill. A dry, deep wine of substance.

Marques de Grinon Valdepusa Syrah 1996 16.5 E

One of the classiest under-a-tenner reds in Spain. It's dry, spicy, savoury, balanced, rich and very deep. Hugely lingering flavours.

Navarra, Sainsbury's 15 B

Navarra Tempranillo/Cabernet Sauvignon Crianza 1995, Sainsbury's 16 C

Wonderful mature fruit here: tobaccoey, ripe, rich, deep, woody, balanced and very eager to please. Loads of class.

Old Vines Garnacha, Navarra NV 15.5 C

Loads of earthy rich fruit here. Real barrow loads of it. Selected stores.

Rioja Reserva Vina Ardanza 1989 14 F

Expensive, dry, rich, old-style but has elegance on the finish. Seventy-five selected stores.

Stowells Tempranillo La Mancha NV (3-litre box) 13.5 B

Dry and fruity and has some character, not conspicuously tempranillo-like but most acceptable. Price bracket has been adjusted to show bottle equivalent.

Valencia Oak Aged, Sainsbury's 14.5 B

Vinas del Vero Tempranillo/Moristel 1997 14.5 C

Soft and so utterly slurpable it's nearly a sin. Selected stores.

SPANISH WINE WHITE

Lagar de Cervera, Rias Baixas Albarino 1997 15.5 D

Unusually vibrant fruit, hint of spice, touch of subtle mango, but it's the crisp, nervous acidity which carries these nuances so well. Ninety-five selected stores.

Navarra Rosado NV, Sainsbury's 15 C

An impressive rose of real depth and flavour. 150 selected stores.

Santara Chardonnay 1996 16 C

Such lovely texture to the lemony fruit. It's real class. Selected stores.

USA WINE RED

California Estates Old Vine Zinfandel 1996 16 D

Individual, rich, vibrant, sexy, deliciously full, deep and softly structured, this wine is a wonderful zinfandel with loads of juicy raspberry, plum and black cherry flavour. The perfume and the finish are lingering and very complex. Ravishing stuff, gooey but huge fun. Not at all stores.

Fetzer Bonterra Cabernet 1995 (organic) 15 E

Rich, rounded, full, Californian in ripeness and tannic cosiness from nose to throat.

USA WINE — WHITE

Byron Chardonnay, Santa Barbara County 1994 14 G

Has a certain sensuality. Very rich and clinging. Available at the fifty Fine Wine stores.

Fetzter Bonterra Chardonnay 1995 (organic) 14.5 E

Sutter Home White Zinfandel 1997 13.5 C

Has some raspberry-edged and somewhat boyish charms. Not at all stores.

FORTIFIED WINE

1985 Vintage Port Quinta Dona Matilde, Sainsbury's 15 G

Aged Amontillado, Sainsbury's (half bottle) 13.5 B

Blandy's Duke of Clarence Madeira 15.5 E

Fruit cake companion and old buffer's friend. Selected stores.

Cantine Pellegrino Superiore Garibaldi Dolce Marsala (half bottle) 14 D

Cream Montilla, Sainsbury's 14.5 B

Rich and ripe, like a light oloroso. Good with chocolate biscuits at tea time. Not at all stores.

Fino Sherry, Sainsbury's 14 C

Gonzales Byass Matusalem Old Oloroso (half bottle) 14 E

Medium Dry Montilla, Sainsbury's 13.5 B

An aperitif for off-dry sherry drinkers.

Mick Morris Rutherglen Liqueur Muscat (half bottle) 17 C

A miraculously richly textured pud wine of axle-grease texture and creamy figginess. Huge, world class. Sixty selected stores only.

Old Oloroso, Sainsbury's (half bottle) 16 B

Pale Cream Montilla, Sainsbury's 14 B

A glass with fresh fruit is a great idea after lunch or dinner.

Pale Cream Sherry, Sainsbury's 15.5 C

Sweet with a hint of delicious cream caramel and butterscotch.

Pale Dry Amontillado, Sainsbury's 15 C

Richer textured than many with a hint of ripe baked fruit. Superb aperitif for serious friends. Selected stores.

Pale Dry Manzanilla, Sainsbury's 15 C

A dry, nutty, aperitif-style sherry with a hint of tea-leaf. For aficionados. Selected stores.

Pale Dry Montilla, Sainsbury's 14 B

A lovely dry glass of it, chilled, with nuts and olives is a great treat. Selected stores.

Palo Cortado, Sainsbury's (half bottle) 

Be different. A winter warmer of quirkily nutty richness yet not sweetness. Not at all stores.

Ruby Port, Sainsbury's 13 D

Rich, warming.

Sainsbury's LBV 1990 15 E

A beautifully plump, rich port of deliciously sinful drinkability.

Tawny Port, Sainsbury's 13.5 D

Rousingly sweet yet not sickly.

SPARKLING WINE/CHAMPAGNE

Angas Brut Rose (Australia) 15 D

Asti, Sainsbury's (Italy) 13 C

Very sweet and innocent. Maud might like it in the garden but not I.

Blanc de Blancs Vintage Champagne 1991, Sainsbury's 15 G

Very elegant, mature, gently rich, classic. The '92 might be coming into store as this book is published but I haven't had a chance to try it yet. Not at all stores.

Blanc de Noirs Champagne Brut, Sainsbury's 14.5 F

Cava Rosado, Sainsbury's 15 C

Cava, Sainsbury's 16 D

Champagne Extra Dry, Sainsbury's 14 F

Chardonnay Brut, Methode Traditionelle, Sainsbury's (France) 14 D

Not especially chardonnay-like in its crispness and pace.

Demi Sec Champagne, Sainsbury's 10 E

Freixenet Cava Rosado NV 14 D

Great fun. 140 selected stores.

Gallo Brut 10 D

Graham Beck Brut, Robertson (South Africa) 13.5 D

Jules Camuset Champagne Brut NV 14 E

Not bad. Under-a-tenner champagne. There should be more of it.

Lindauer Special Reserve NV (New Zealand) 14 E

An echo of peach but it's essentially dry and very stylish. Seventy selected stores.

Seaview Brut NV (Australia) 14 D

Dry and wry. Selected stores.

Seaview Brut Rose NV (Australia) 14 D

Saucy. Selected stores.

Segura Viudas Brut Reserva (Spanish) 13 D

Selected stores.

Sekt, Medium Dry, Sainsbury's (Germany) 13 C

Seppelt Pinot Noir/Chardonnay NV 16 D

Has the classic dryness of fine bubbly with that urge-to-return-to-the-glass hint of steely fruit. Delicious charmer. Selected stores.

Sparkling White Burgundy, Sainsbury's 13.5 D

Sixty-eight selected stores.

Vin Mousseux Brut, Sainsbury's (France) 13 C

Dry and appley.

SOMERFIELD

ANGIE CONTINUES TO SPIT IN THE BIG BOY'S EYES!

Somerfield may claim that its computer systems will be ready for the Millennium and will be able to accept the double-nought digits (in the face of the dire predictions of computer experts who have suggested that retailers will face cataclysmic computing problems once 1/1/00 rolls around), but I feel much more of an achievement has been the rise and rise of its wine buyer Mrs Angela Mount, who has significantly helped make this supermarket chain face the coming of the Millennium with increasing confidence. Her price cutting policy has promoted wines at deliciously absurd levels every month and although such antics get right up the noses of the store's competitors, some of whom feel selling a wine at cost or at a loss is not playing the game, the wines delight the pockets of Somerfield's increasing customer base.

In other respects, Somerfield is not so dynamic. It finally rolled out the Catalina EPOS-driven coupon system after trials dating back to 1994. A five year trial for such comparatively unadventurous technology seems a touch constipated to me. On the other hand, Somerfield abandoned plans to roll out to its branches ostrich, kangaroo and crocodile meat (research apparently showing that consumers were concerned about how the meat was farmed). This announcement followed Tesco's earlier one that it was to stop selling similar exotic meats owing to a lack of demand. My local Sainsbury's meat counter, however, one afternoon earlier this year had a counter with these meats on display around which was an enraptured crowd of French children on a school trip, their planned excursion to London Zoo apparently having been rained off.*

In January, Somerfield sponsored the 'Scoop of the Year' prize at this year's British Press Awards. The City reporter who broke the news of the merger of Somerfield and Kwik Save must be in the running.

Extending its new-found confidence in the computer, Somerfield set up a pilot home shopping service – one of the most 'personalised of such services introduced by major retailers in the last year or so' so I was informed. The retailer is also planning a home shopping service on CD-Rom. Can I make a plea here that such shoppers can at least get to move a little trolley cursor around their screens? (It might also be fun to introduce random on-screen trolley collisions. Just a thought.)

Then the big news was finally confirmed. A £1.26 billion merger was announced between Somerfield and Kwik Save. Within months, it was reported that Somerfield's 28 Food Giant stores would now trade under the Kwik Save fascia.

The future of the dynamic wine buyer of this now bullish supermarket operator is extremely rosy it seems to me. More spits in competitors' eyes are doubtless being planned.

* this is almost a complete lie. I have never encountered a French school child in a British supermarket.

Somerfield
Gateway House
Hawkfield Business Park
Whitchurch Lane
Bristol BS14 OTJ
Tel: 0117 935 9359
Fax: 0117 978 0629

SEE STOP PRESS SECTION AT END OF BOOK FOR LAST-MINUTE ADDITIONS OR UPDATES TO THIS RETAILER'S RANGE.

ARGENTINIAN WINE RED

Argentine Red 1997, Somerfield 14 B

Good confident glugging.

Bright Brothers Argentine Tempranillo 1997 15 C

Rather haughty in its own dry way. It's a delicious sipping wine, perhaps too dry for some, but the rich plum fruit is great with food.

Bright Brothers San Juan Cabernet Sauvignon Reserve 1997 17 C

Magnificent breadth of lingering fruit here, simply cavernous in its embrace, and with the tannins in superb form. A fabulous fiver's worth here. World class luxury. At larger stores.

Santa Julia Argentine Tempranillo 1997 16 C

Rich ripe fruit of consummate drinkability and style. Very lingering flavour, with deftly interwoven fruit and acidity and a textured finish of subtle tannins.

ARGENTINIAN WINE WHITE

Argentine White 1997, Somerfield 13.5 B

Bright Brothers Chardonnay/Chenin 1998 14.5 C

Dry, assertive, sophisticated, hard-nosed, food friendly.

Bright Brothers San Juan Chardonnay Reserve 1998 15 C

Very rich creamy edge to dry fruit which makes for impressive quaffing. The fruit has a subtle smoky quality and it lingers lovingly. Top 200 stores.

AUSTRALIAN WINE RED

Australian Cabernet Sauvignon 1997, Somerfield 14 C

Cabernet with tannin and lots of jammy fruit.

Australian Dry Red, Somerfield 13.5 B

Australian Shiraz Cabernet 1997, Somerfield 14 C

Quaffing with a hint of black cherry and chocolate.

Hardys Banrock Station Mataro/Grenache/ Shiraz 1997 14 B

Quaffing of very high quality quaffability. (After a bottle you may not find this so easily quickly to utter.)

Hardys Nottage Hill Cabernet/Shiraz/ Merlot 1995 14.5 D

Free flowing and full of itself – but charming company. Top 250 stores.

Hardys Stamp Cabernet Shiraz Merlot 1996 15.5 D

Yes, it's juicy but there are tannins and tenacity. So: you get backbone!

Hardys Stamp Shiraz Cabernet 1997 14 C

Juice! Juice! Juice! (But it has some wit too.)

Nottage Hill Shiraz/Cabernet Sauvignon 1996 14.5 C

Penfolds Coonawarra Bin 128 Shiraz 1994 15.5 E

Unrestrained hedonistic richness and vivacity. At larger stores.

Penfolds Koonunga Hill Shiraz Cabernet Sauvignon 1997 14 D

Usual smooth tannin and fruit artefact at this price from Penfolds. Highly competent if a touch soulless.

Penfolds Rawsons Retreat Cabernet Sauvignon/Shiraz/Ruby Cabernet 1997 14 D

Again the princedom of soft manners sends out its rich, gooey ambassador.

Rosemount Estate Shiraz Cabernet 1997 14.5 D

Got a bit of oomph and style to the finish – which is soft, rich, savoury.

Rosemount Shiraz 1995 15.5 D

Very fruit-cakey flavour of such exuberance of richness. There's a good savoury edge, though.

AUSTRALIAN WINE WHITE

Australian Semillon/Chardonnay 1997, Somerfield 15 C

Hardys Banrock Station Chenin Blanc/Semillon/Chardonnay 1997 15 C

Shows the real elegance of the '97 Aussie whites.

Hardys Chardonnay Sauvignon Blanc 1997 14 D

A warm, rich, almost cloying sauvignon. Great for rich fish dishes with impertinent sauces. Top 200 stores.

Hardys Padthaway Chardonnay 1996 16 E

Do you like Meursault? You'll like this, then. This kind of woody, hay-rich, vegetal fruitiness is a miracle under eight quid. Top 200 stores.

Hardys Stamp Semillon Chardonnay 1997 14.5 C

Stylish richness and flavour.

Jacobs Creek Semillon/Chardonnay 1997 14 C

A brand but not taking its fruit (or its fans) for granted. Shows some fresh '97 fruit.

Penfolds Australian Chardonnay 1997, Somerfield 14 C

Penfolds Australian Dry White 1997, Somerfield 13 B

Penfolds Bin 202 Riesling, South Australia 1997 15 C

I think it needs a year to eighteen months to develop character but it's classy and fine for all that.

Penfolds Koonunga Hill Chardonnay 1997 15.5 D

The '97 Aussie whites are on song and no branded chardonnay hits a sweeter (yet drier) top note than this one.

Penfolds Rawsons Retreat Semillon/Chardonnay/Colombard 1997 15.5 C

Gorgeous harmony struck up here between rich fruit, quite thick, and lithe pineapple acidity.

Rosemount Estate Semillon/Chardonnay 1997 14.5 E

Elegant and worldly. Serve it with grilled white fish.

BULGARIAN WINE RED

Bulgarian Cabernet Sauvignon, Somerfield 15.5 B

Juicy and ripe, fresh and full of itself, but held back from frivolous embrace by excellent tannins, overall balance of elements, and a flavour-packed dry edge.

Country Red Merlot/Pinot Noir, Somerfield 15 B

Domaine Boyar Merlot, Iambol 1996 15.5 B

Dry, somewhat stern, tannic merlot of great food compatibility. Superb value for money.

Iambol Cabernet Sauvignon 1996 15 B

Brilliant candied blackcurrant glugging.

Oriachovitza Cabernet Sauvignon 1992 16 C

Rich, warm, almost meaty but perfect weight of alcohol (12%), soft tannins and a lovely floral-edged presence to the leather and coffee fruit. Fantastic value here.

BULGARIAN WINE — WHITE

Bulgarian Barrel Fermented Chardonnay, Pomorie 1996 15 C

Chewy, subtle lemon sherbet.

Bulgarian Chardonnay, Somerfield 13.5 B

Suhindol Aligote Chardonnay Country White, Somerfield 13.5 B

Suhindol Barrel Fermented Bulgarian Chardonnay 1996, Somerfield 15.5 B

CHILEAN WINE — RED

Canepa Reserve Merlot 1995 13.5 D

Chilean Cabernet Sauvignon 1996, Somerfield 15.5 C

Hauntingly fruity in the sense that there's a black cherry and chocolate undertone, very subtle, to the full-throated, soft fruit.

Chilean Red 1997, Somerfield 15.5 B

Gorgeous ripeness of fruit, readiness of texture, raunchiness of tone. A lovely balance of elements, luxurious in feel and style.

Cono Sur Pinot Noir 1997 13 C

Top 250 stores.

Terra Noble Merlot 1997 17.5 C

What a tremendous price for such wonderfully soft leathery fruit (cherries, blackcurrants and plums) and such superb warmth and texture to it. It's a wonderful wine of huge class and depth. It'll manage either food or mood magnificently. Top 100 stores.

CHILEAN WINE WHITE

Chilean Chardonnay 1997, Somerfield 14.5 C

It's the texture which so marks its Chilean-ness out: soft, silky, rich, finely woven.

Chilean Sauvignon Blanc 1997 16 C

Such effortless class and high quality fruit is seems unfair on other grape growers. Lovely understated richness and charisma.

Chilean Sauvignon Blanc 1997, Somerfield 15 C

Has more fatness but less fleet-of-foot acidity.

Chilean White, Somerfield 13 B

Valdivieso Reserve Chardonnay 1997 16.5 D

Not classic sophistication here – it's too vanillary and rich for that. But the sheer impudence of its vegetality and fruitiness, the lazy lush texture, the aplomb of the finish – it's all there. Top 100 stores.

FRENCH WINE RED

Beaumes de Venise Cotes du Rhone 1995 13.5 C

Beaumes de Venise, Cotes du Rhone Villages 1996 14 C

Very smoothly shaven – as a baby's bum.

Bourgogne Hautes Cotes de Beaune, Cottin 1995 12.5 D

Brouilly, Selles 1996 13 D

Juicy. And most gluggable. But the price . . ! ? At larger stores.

Buzet Cuvee 44 1996 13 C

Cabernet Sauvignon VdP d'Oc 1997, Somerfield 15 B

Lovely plump fruit here with handsome tannins and a great finish. Terrific value.

Chateau de Caraghuiles, Corbieres 1995 (organic)  

Fabulous organic and of such lovely fruit you wonder if Corbieres is really where it's grown. More like Aus. with attitude.

Chateau La Rose Boyer, Premieres Cotes de Blaye 1995 

Approachable claret yet still with the classic hints of charcoal dryness.

Chateau Pierredon, Bordeaux Superieur 1995 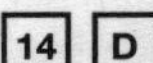

Hints of fat to the fruit gel nicely with the well-defined tannins. Good food claret.

Chateau Plaisance, Montagne St Emilion 1996  

Sheer silky class in a glass. At larger stores.

Chateau Saint Robert, Graves 1994 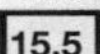 

Gorgeous richness and texture. Toothsome and classy.

Chateau St Benoit Minervois 1995  

Wonderful value for such rich, dry, energetic fruit of character, charm and utter class.

Chateau Talence, Premieres Cotes de Bordeaux 1996 

Soft, rich, most quaffable – not always Bordeaux's strong suits. At larger stores.

Chateau Valoussiere, Coteaux du Languedoc 1995 16.5 C

Fabulous herby fruit of huge sunniness, richness, earthy friendliness and great gripping texture.

Claret, Somerfield 13.5 B

Pleasant sippin' claret.

Corbieres Val d'Orbieu, Somerfield 12.5 B

Cotes de Gascogne Rouge 1997, Somerfield 14.5 B

Dry, energetic, rich, lively, full of personality and flavour.

Cotes de Roussillon Jeanjean 13 B

Cotes du Rhone 1997, Somerfield 14.5 B

Modern, rounded, rich, very fat and exceedingly mouth-filling. Astonishing, fleet-of-foot red Rhone for the money.

Cotes du Rhone Villages, Lucien de Nobleus 1996 14 C

Cherries and blackberries – a vague hint of earth.

Domaine de Bisconte, Cotes du Roussillon 1995 16 C

What a price to pay for such cosiness and warmth. Beautifully well developed tannins and fruit. At larger stores.

Fitou, Rocher d'Ambree 1996, Somerfield 15 C

Very soft earth here with plump fruit of vibrancy and style. Great stuff.

Gigondas Chateau Saint Andre 1996 13 D

Hautes Cotes de Beaune, Georges Desire 1996 12 D

James Herrick Cuvee Simone VdP d'Oc 1995 16 C

Earthy edge to some very stylish blackcurrant/plum fruit of elegance and richness.

Medoc NV, Somerfield 13 C

Medoc, Somerfield 14 C

Medoc as if made in Argentina. A most lively piece of geographical cross-dressing!

Merlot VdP d'Oc 1997, Somerfield 14 B

Blackberries and cherries essentially. Plus a hint of earth. Great with pasta.

Oak Aged Claret, Somerfield 12.5 D

Red Burgundy 1996, Somerfield 12 C

Sirius Bordeaux 1994 13 D

St Emilion P. Sichel 13.5 C

Vacqueyras Selles 1996 16 C

Gorgeous richness of tone, like cassis-edged liqueur cherry. But the acid and tannin balance things out. Yummy stuff.

Vin de l'Ardeche Rouge 1997, Somerfield 14 B

Cherry ripe, dry, hints of the sunny south.

Vin de Pays des Bouches du Rhone, Selles 1997 15 B

Wonderful subtle touches of farmyard gates and barn doors but the fruity exuberance subsumes it. Great value.

FRENCH WINE WHITE

Anjou Blanc 1997, Somerfield 12 B

Sort of off-dry. Can't quite make its mind up.

Bergerac Blanc 1997, Somerfield 13 B

Coarse and earthy with the fruit only asserting itself on the finish.

Bordeaux Clairet, Sichel 1997 12 C

Bourgogne, Hautes-Cotes de Bourgogne 1996 12.5 C

Very lemony. Modern? A touch.

Chablis 1995, Somerfield 12 D

Chardonnay VdP d'Oc 1997, Somerfield 14.5 C

Plump, ripe, handsome, nicely finished off (fresh yet fruity) and altogether a splendid little tipple. Lemony, melony, textured, joyous.

Chardonnay VdP du Jardin de la France 1997 14 C

Very fruity but with enough freshness to give it a balanced impact. A solid glug of some style.

Domaine du Bois Viognier VdP d'Oc, Maurel Vedeau 1997 15.5 C

Deliciously controlled plump apricot fruit. Top 250 stores.

Domaine Sainte Agathe Oak Aged Chardonnay, VdP d'Oc Maurel Vedeau 1997 15.5 C

Textured, finely wrought, beautifully warm yet fresh, it has a delicious charm of its own. Nice nutty finish, too. Top 300 stores.

Entre Deux Mers 1997, Somerfield 13.5 C

Some freshness and flavour here.

Gewurztraminer Alsace, Caves de Turckheim 1997 15.5 D

Great vintage for this grape: aromatic, rich, insistent, very stylish and great with oriental food. Lovely crushed rose petal fruit.

James Herrick Chardonnay 1996 15 C

Good age for a wine not designed to grow old with any great grace. Here it's perfectly mature, melony and lemony and strikes home with style.

Muscadet de Sevre et Maine sur Lie 1997 

Touch dull. At this price, Chile invades Nantes, slaughters the entire citizenry and razes the place to the ground.

Muscat de Frontignan NV 

Another brilliant screw-capped bottle of honey (qv Moscatel de Valencia) but this one is even raunchier, riper and more dazzlingly rich. At larger stores.

Pinot Blanc Alsace, Caves de Turckheim 1997 

Excellent pinot with a hint of very dry peach and nuts.

Rivers Meet Sauvignon/Semillon, Bordeaux 1997 

Crisply turned and well tuned in to modern fish dishes.

Sancerre 1996, Somerfield 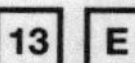

A delicious wine – at £3.99. At £7.49 can I have more thrills please?

Sauvignon VdP du Jardin de la France 1997 

Fresh and clean – perhaps not quite as a whistle but near enough to give it appeal with a squid stew or somesuch.

Syrah Rose Vin de Pays 1997 

An excellent rose of rich cherry fruit, good texture, yet dry and stylish enough to go with food.

Vin de Pays de l'Ardeche Blanc 1997, Somerfield 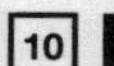

Perfectly dull – indeed I have not encountered such perfection in a twelvemonth of slurping and gargling and spitting and am wondering if God really intended me for this missionary work.

Vouvray 1997, Somerfield 14 C

Real semi-sweet chenin with the taste of raspberry and glucose impregnated wet wool. Lovely with grapes and goat's cheese.

White Burgundy 1997, Somerfield 13 C 

Some richness here.

GERMAN WINE — WHITE

Baden Dry NV, Somerfield 10 C 

Baden Gewurztraminer NV 13.5 C  

Hock, Somerfield 14 B 

What's wrong with a chilled glass of this sat on the patio in July?

Morio Muskat, St Ursula NV 14 B  

Serve it with a minted pea dish – it's wonderful (also good with asparagus).

Mosel Riesling Halbtrocken NV 14 B  

A lovely crisp aperitif.

Niersteiner Spiegelberg, Riesling Kabinett Rudolph Muller 13 B

Rheingau Riesling 1996 13 C

Rheinhessen Auslese NV, Somerfield 13 C

Rudesheimer Rosengarten NV 14 B

An elegant label leading to elegant, crisp, off-dry fruit. Delicate and efficient.

Schloss Schonborn Riesling Kabinett 1987 15.5 D

Perfect, paraffin-edged maturity with the added wit of middle-aged riesling's wrinkled minerality. An exceptionally well-priced aperitif. Be daring! Offer it!

St Johanner Abtey Kabinett, Rudolph Muller NV 13.5 B

Apple-cheeked, faintly honeyed.

St Ursula Devil's Rock Riesling 1996 14 B

Brilliant price, brilliant vintage. A dry, flinty, fresh German of such style as to make you think again about this country's cheaper whites.

St Ursula Dry Riesling 1996 13.5 C

Chile, South Africa and Italy crush it to death at this price level.

GREEK WINE — WHITE

Samos Sweet White Wine NV (half bottle) 15.5 B

HUNGARIAN WINE — WHITE

Castle Ridge Sauvignon Blanc 1997

Lovely clean, crisp fish wine of no little distinction and varietal typicity.

Gyongyos Chardonnay 1996

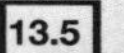

Starting to lose its freshness, but needs food.

ITALIAN WINE — RED

Bright Brothers Nero di Troia Primitivo 1997

Great trick of wine-making skillduggery to combine racy fruitiness with rich tannins.

Cabernet Sauvignon delle Venezie, Pasqua 1997, Somerfield

Caramia Primitivo del Salento 1996

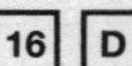

The bonniest Italian in the store. Rich, fresh, ripe, yet with character, a typicity of regional humour and warmheartedness. A lovely wine for food and conversation over it. At larger stores.

Cascine Garona Barbera d'Asti 1996

Chianti Classico Montecchio 1994

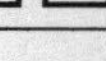

Chianti Serristori 1996, Somerfield 12.5 C

Copertino 1994 14 C

d'Istinto Sangiovese/Merlot 1997 (Sicily) 15.5 C

Great gobbets of earthy rich tannins. Gorgeous bristly fruit here. Great for food.

I Grilli di Thalia 1996 (Sicily) 15.5 C

Delicious rich earthy fruit, not one whit cloddish. A lovely food wine.

Isola de Sole Sardinian Red NV 13 B

L'Arco Cabernet Franc, Friuli 1996 15.5 C

Delicious Italianate Loire-style red with dark-cherry fruitiness, earthy tannins and a lovely cigar-edged finish. Real style and flavour here. Top 200 stores.

Lazio Rosso 1997, Somerfield 12 B

Paul Gascoigne played locally here, so I'm told. Left his boots behind.

Le Trulle Primitivo del Salento 1996 13.5 C

Merlot del Veneto 1997, Somerfield 12 B

It floats.

Montepulciano d'Abruzzo, Illuminati 1995 15 C

Getting better and more tetchy as it matures. Added to the softness of last year is some development in texture, perfume and finish.

Montepulciano del Molise 1996 11 B

Montereale Sicilian Red 1997, Somerfield 14 B

Dry, earthy, but freshly orchard-plucked.

Piccini Chianti Classico 1996 11 D

Soltero Rosso, Settesoli 1995 (Sicily) 14 C

Squinzano Mottura NV 13.5 C

Terralle Primitivo di Puglia 1996, Somerfield 15 C

Lovely ripeness of the controlled rustic variety. Plummy and deep with a well-formed dry finish.

Valpolicella 1997, Somerfield 12 B

Light.

Valpolicella Classico, Vigneti Casterna, Pasqua 1995 13 C

Quaffable, certainly.

ITALIAN WINE WHITE

Bidoli Pinot Grigio, Friuli 1997  14 C

Yet another surprisingly well organised, fruity, classy Italian white at Somerfield (larger stores only). As ever, it's a food wine.

Bright Brothers Greganico/Chardonnay 1997 (Sicily) 14.5 C

Superb little fish wine with its dryness, cleanness, and hint of earthy minerality.

Chardonnay Histonum 1996 14 C

Hints of a nutty edge to the perfumed fruit which is balanced, soft and controlled.

---

d'Istinto Insolia Trebbiano 1997 (Sicily) 11 B

Touch cabbagey and old hat.

Frascati 1997, Somerfield 14 C

Seems expensive? Perhaps, considering Frascati's dull reputation, but this has some classy hints and genuine Italian fish friendliness.

Le Trulle Chardonnay del Salento 1997 15.5 C

More lemony and crisp than previous vintages.

Marche Bianco 1997, Somerfield 14 B

Dry, crisp, pleasant, engagingly simple and refreshing. In no way coarse or ill-refined.

Montereale Sicilian White 1997, Somerfield 15.5 B

Brilliant new vintage of an old favourite – this year a touch richer and more textured.

Salice Salentino Bianco 1996 14 C

Soave 1997, Somerfield 14 B

Fresh and nutty – little wrong with that.

Tuscan White 1996, Somerfield 

MOLDOVAN WINE — WHITE

Kirkwood Moldovan Chardonnay 1996 

Texture and fruit, balance and personality – yet in no way are any of these virtues overplayed or too strident. A wine of elegance.

NEW ZEALAND WINE — WHITE

Coopers Creek Chardonnay, Gisborne 1996 14.5 E

The cool side of the chardonnay grape. Whispers rather than shouts. At larger stores.

Coopers Creek Sauvignon Blanc, Marlborough 1997 16 E

One of the classiest sauvignons NZ has to offer: fresh, not one whit herbaceous, and very elegant. At larger stores.

Montana Sauvignon Blanc 1997 15 D

Restrained, confident, gently citrussy.

Timara Dry White 1997 13 C

PORTUGUESE WINE RED

Alta Mesa Red, Ribatejo 1997 14 B

Dry ripe cherries with a hint of twig.

Atlantic Vines Baga 1995 12 C

Bright Brothers Trincadeira Preta, Ribatejo 1997 13.5 C

Bit soft and juicy for a fiver. Top 200 stores.

Fiuza Cabernet Sauvignon, Bright Brothers 1995 15.5 C

Delicious hedgerow fruit with a hint of refined earth.

Leziria, Almeirim NV 15 B

Gorgeous unabashed fruit here of rich plum with a hint of baked apple and peach – curious? You said it!

Portuguese Red 1997, Somerfield 14 B

Basic baked plum fruit, nicely thick and warm out of the oven.

PORTUGUESE WINE WHITE

Fiuza Bright Chardonnay, Ribatejo 1996 16 C

Wonderful aroma of ripe warm fruit as it wafts off the barrows in some southern European street market. The edge of this fruit is spring-fresh and crisp. A delicious classy wine. Top 100 stores.

Portuguese White 1997, Somerfield 14 B

Crisp, gently fruity, food friendly, quaffable. More than this the £2.99 white wine rarely provides.

ROMANIAN WINE RED

Pietroasa Young Vatted Cabernet Sauvignon 1996 15.5 C

Delicious chirpy, cheeky brew smelling and tasting of gently peppery blackcurrant, as cab. sauv. is classically supposed to. But underlying it is warmth and personality.

SOUTH AFRICAN WINE RED

Bellingham Pinotage 1996 14 D

Almost prissy compared to Somerfield's own-label pinotage. Top 100 stores.

Kumala Cinsault Cabernet 1997 14 C

Sheer naked sensuality.

Kumala Cinsault Pinotage 1998 14.5 C

Rich, well-baked fruit, hint of exotic hedgerow on the finish (some kind of alien redcurrant) and a lovely textured warmth and wit.

Kumala Reserve Cabernet Sauvignon 1996 14 E

Fresh and jammy but with enough rich, dry tannins to save it from soppiness. But eight quid is a lot of money. Top 100 stores.

South African Cabernet Sauvignon 1997, Somerfield 15.5 C

Juicy and ripe yet friendly, dry, rich and lingering. Some wit here.

South African Cabernet Sauvignon NV 13.5 B

Fruity and warm but it's a touch too overripe and eager on the edge to rate 14.

South African Cape Red 1997, Somerfield 13 B

South African Pinotage 1998, Somerfield 16.5 C

Baked rubber, cheroots, plum – a classic dry pinotage!!! Drink it all before Christmas! It's too wonderfully youthful to appreciate middle age – except with the throat it will pour down. A terrific pinotage of depth and deftness.

SOUTH AFRICAN WINE WHITE

Bellingham Sauvignon Blanc 1997 15 C

Kleinbosch Chenin Blanc/Chardonnay 1997 14.5 C

Nice creamy and nutty finish. Very attractive.

Kleinbosch Early Release Chenin Blanc 1998 15.5 B

Brilliant zippiness and richness here. Lovely glugging!

Kumala Colombard Sauvignon 1997 13.5 C

South African Chardonnay 1998, Somerfield 13 C

Dry and nervous.

South African Dry White 1998, Somerfield 14 B

Fat frowsty Rubenesque fruit of embracing fruitiness and rich colour.

SOUTH AMERICAN WINE RED

Two Tribes Red 1997 (Chile/Argentina) 13.5 C

SOUTH AMERICAN WINE WHITE

Two Tribes White 1997 (Chile/Argentina) 13.5 C

Two tribes which can't quite agree. Should be a quid cheaper.

SPANISH WINE RED

Berberana Rioja Tempranillo 1996 15 C

Vanilla warmth with a hint of soft textured vegetality cutting across the blackcurrant/plum (cherry edge). Delicious stuff.

Bright Brothers Old Vines Garnacha NV 15.5 C

Dry, rich, fulsome.

Las Campanas Navarra Garnacha 1996 14.5 C

Med Red 1997 14 B

Dry and a touch old-fashioned-Claret-like in the earthiness of the finish. But the cheerful sunny smile never leaves the scene . . .

Pergola Tempranillo, Manchuela 1997, Somerfield 15.5 B

Gorgeous joyful fruit here. Warm, biscuity, plum ripe, hugely gluggable.

Rioja Tinto Almaraz NV, Somerfield 14 C

Rioja in its chummy, fruity mode. Hint of dried cherry.

Sierra Alta Cabernet Sauvignon 1997 16 C

Tannins, texture, richness, ripeness and a lingering fruitiness of great depth. Rioja meets Bordeaux with a hint of Chianti. Top 300 stores.

Sierra Alta Tempranillo 1997 15.5 C

Lovely combination of warmth, earthiness, plum/cherry fruit, and rousing finish.

Valencia Red, Somerfield 14 B

Load of old bull. But that's just the label. The fruit spins a fruitier yarn.

SPANISH WINE WHITE

Almenar Barrel Fermented Rioja Blanco 1995, Somerfield 14 C

Vanillary and very subtle coconutty fruit which augurs well for this wine with a Thai fish or chicken dish. At larger stores.

Castillo Imperial White NV 14.5 B

Brilliant edge of bright fruit to fish-wine style freshness and pace.

Gandia Chardonnay, Hoya Valley 1996 14 C

Moscatel de Valencia, Somerfield 16 B

Superb, rich fruit here, great with dessert, of cloying texture, candied melon, honeyed fruit. And a screw-cap too! No filthy tree bark!

Pergola Oaked Viura, Manchuela 1997, Somerfield 15 B

Lovely clash of ripe melon and fresh citric acidity. Some delicious tension here: a taut, creative wine.

Santa Catalina Verdejo/Sauvignon 1997 15.5 C

Top notch sauvignon here of a gooseberry-and-grass vein which shames many a Sancerre at twice the price.

USA WINE RED

Californian Dry Red, Somerfield 14 C

Gallo Turning Leaf Cabernet Sauvignon 1995 15 D

Very approachable, soft, ripe, and in the Aussie mould. At larger stores.

Laguna Canyon Zinfandel 1997 15 C

Huge gobbets of richly smoked fruit and tannin fill the mouth. And the texture is likewise deep and engaging. Big, bonny, modern.

Redwood Pinot Noir 1995 14.5 D

USA WINE WHITE

Californian Colombard/Chardonnay, Somerfield 13.5 C

Fetzer Sundial Chardonnay 1996 15.5 D

Redwood Chardonnay 1996 15 D

Talus Chardonnay 1997 16 D

So warm and rich, yet dry and balanced, that you do wonder at the price. Not, perhaps, as Californian-elegant as some – but the neo-rusticity of this is terrific. Top 200 stores.

FORTIFIED WINE

Fine Old Amontillado Sherry, Somerfield 14.5 C

Fino Luis Caballero, Somerfield 15 C

Manzanilla Gonzales Byass, Somerfield 14.5 C

Superior Cream Sherry, Somerfield 12 C

SPARKLING WINE/CHAMPAGNE

Angas Brut Rose (Australia) 15.5 D

Asti Spumante, Somerfield 12 D

Baron Edward Masse Brut NV 13 G

Cordoniu Chardonnay Brut 14 D

Cremant de Bourgogne, Caves de Bailly NV 14 D

Devauzelle Champagne NV 12 F

Lemony and not as exciting as an eleven quid wine – even a champagne – could be.

Huguenot Hills Sparkling (South Africa) 14 D

Lindauer Brut 13 E

Masse Brut, Lanson Pere et Fils 13 G

Moscato Fizz, Somerfield 14.5 C

Mumm Cuvee Napa Brut (California) 15 E

Nottage Hill Sparkling Chardonnay 14.5 D

Soft, rather than classically dry bubbly.

Prince William Blanc de Blancs Champagne 13 G

Prince William Champagne NV 13 F

Seaview Brut 14 D

Seaview Brut Rose 14 D

Engaging rosiness without flushness. Nicely rebuking of champagne prices.

Seaview Pinot Noir Chardonnay 1994 15 E

Seaview Pinot Noir/Chardonnay 1994 (Australia) 16 E

One of Australia's strongest and tastiest challenges to Rheims' hegemony.

Seppelts Quality Australian Sparkling, Somerfield 14 C

Somerfield Cava Brut NV 

Elegant, not coarse, taut, wimpish or blowsy, but has hints of ripe fruit and a restrained edge. Fantastic value.

Somerfield Rose Cava NV 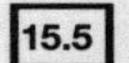 

TESCO

ANNE-MARIE LEADS THE ASSAULT ON CORK & TELLS IT TO GET SCREWED!

The thing about Tesco's wine department is that it is run by women and women are very sensible where corks are concerned. They hate them. Corkscrews get in the way of a sensible relationship with a bottle of wine. Do you know Wendy Cope's heart-rending poem on the subject?

Loss

The day he moved out was terrible –
That evening she went through hell.
His absence wasn't a problem
But the corkscrew had gone as well.*

The answer is not 'Who needs men?' – an interesting question I am happy to debate but not just now – but 'Who needs corks?' Tesco has been one of the leaders of the retail assault on the problem of corks. The failure of the cork industry to manufacture a 100% taint-free guaranteed product leads to a small but significant percentage of wines being spoiled. Tesco has reacted by introducing a range of screwcapped wines. Following a somewhat tongue-in-cheek competition I set in my Saturday *Guardian* column, Tesco also went along with a reader's suggestion and also placed a 'What No Cork' collaret on each bottle. The result was that half-a-million bottles disappeared

* from *Serious Concerns*, published by Faber & Faber, £6.99.

from the shelves, went through the checkouts, and gushed down customers' throats, within several months. Anne-Marie Bostock's wine buying department can feel justified in patting themselves several times on the back. (This department has developed a rather impish sense of humour and insouciant confidence over the past year. Both Helen Robinson and Judith Candy, as well the department's PR executive Nicki Walden, handle themselves with refreshing ease; and with a charm which is often, I notice, in striking contrast to the old farteries certain self-obsessed attendees at wine tastings are wont to come out with.)

Tesco took many other initiatives as well. It was the first UK retailer to flog non-vintage champagne with an age statement (Charles Heidsieck 1994 Mise en Cave). This is the cause of some controversy among the Champenois who are trenchant traditionalists; a Kentucky hill-billy is a hip modernist compared to some stuffed shirt champagne makers. Fragrances like L'Air du Temps were also sold cheaper than the manufacturers approve of and prices of women's magazines were slashed by 20%. The store also, as the *FT* put it, 'stepped on the toes of running shoe giant' when it flogged Adidas sportswear cheaper. The *FT* report quoted Adidas as saying '. . . having our products sold between baked beans and loo rolls is not the image we want.'

You have to laugh. Maybe someone at Adidas should ring up the chaps at Chateau Giscours, the snotty so-called *grand cru classe* Margaux which Tesco sells the 1993 vintage of for £14.99, and ask how *they* feel about being seen under the same roof as the loo rolls and baked beans. On second thoughts, the chaps at Chateau Giscours have other things on their hands at the moment (and these could be handcuffs if they're not acquitted of the allegation of adding illegal substances to some of their wines). This latter tale of pretension and woe, deception and skullduggery, was the big wine scandal story of the year; which I happened upon by sheer accident when I passed a Paris newstand the day the story broke and caught the whole sorry tale in *Le Monde*.

More prosaically, Tesco refitted its fleet of 200,000 trolleys, at a cost of £4 million, with simple state-of-the-art gadgetry on the wheels so that an unswerving course can be maintained even if the trolley in question is stuffed, of wine perhaps, and its pusher, also stuffed full of wine perhaps, is negotiating the tricky corner of a crowded aisle.

Tesco also introduced a scheme, so I read, of which I have yet to see any evidence. This was a so-called Bike & Trailer idea which for a £5 deposit brings customers a bag for their groceries which can be attached to the back of a bike. My own bike is ready and waiting (to nip off to my local Tesco to try the new range of organic milk cheeses which as long as the milk's not been pasteurised I'm looking forward to eating).

Earlier this year, Tesco did another brave thing. It permitted BBC-2 to make a superstore fly-on-the-wall documentary. Among many other things, it revealed that Tesco's Banbury store throws away £3,500-worth of food past its sell-by date *per week.* £6.7 million's worth of food is, apparently, thrown away every week by the supermarkets. There is no record of a single drop of wine being included in this disposal which is, I would have thought, a faintly shocking indictment of the way we live today. Tesco has run computer training sessions for teachers at its stores, so can't one of the bright sparks attending such events work out an answer to this appalling waste? Computers have the answer to everything don't they?

Following Budgens lead, Tesco introduced in-store polling stations (at Purley and Thornton Heath) during the London mayoral referendum in May 1998. It also agreed a deal with the union USDAW. There are 150,000 Tesco employees and the company is the largest private employer of a unionised workforce in the country. Tesco also announced it was to offer up to 1,500 jobs to unemployed young people as part of the government's Welfare to Work scheme.

In June this year, Tesco made its boldest move yet to strengthen its lead as the nation's leading wine merchant. It announced the basing of a full-time wine product development manager, Mr Phil Reedman, in Adelaide. This is the furthest any supermarket has yet gone in developing ties with a wine-producing country and it is a superb, and possibly long-overdue, initiative. Anne-Marie Bostock said the appointment was necessary because 'of the difficulty of visiting key Australian suppliers on a regular basis. No other supermarket or multiple specialist has a permanent wine buying presence in Australia and this appointment has the backing of the Tesco board.'

I'm sometimes asked if I care about what supermarkets do beyond what happens on the wine shelves. The answer to this question is, I would have thought, fully answered above.

Tesco
Tesco House
P O Box 18
Delaware Road
Cheshunt
Herts EN8 9SL
Tel: 01992 632222
Fax: 01992 644235
Customer Care Line: 0800 505555
e-mail www.tesco.co.uk

SEE STOP PRESS SECTION AT END OF BOOK FOR LAST-MINUTE ADDITIONS OR UPDATES TO THIS RETAILER'S RANGE.

ARGENTINIAN WINE RED

Picajuan Peak Bonarda NV 14.5 C

Quite simply, a stickily rich bangers and mash plonk of great charm, texture and depth. As Nietzsche once said, 'By gum, it's yum.'

Picajuan Peak Malbec NV 15 C

Has a serious edge to it, thanks to the dry tannins, but it's also, for the true malbec lover (which roughly equates, *mutatis mutandis*, with Beckett on stage), wonderfully rich and quaffable. Worth waiting for (and with food, even normal mortals might love it). About 209 selected stores.

Picajuan Peak Sangiovese NV 15 B

Brilliant value. Alert, rich, dry, incisive, firm and fruity to finish, this has echoes of baked soil and cherry/plumminess which Chianti often fails to provide at twice the price. About 360 selected stores.

ARGENTINIAN WINE WHITE

Picajuan Peak Chardonnay NV 16 C

Picajuan Peak Viognier NV 15.5 C

Great price for such classy stuff, hinting at dry apricot with a nutty, dry undertone. Individual, decisive, gluggable, gently quirky, great with a wide range of fish and light poultry dishes. Another terrific improvement in bottle since last autumn. Top eighty-five stores.

AUSTRALIAN WINE RED

Australian Cabernet/Merlot NV, Tesco 14 C

Handsome edge to the ripe fruit, perhaps the peppery cab gives the ripe merlot some character.

Australian Red, Tesco 14.5 B

Australian Ruby Cabernet, Tesco 

An excellent alternative to Beaujolais: fresh, flowing, fruity, juicy and fun to quaff.

Australian Shiraz NV, Tesco 13 C

Juicy, very juicy.

Australian Shiraz/Cabernet NV, Tesco 14 C

Jammy and a touch baked (but not half), this has a handsome texture to its richness. Fine Aussie plonking here.

Baileys Shiraz 1995 15 D

Improving nicely in bottle. The maker understands tannin and the character it can bequeath to wine. Top eighty-five stores.

Barramundi Shiraz/Merlot NV 

A richly endowed duo, this blend, combining savouriness with wryness.

Best's Great Western Cabernet Sauvignon 1994 

Expensive dive-in quality juice. Needs food. The tannins take time to grip. Top eighty-five stores.

Bleasdale Langhorne Creek Malbec 1997 

Wonderful warmth and richness. Very savoury and ripe but the thickness of the fruit is nigh spreadable on toast. Top 205 stores.

Brown Brothers Tarrango 1997 

Got more tannin than previous incarnations and so the cascade of fruit is strewn with interesting rocks which the weary traveller strikes with delight. Top eighty-five stores.

Chapel Hill Coonawarra Cabernet Sauvignon 1996  

Stylish tannins here and they give the fruit character and backbone.

Cockatoo Ridge Grenache/Shiraz 1996 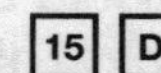

Ripe and very ready, rich and juicy and gushing – but the gush is also eloquent and easy. The wine is soft, lush and lovely. About 200 selected stores.

Hardys Nottage Hill Cabernet Sauvignon/ Shiraz 1996 15 C

Elegant, rich, aromatic, balanced, most compellingly well priced, and more stylish than other vintages of the same brand.

Ironstone Shiraz Grenache, Margaret River and Swan Valley 1996 16.5 D

Takes shiraz into a new dimension of such balance of fruit, acid and tannin, all so deftly interwoven and gorgeously textured, that it makes offerings from other Oz regions seem either mean or too expensive. It's a terrific wine with a hint of wildness. Top 205 stores.

Kingston Estate Murray Valley Shiraz 1994 14 D

Goodness, how action packed this juicy wine, in a cartoonish sort of way, is. It really is colourful and expletive.

McLaren Vale Grenache 1997, Tesco 13.5 D

Juicy, very juicy.

McLaren Vale Shiraz 1995, Tesco 16.5 D

Superb own-label Aussie red here. Really does show how to get the best from spicy shiraz. The wine combines very typical softness and ripeness but there are lovely tannins to the herby fruit and great warmth with the impactful finish.

Oxford Landing Cabernet Sauvignon and Shiraz 1997 15.5 D

Delicious tobacco-scented fruit which though dry has a flowing, juicy finish to it. Well-behaved but has a hint of a dark past. Top 205 stores.

Rosemount Merlot 1997 

Juicy and ripe but with just enough dry, tannic character to save it from flopping. Not at all stores.

Rosemount Shiraz 1997 

Rather raunchy and sensual in its aromatic richness and texture. At most stores.

SE Shiraz 1996 

Totally at its peak of soft, ripe, utterly giving drinkability. About 200 selected stores.

St Hallett Faith Shiraz 1995 

Intensely sure of itself, this character is brusque to begin but finishes being soft as a pussy cat. Top eighty-five stores.

Stonyfell Metala, Shiraz/Cabernet Sauvignon 1995 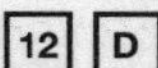

Soft, soppy and as daft as its label – like invalid juice. Top eighty-five stores.

Temple Bruer Langhorne Creek Shiraz/Malbec 1996 16 D

My goodness! Talk about fruit juice with attitude! This wine seems so juicy at first, revealing every soft hedgerow fruit in a shameless degree of ripeness, but then it strikes tannically and characterfully on the throat. Top 205 stores.

Temple Bruer Reserve Merlot 1996 15.5 E

Impressive tannins here, well developed and rich. An unusually well developed Aussie and unusually well suited to food.

AUSTRALIAN WINE WHITE

Australian Chardonnay, Tesco 14 C

Cute little number which packs in fresh crisp fruit with a delicious underlying ripeness.

Australian Colombard/Chardonnay, Tesco 13.5 C

Touch and go on the finish.

Australian Rhine Riesling, Tesco 15 C

Fine example of classic riesling freshness of tone, steely crispness, hint of paraffin (usually only detected in well-aged specimens) and a nutty edge to a slightly creamy finish. An excellent workhorse riesling for smoked fish platters.

Australian White NV, Tesco 14 B

Azure Bay Chardonnay/Semillon 1997 14.5 C

Here, in spite of the blue bottle, the sting is benign and delicious. A shrewd blend of richness and elegance. Not at all stores.

Blues Point Semillon/Chardonnay 1997 12 D

Lot of dosh for a flashy blue bottle. Stings you for six quid. Not at all stores.

Brown Brothers Late Picked Muscat 1996 16 D

Gorgeous aperitif, not for one second is it too cloying or

oversweet. The acidity bites into the rich honey/melon/pineapple tones to provide balance and style. The texture is lovely, too.

Chateau Tahbilk Marsanne 1997 16 D

Combines hints of rich, sticky toffee with incisive, fresh acidity derived from some sort of pineapple/honey equation. Has a floral hint, too. Delicious food wine. Not at all stores.

Clare Valley Riesling 1997, Tesco 14.5 C

Delicious hints of mineralised acidity gleam through the typically sullen (moody, teenage, difficult) fruit of the riesling, but this is its spiky charm. Will age well for eighteen months if not more.

Hardys Stamps of Australia Grenache/ Shiraz Rose 1997 12 C

Hunter Valley Semillon 1997, Tesco 16 D

Such an undervalued grape! Here it shows vivacity and style, richness yet freshness and a lovely lilt on the finish as it oozes down the throat.

Ironstone Semillon/Chardonnay, Margaret River 1997 15.5 D

A rich, dry, crisp food wine of compelling double-faced furtiveness. It shows one side of itself which is soft and almost creamily fruity and then a crisp, raw delicious fresh face. Top 205 stores.

Langhorne Creek Verdelho 1997, Tesco 14 D

Curious wine, rich and dry with a thick texture and a hint of bitterness, and probably at its best with Thai food.

Lindemans Bin 65 Chardonnay 1998 

Supremely sure of itself, this well-established brand showing, in its '98 manifestation, what a great year this is for Aussie whites from the region (Hunter Valley). This has great hints of warm fruit balanced by complex crispness and acidity. A lovely under-a-fiver bobby dazzler. Top 205 stores.

Lindemans Padthaway Chardonnay 1997 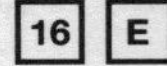

Smacks of fresh melon, pineapple and with a hint of toasted nuts with a touch of butterscotch. Enough for you? Top 205 stores.

McLaren Vale Chardonnay 1997 

Very underripe melon, a hint of smoky pear, lime and pineapple – it packs 'em in, this wine, yet manages to achieve balance, freshness and texture. Has an impish sense of humour, too.

Normans Unwooded Chardonnay 1997 

Rather austere but friendly with food. Not at all stores.

Oxford Landing Sauvignon Blanc 1997 

Hints of clean classiness.

Pewsey Vale Eden Vale Riesling 1997 15.5 D

Gorgeous delicacy yet fire-in-its-belly fruitiness which blends fresh and baked fruit, soft and hard, along with steely acidity. A lovely, genuinely fish-friendly wine – and classy. About 300 selected stores.

Rosemount Chardonnay 1997 16 D

Rich yet restrained, deep yet fathomable, turbulent yet affordable. This wine is packed with civilised incident. Available at most stores.

Rosemount Semillon/Chardonnay 1997 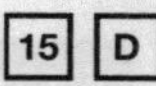

Very calm and collected, elegant and unruffled. The fruit is fresh, underripe and classy. Not at all stores.

Rosemount Semillon/Sauvignon 1997 

A classy blend of some substance.

Rymill Coonawarra Sauvignon Blanc 1997 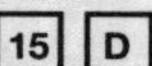

If you like gooseberry jam this wine will really tickle your palate. Thick and rich, too. Top twenty-two stores.

Shaw & Smith Sauvignon Blanc 1997 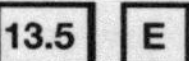

Lot of money for a lack-lustre finish. Top eighty-five stores.

Shaw & Smith Unoaked Chardonnay 1997 

Like an outstanding Chablis in an exceptional year, this hugely elegant chardonnay shows rich mineralised acids combined with underripe melon fruit and a hint of soil. Lovely stuff. Top eighty-five stores.

St Hallett Poachers Blend 1997 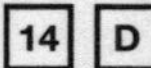

Tim Adams Riesling 1997 15.5 E

Nutty finish to a deliciously complex wine of ripe charms and open-hearted fruitiness of purpose. It has a faint petrol tinge to the edge of this fruit and a hint of lemon drop. Elegance and style here.

AUSTRIAN WINE RED

Lenz Moser Blauer Zweigelt 1996 

AUSTRIAN WINE WHITE

Lenz Moser's Prestige Beerenauslese 1995 (half bottle) 15.5 D

Sweet, gently candied edge of satsuma.

BRAZILIAN WINE RED

Brazilian Cabernet Sauvignon/Merlot, Tesco 14 

BULGARIAN WINE RED

Bulgarian Cabernet Sauvignon Reserve 1993, Tesco 15 C

Interesting oxidised edge giving a ripe raisiny quality to some pretty firm earthiness and dryness (tannins). A great meaty food wine.

Noble Oak Premium Lyaskovets Merlot 1995 15.5 C

An excellent merlot of immense quaffability. Has nice easy-going, soft (yet juicy) leather undertones to the fruit and it's sheer fun to drink.

Reka Valley Bulgarian Cabernet Sauvignon, Tesco  B

CHILEAN WINE — RED

Canepa Oak Aged Zinfandel 1996  C

Dry, zippy, fruity, fresh, cheeky – pity it's so close to a fiver. Top eighty-five stores.

Chilean Cabernet Sauvignon Reserve 1996, Tesco 16 C

Chilean Cabernet Sauvignon, Tesco 16 C

Chilean Red, Tesco 14.5 B

Errazuriz Cabernet Sauvignon Reserve 1995 16.5 E

Smells like tobacco and a ripe warm saddle – so the lonesome cowboy makes the first impression – but the pace of fruit, the texture, the tannins and the lingering finish make for a long-drawn-out death of moving sublimity.

Errazuriz Merlot El Descauso Estate 1997 16.5 D

Soft leather, cherries and blackberries and hints of earth, ripe yet cuddly tannins, and a rich, warm finish. An admirable merlot of class and cosiness. At most stores.

Great With Indian 1997, Tesco 15.5 C

As a wine, its rating is correct. For so is the fruit – rich, dry, classy and typically Chilean in its lovely, textured blackcurrantness – but is it robust enough for Chicken Dansak? I have my doubts. I love it as a great quality quaffing wine. About 300 selected stores.

Luis Felipe Edwards Reserva Cabernet Sauvignon 1996 16.5 D

A cabernet lover's dream: tannic pertness, rich vegetal fruit with hints of green pepper and white pepper, balance, tenacity on the palate, and huge drinkability. One of the most classic Bordeaux style of Chilean cabs, it provides a smooth yet eventful ride. Not at all stores.

Montgras Merlot 1997 16 C

Utterly disgraceful! How is the honest wine snob, who regards under-a-fiver wines as anathema, to keep his prejudiced pecker up when he can spend £4.50 on a merlot as aromatic, textured and thrilling as this? The authorities should be alerted. About 200 selected stores.

Santa Ines Cabernet/Merlot 1996 14.5 C

Santa Ines Carmenere 1997

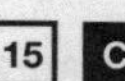
15 C

Rich and soupy, with a compelling finish. Selected stores.

Santa Ines Malbec 1997

16.5 C

What vim here displayed! The fruit is full of life and lushness yet it's also herby, deep, tannic and tenacious, and very very lingering. Great class here and fantastic value. Not at all stores.

CHILEAN WINE — WHITE

Chilean Chardonnay, Tesco

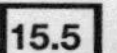
15.5 C

Bargain softness and subtle richness, though it's losing, slightly, its grip.

Chilean White NV, Tesco

15 B

Terrific value. Lip-smackingly fruity yet the hints of real class shine through that tiny price tag and it accomplishes refreshment and thought-provocation at one quaff.

Errazuriz Chardonnay 1997

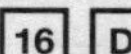
16 D

I love the nutty, baked fruit aroma and the gentle fumaceous edge to the fruit as it descends, plump, ripe yet elegant, down the throat. Utterly delicious. About 400 selected stores.

Errazuriz Chardonnay Reserva 1996

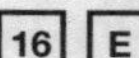
16 E

Big edge to the keenly fresh fruit which gives it bulk. The

creamy, smoky edge is very fine. Not a full wine, it's better mannered than that, but it has oodles of class. Top 205 stores.

Luis Felipe Edwards Chardonnay Reserve 1997 16.5 C

Superb value here. Shows such richly knitted fruit and acidity it seems the wine must cost twice what it does. Not a block-buster, nor overly vegetal, just classy and sure of itself. Top eighty-five stores.

Santa Ines Sauvignon Blanc 1997 16 C

Makes you wonder if Sancerre producers shouldn't turn to farming beetroot. This sauvignon is tightly priced, balanced and handsomely packed with crisp fruit, of vaguely gooseberryish concentration. About 200 selected stores.

Undurraga Gewurztraminer 1997 13.5 C

Pleasant light style.

ENGLISH WINE — WHITE

Chapel Down Bacchus 1996 11 C

Finishes with a bit of a limp. Not at all stores.

Chapel Down Summerhill Oaked NV 12 C

Touch tart. Not at all stores.

Three Choirs Estate Premium Medium Dry 1996 11 C

Top twenty-two stores.

Three Choirs Estate Reserve 1996 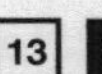 

At this close to a fiver, I want more thrills. This is only medium thrilling. Not at all stores.

FRENCH WINE RED

Baron de la Tour Fitou 1996 15.5 C

Lovely herby, sunny fruit redolent of lavender, thyme and cracked earth. A mouthful of the Midi! Not at all stores.

Baron Philippe Rothschild Merlot VdP d'Oc 1996 13.5 

Boisset Bourgogne Pinot Noir 1996 12.5 

Top eighty stores.

Bourgogne Hautes Cotes de Beaune Grande Cuvee 1996 11 D

A pre-fab at the price of a Victorian semi. About 360 selected stores.

Bourgueil 1995 12 

Very juicy on the finish and has only a hint of the Rabelaisan cabernet franc grape. Top eighty-five stores.

Buzet Cuvee 44 1997 14.5 

Best vintage yet for this 44 label. Great tannic control to the firm, rich fruit. Real class emerging at last. Top eighty-five stores.

Chateau de Cote de Montpezat, Cotes de Castillon 1996 15.5 D

Most approachable yet serious-sided claret. Lovely wood/fruit balance, great fresh acids, and terrific tannins. Recipe for happiness and health. Top 205 stores.

Chateau La Raze Beauvalet Medoc 1996 13.5 D

Dry, austere, classically standoffish.

Chateau Maurel Fonsalade, St Chinian 1996 15.5 C

Very soft with a juicy undertone but there are tannins and thus backbone and muscle. Very drinkable, it has a curiously serious cigar-box undertone. Top eighty-five stores.

Chateau Soudars Haut-Medoc 1995 14 F

Very classy and full of style (tannins/fruit/acidity) and so it should be for eleven quid. It might repay four or five years cellaring. Not at all stores.

Corbieres, Tesco 14.5 B

Cotes du Rhone, Tesco 13 B

Cotes du Rhone Villages 1997, Tesco 14.5 C

A delicious jammy red with not one whit of the earthy herbiness of the breed. But what drinkability!

Domaine de Lanestousse Madiran 1994 16 D

Oh yes! The tannin here is well held by the earthiness of the fruit – tobacco-scented and ripe – and the finish is rousing. Not at all stores.

Fleurie Louis Josse 1996 11 D

Oh, come on Beaujolais. Seven quid is ridiculous. About 300 selected stores.

French Cabernet Sauvignon Reserve, Tesco 14 C

French Cabernet Sauvignon, Tesco 15.5 B

French Grenache, Tesco 14 B

Shallow, gently rough, unshaven, vulgar, uncollared and proud of it, this is a genuine quaffing bumpkin of a bottle with the wit not to be something it isn't except easy to drink, if you don't mind its refusal to doff its cap or wipe its boots, and it'll cheerfully put up with abuse from food.

French Merlot Reserve, Tesco 14.5 C

French Merlot VdP de la Haut de l'Aude, Tesco 15 B

Gamay, Tesco 10 B

Bit feeble for three quid.

La Bareille Beaujolais 1997 10 C

Defies belief at a fiver – well, even at £1.99. About 200 selected stores.

La Dame de Montrose, St Estephe 1993 15 F

Laperouse VdP d'Oc Red 1995 15.5 C

Les Estoiles Organic Grenache/Syrah (organic) 15.5 C

Big, chewy, rich, muscular yet lithe, this is a terrific organic wine of immensely dry fruit. It has character and bite but also freshness, pertness, flavour and brilliant versatility with food.

Louis Jadot Moulin a Vent 1996 11 E

Some texture. Top eighty-five stores.

Margaux 1995, Tesco 14 E

Heavily woody, very dry classic claret with a no-holds barred fruitiness and rich tannicity which is best left for three of four years to soften – or drink it now with rare meat.

Minervois, Tesco 14 B

Moulin de la Doline Fitou 1996 13.5 C

Oddly dry and juicy.

Mourvedre VdP d'Oc 1995 13 B

Extremely juicy and fresh. It seems to lack an element of tannicity which the mourvedre usually flaunts in spades. About 300 selected stores.

Oak Barrique Shiraz 1995 15.5 C

Lovely, rich, textured, dry yet soupy and savoury, with a lot of Midi warmth to it, levelling backbone to the softness of the fruit. A real competitor to, and vanquisher of, many more expensive Australian shirazes.

Pauillac 1994, Tesco

Raisin d'Etre, Rhone Valley 1997

Yes, it's juicy and full of itself (eager and deep) but the tannins buttress the fruit marvellously so you get quaffability with food compatibility. About 200 selected stores.

Savigny Les Beaune 1996

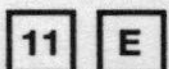

Nice pong, but not on song on the finish. Top eighty-five stores.

St Emilion, Tesco

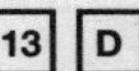

Syrah VdP d'Oc, Tesco

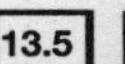

Good value here for a party and blunt palates. Not at all stores.

Vintage Claret 1996, Tesco

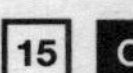

Delicious richness and texture – combines classic dryness and earthiness with lovely fruit of depth and decisiveness and style, savour, wit and warmth. About 360 selected stores.

FRENCH WINE — WHITE

Alsace Gewurztraminer 1997, Tesco

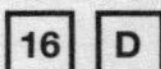

Here's your real 'Great with Chinese' wine (c.f. entry later in this section)! Spicy, rich, rosy and nutty, with loads of personality and punch, texture and tension. This is a great vintage for this great Alsace grape.

Alsace Riesling Graffenreben 1995 11 D

Boisset Bourgogne Chardonnay 1996 13 D

Top eighty stores.

Cabernet de Saumur Rose, Tesco 13.5 C

Chablis 1996, Tesco 12 D

More expensive than it is wise to be (when your fruit's so loose and wobbly). It needs more bite to be classic Chablis.

Chablis Grand Cru Les Preuses 1994 12 G

Top eighty-five stores.

Chateau de la Grange Muscadet 1996 12 C

Top eighty-five stores.

Chenin Blanc, VdP du Jardin de la France, Tesco 15 B

Cotes du Rhone Blanc NV 14 C

Domaine de la Done Syrah Rose, VdP d'Oc 1997 12 B

A touch austere as it finishes. About 300 selected stores.

Domaine de la Jalousie Cuvee Bois VdP des Cotes de Gascogne 1995

Astonishing maturity yet vigour here. Has wood, vegetality, richness and that typical Gascogne touch of ripe pineapple.

Here it's a hint – subsumed under more serious fruit. Top eighty-five stores.

Domaine de la Jalousie VdP des Cotes de Gascogne 1997, Tesco 15 B

Love the impish, pineapple/pear fruit. A terrifically welcoming wine of crispness and fruit. Top eighty-five stores.

Domaine de Montauberon Marsanne 1996 12 C

Domaine du Soleil Chardonnay VdP d'Oc NV (vegetarian) 15.5 C

Domaine du Soleil Sauvignon/Chardonnay NV (suitable for vegetarians & vegans) 14 C

Domaine Saubagnere, VdP des Cotes de Gascogne, Tesco 13.5 C

Entre Deux Mers, Tesco 13 C

Fait Accompli Rhone Valley 1997 13 C

A quid cheaper and I'd like it more. About 200 selected stores.

Four Corners Bordeaux Sauvignon Blanc 1997 14 C

An elegant, restrained yet decisively balanced and fruity/crisp shellfish wine. Not at all stores.

Four Corners Chenin/Chardonnay 1997 13.5 C

French Chardonnay, VdP d'Oc, Tesco 12 C

French Oak-aged Chardonnay 1996, Tesco 13.5 C

Slight muddiness of tone on the finish fails to win it more points.

French Semillon, Tesco 10 B

French Viognier 1996, Tesco 14 C

Great With Chicken 1996 12 B

Great With Chinese Muscat/Sauvignon Blanc 1997, Tesco 

Did Vin de Pays d'Oc ever dream of ending up in this situation? An imaginative idea, especially the blending of the grapes, but again I question the wine's fortitude in the face of oriental fodder. More muscat is needed and viognier – not sauvignon. About 300 selected stores.

Great With Fish 1996 13 B

James Herrick Chardonnay 1996 15 C

Good age for a wine not designed to grow old with any great grace. Here it's perfectly mature, melony and lemony and strikes home with style.

La Cote Chery Condrieu 1996 13 G

I am a great fan of certain wines of this bijou appellation. But this specimen, if it is to charm my socks off at £15, needs to grow up a bit. Three years? Maybe four. But it needs time in bottle to stagger our palates with the typical old hay, sesame seed and apricot fruit of classic Condrieu. Available at Wine Advisor Stores.

Laperouse VdP d'Oc White 1995

Macon Blanc Villages 1996, Tesco

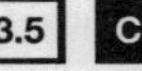

Meursault Louis Josse 1995

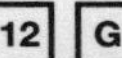

Good aroma, certainly typical – and typical of decent Meursault. But thereafter the wine lags. It is true it'll be more emphatic, crustier, mouldier and tastier in ten years. But I can think of much better uses for £15 for a decade than this wine.

Muscadet de Sevre et Maine sur Lie 1997, Tesco

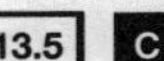

Getting better, Muscadet, after years of doldrumic stagnation, and this example is plump yet crisp and shows some fleet turn of foot.

Muscat Cuvee Jose Sala 1996

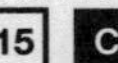

Muscat de Rivesalte, Tesco (half bottle)

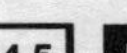

Premieres Cotes de Bordeaux, Tesco

Puligny Montrachet Premier Cru 'La Mouchere' 1996

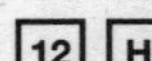

Begins wonderfully, ends woefully. Top twenty-two stores.

Sancerre 1997, Tesco

Tough to like. It's tart rather than taut.

Saumur Blanc, Tesco

Sauvignon Blanc Bordeaux, Tesco 14 B

Vouvray, Tesco 13 C

GERMAN WINE WHITE

Black Soil Rivaner Riesling 1996 14 C

Carl Ehrhard Riesling 1997 13 C

Good stab at a new way to grow, vinify and package riesling. Top eighty-five stores.

Castle Rock Riesling 13 C

Riesling fails to excite completely or convince at this price when it tries so hard to be dry *and* to please.

Fire Mountain Riesling 1996 14 C

Getting there, this new style riesling. Dry, classic edge, but still too austere for New World fruit lovers.

Liebfraumilch, Tesco 12 B

A new blend, using modern vinification techniques.

Nierstein Kabinett, Tesco 12.5 B

A new blend, using modern vinification techniques.

Nierstein, Tesco 13.5 B

Scharles Kerner Kabinett Halbtrocken 1995 (50 cl) 12 C

St Johanner Abtey Spatlese 1995, Tesco 13 B

Steinweiler Kloster Liebfrauenberg Kabinett, Tesco 13.5 C

Steinweiler Kloster Liebfrauenberg Spatlese, Tesco 12.5 C

Villa Baden Chasselas 1996 13 C

HUNGARIAN WINE RED

Reka Valley Hungarian Merlot, Tesco 13.5 B

HUNGARIAN WINE WHITE

Hungarian Oak Aged Chardonnay, Tesco 13 C

King Mountain Chardonnay/Furmint 1996 12.5 B

Doesn't quite come alive as a blend of two distinct grape varietal styles.

Reka Valley Hungarian Chardonnay, Tesco 12 B

Reka Valley Hungarian Sauvignon Blanc, Tesco 13.5 B

Plain, simple and clean with a hint of underripe hard fruit.

ITALIAN WINE RED

Argiolas Cannonau di Sardegna 1996 (Sardinia) 14 D

Dry but soft, hint of jam, and a soft yet strident finish.

Barrique Aged Negroamaro del Salento 1995 16 D

Real brilliance which southern Italy has made its own: a wine with figgy ripeness and raisiny richness yet with terrific compensating, earthy tannins. Top eighty-five stores only.

Chianti Classico 1996, Tesco 13.5 C

Lightness of tone fails to get it a higher rating but it does have some good earthy fruit.

Chianti Colli Senesi 1997, Tesco  C

The Colli Senesi showing the posher Chianti areas it can produce deliciously ripe, earthy, gently baked fruit of freshness and flavour. At most stores.

Chianti Rufina 1996, Tesco 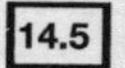 C

Very earthy yet ripe with fresh cherries. Great pasta wine.

L'Arco Cabernet Franc, Friuli 1996 15.5 C

Delicious Italianate Loire-style red with dark-cherry fruitiness, earthy tannins and a lovely cigar-edged finish. Real style and flavour here. Not at all stores.

Merlot del Piave, Tesco 14 B

Merlot del Trentino, Tesco 15.5 C

Monvigliero Barolo Riserva 1990 12 G

Well, it's earthy and ripe, and has echoes of licorice and figs, but it's three times the price of comparable reds from elsewhere. Available in Wine Advisor Stores only.

Morellino di Scansano 1996 15 D

A dry wine with a hint of cherry jam. This seeming paradox is most attractive.

Pinot Noir del Veneto, Tesco 14 C

Rosso Conero Riserva 1994 16 C

Manages to combine the juiciness of Australia with the herby fruit of the warm south, with a sprinkling of profound tannins. Excellent balance and rich finish. Selected stores.

Sicilian Red, Tesco 13.5 B

Tuscan Red, Tesco 14 C

Juicy, earthy, exceedingly drinkable. Chianti in a playful mood. Not at all stores.

Villa Pigna Cabernasco 1996 15.5 D

One of Tesco's most food-friendly reds. This is due to the

briskness of the deep fruit – and pace is rare with profundity – and the richness of the tannins. You can quaff it with a wide smile (width necessary to cram all the fruit in) and sip it elegantly, little finger crooked, with roast sheep. About 360 selected stores.

Villa Pigna Rosso Piceno 1994

That curious quirky freshness makes it wonderful with food.

ITALIAN WINE WHITE

Le Trulle Chardonnay del Salento 1996

Subdued chardonnay character but this is not a criticism. It's still a fleshy, well-formed wine with a good deal of soft fruit – not overrich or overripe but calm, collected, cooling.

Orvieto Classico Abbocato 1997, Tesco 13.5 C

Interesting (and daring) to stock this wine. It's sort of dry/sweet with its hint of honey and nuttinesss yet its richness means it might stand up well to Thai food.

Pinot Grigio/Chardonnay delle Venezie 1997

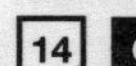

Nutty and fresh. Delicious with grilled prawns.

Verdicchio dei Castelli di Jesi Classico 1997, Tesco

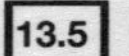

Good nutty theme here, but seems shy on the finish.

NEW ZEALAND WINE RED

Montana Reserve Merlot, Marlborough 1996 16 E

Superb balance of tannins and fruit: elegant, rich, dry, hints of spicy earth, a touch of chocolate. Lovely stuff.

New Zealand Cabernet Sauvignon NV, Tesco 13.5 C

Very juicy on the finish. Loses its grip here. Not at all stores.

NEW ZEALAND WINE WHITE

Cooks New Zealand Chardonnay 1997 13 D

Bit bony for an over-a-fiver chardonnay. Not at all stores.

Jackson Estate Sauvignon Blanc 1997 16 E

Richness and flavour, fatness of fruit yet knife-clean acidity which balances the whole effect into one long stream of pleasure. Not a typical Marlborough sauvignon, but this is a virtue.

Montana Marlborough Riesling 1997 13.5 C

Montana Reserve Chardonnay 1997 14.5 E

Classy, grassy, rich, confident, voluptuous.

New Zealand Chardonnay, Tesco 15 C

Showing great maturity and bruised, wrinkly fruit. But this richness makes it vegetally impactful and great with food. Not at all stores.

New Zealand Dry White, Tesco 13.5 C

At this price, it competes with more complex, richer fruit and though respectable this wine isn't quite as forceful as it might be. A £2.99 wine?

New Zealand Sauvignon Blanc 1997, Tesco 14 C

Stoneleigh Chardonnay 1996 16 D

The gorgeous restraint of the wood lets the fruit sing its heart out and the result is class, composure and consummate drinkability. Top eighty-five stores.

PORTUGUESE WINE RED

Borges Douro Premium Red 1995 16 C

Bright Brothers Atlantic Vines Baga 1997 13 C

Intensely fruity and ripe. Top eighty-five stores.

Bright Brothers Douro 1996 16 C

Very juicy and ripe yet, astonishingly, dry and tannic to finish. Lovely trick to pull off here – great with food and for quaffing with serious company. Not at all stores.

PORTUGUESE WINE — WHITE

Dry Vinho Verde, Tesco 13 B

Fiuza Bright Brothers Sauvignon Blanc 1997 15 C

Leafy, crisp, herbaceous, very stylish as it finishes. Excellent shellfish wine. Selected stores.

ROMANIAN WINE — RED

Reka Valley Romanian Pinot Noir, Tesco 15.5 B

Special Reserve Barrel Fermented Merlot 1996 16.5 C

Gorgeous ripeness of plummy, raspberry and cherry fruit, a hint of earth, a coating of tannin, and a real soul. A witty, brilliantly priced red of great style.

SOUTH AFRICAN WINE — RED

Beyers Truter Pinotage NV, Tesco 15.5 D

Pinotage in its Sunday best. The tannins give it presence and persistence but there's none of the burnt rubber juiciness of the grape. Instead, we get well pressed and neatly pleated fruit of style and flavour.

Cape Cinsaut NV, Tesco 15.5 B

Brilliant value. Really terrific well-baked fruit, rich and ready, but there is a dry, tannic presence which gives the cherry/black-currant fruit real weight, quaffability and class.

Cape Cinsaut/Pinotage NV, Tesco 15.5 C

The rampaging elephant of the label carries on his way over the taste buds where thick-skinned gobbets of earthy fruit mingle with cherries and prunes. Great glugging stuff and great with food. Not at all stores.

Diemersdal Merlot 1996 14 D

Diemersdal Shiraz 1997 15 D

Now this is juicy, yes, but it's serious fruit juice with a deep, dry edge. High class quaffing for Sunday celebrations. About 300 selected stores.

Fairview Gamay Noir 1998 15 C

Black cherries with a hint of tobacco. A terrific quaffing wine here. Splendid chilled with rich fish dishes. Not at all stores.

Fairview Merlot 1996 16 D

Such high minded fruit here it's more a libation than a mere quaffing beauty. It offers rich, soft, leathery fruit, great aroma and stylish presence, and tannins in fine array on the finish. Not at all stores.

Fairview Shiraz 1996 14.5 D

Juicy and ripe on the finish, rich and firm up front. Not at all stores.

Goiya Glaan 1997 14 C

Drink like Beaujolais.

International Winemaker Cabernet Sauvignon/Merlot, Tesco 13 C

Leopard Creek Cabernet/Merlot 16 C

Long Mountain Cabernet Sauvignon 1997 13.5 C

Very juicy and ripe. Not at all stores.

Oak Village Pinotage/Merlot 1996 16 C

Oak Village Vintage Reserve 1997 13.5 C

Burnt rubber on the finish gives it a coarse edge.

Paarl Cabernet Sauvignon, Tesco 15 C

Pinnacle Cabernet Sauvignon/Shiraz 1996 12.5 D

Another juicy red.

Plaisir de Merle Cabernet Sauvignon, Paarl 1995 15 F

One of the classiest Cape cabernets. Has lush fruit with active tannins.

Robertson Cabernet Sauvignon 1997, Tesco 15 C

Lovely juicy, dry fruit here, like savoury jam.

Rosemount Estate Shiraz/Cabernet 1998 15 D

Rosemount reds are always pricey but this new vintage has some tannins to it. Drink it young! Before the tannins ameliorate and make the wine useless with food.

South African Red, Tesco 15 B

South African Reserve Cabernet Sauvignon 1996, Tesco 15 C

Stellenbosch Merlot, Tesco 15 C

Swartland Cabernet Sauvignon/Shiraz 1996 14 C

Wamakers Cabernet Sauvignon 1997 13.5 C

Soft, squashy, very adolescent, beaujolais style soppiness.

Wamakers Pinotage 1997 13.5 D

Better than many a cru Beaujolais, which it winsomely resembles.

Woodlands Cabernet Sauvignon 1997 15.5 E

Unusually rich and ripe Cape red with such alert and mature tannins. Highly drinkable and deftly balanced. Top eighty-five stores.

SOUTH AFRICAN WINE WHITE

Barrel Fermented Franschoek Semillon 1997, Tesco 14 C

Woody stuff here. Needs a roast chicken to set it off.

Cape Chenin Blanc, Tesco

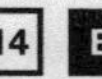

Cape Colombard/Chardonnay, Tesco

Freedom Road Sauvignon Blanc 1998

A historic Cape white since it is almost exclusively black by birth and nurture. But in spite of my personal excitement that such things have come to pass I have not let sentiment cloud my judgement. This is classily rich and elegant sauvignon of style and impact. Not at all stores.

Goiya Kgeisje Chardonnay/Sauvignon Blanc 1998

As imaginatively fruited as it is packaged. It's a real quaffing delicioso of a wine with hints of pineapple and lemon.

Great With Indian Colombard/Chardonnay 1997, Tesco

Well, I love the idea and the sheer chutzpah of the thing, but what Indian food, however jejunely spiced, would successfully partner this white? Even a poppadum would take the edge off the gentility of the Cape fruit. About 300 selected stores.

Paul Cluver Sauvignon Blanc 1997

Steely, with a hint of crisp lettuce leaf but this is well coated with some textured fruit so the final effect is very, very classy. Top eighty-five stores.

Pinnacle Chenin Blanc 1997

What an improvement since I first tasted it last autumn! Brilliant rich fruit hinting at dryness but so thick that the fruit, vegetal and nutty with a lush edge, is very stylish, very high class chenin and of an impactful generosity.

Plaisir de Merle Chardonnay 1996 13 E

Lot of money for a £3.99 wine (at best). Sure, there's some charm but when a price tag has such sharp edges on it it negates any smoothness the fruit might have. Top eighty-five stores only.

Ryland's Grove Barrel Fermented Chenin Blanc 1997 15 C

Schoone Gevel Chardonnay 1996 16.5 D

I confess to preferring this wine to several hugely more expensive white Burgundies I've encountered recently and the reason is this fruit is so much more honest, and honestly priced. It is aromatic, textured, finely wrought, and polished without obscuring its depth of character and flavour. This is a seriously delicious white wine which is perfectly priced and poised. Selected stores.

South African Chardonnay/Colombard, Tesco 14.5 C

South African White, Tesco

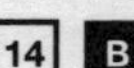

Tasty – nicely restrained richness and flavour here. Terrific value.

Van Loveren Special Late Harvest Gewurztraminer 1996 (half bottle) 14 C

Wamakers Chardonnay 1997 13.5 C

Some engaging gooseberry freshness.

Wamakers Chenin Blanc 1997 14 C

SOUTH AMERICAN WINE RED

Two Tribes Red 13.5 C

A blend of Chile and Argentina, where does Tesco file it? Can you imagine anyone, legally, proposing a merger of France and Germany?

SOUTH AMERICAN WINE WHITE

Two Tribes White 1997 13.5 C

SPANISH WINE RED

Agramont Garnacha 1995 14.5 C

Bodegas Marco Real Garnacha Crianza 1995 14.5 C

Ripe and rich, and the hint of leathery tannins is delightful. Selected stores.

Campillo Rioja Reserva 1988 12 E

Vanillary, but far too expensive for vanilla. Selected stores.

Don Darias 14 B

Marques de Chive Reserva 1991 15 C

Warm, savoury, dry, rounded, supple, lingering and gently lush. Terrific tippling here.

Marques de Grinon Rioja 1996 16 C

The Marques is a real smoothie and so polished, so rich, and with hints of ruggedness under that smart uniform of fruit and tannin. A more civilised yet characterful under-a-fiver Rioja is difficult to imagine. Top 205 stores.

Mendiani Tempranillo/Cabernet Sauvignon Navarra 1996 16.5 B

Perdido Navarra Cabernet Sauvignon Crianza 1995 16 C

Brilliant value here. The rich, textured, warmly tannic fruit has depth and weight and the polish has not obscured the character.

Spanish Cabernet Sauvignon 1996, Tesco 16 C

Unusually dark and mysterious for an under-a-fiver Spaniard with beautifully well-developed, rich fruit and tannins. Very approachable, as Spaniards are, but also serious, literary, food friendly. Selected stores.

Spanish Merlot 1996, Tesco 15 C

Juicy, dry, classy, plump, herby and warm.

Vina Mara Rioja Reserve 1994 16 D

Terrific Rioja: modern, dry, deep, rich, rolling and molar crunching. Great with food or mood.

Vina Mara Rioja, Tesco 14 C

Possibly the least offensive, calmest, least febrile, and most unfussily fruity Rioja you can buy for this money.

SPANISH WINE WHITE

Castillo de Monjardin Chardonnay 1995 14.5 C

Moscatel de Valencia, Tesco 16 B

USA WINE RED

Fetzer Barrel Select Pinot Noir 1995 13 E

Fetzer Barrel Select Zinfandel 1995 16.5 E

Gorgeous hunk of a wine. Yet it's witty with it. Immense depths of cherry/plum/blackberry fruit with a dry tannic edge giving the wine backbone and oomph, this is a terrific, jammily ripe zin with attitude. It's worth every penny – and then some. The finish is lingering and perfumed – you can feel you can smell the brambly fruit even at the back of the throat. Wine Advisor Stores only.

Fetzer Syrah 1996 16 E

Superb cheroot edge to the rich fruit which dazzles with its texture, tension and tannic suppleness. Lovely drinking here. Real class and style. Available in Wine Advisor Stores only.

Gallo Sonoma County Cabernet Sauvignon 1992

USA WINE WHITE

Fetzer Barrel Select Chardonnay 1995 15.5 E

Not as woody as the nomenclature might suggest for the gentle toasty edge is well controlled by the lemon/pineapple subtleties of the fruit. A delicious wine. Available at the thirty Wine Advisor Stores only.

Fetzer Viognier 1997 15.5 E

Shows how firmly fruity viognier can become, warmly encouraged to this level of expression by the Californian sun.

Garnet Point Chardonnay/Chenin, California 1996 14.5 C

Hints of marzipan and nuts, melon and citrus, this is a terrific oriental food wine. Has texture, ripeness and deliciously sprawling fruit. About 300 selected stores.

FORTIFIED WINE

10 Year Old Tawny Port, Tesco 13.5 F

Finest Madeira, Tesco 15.5 E

A delicious nut companion. Therefore, sip it whilst watching

Coronation Street. Every character is a rich nut and so is this off-dry wine.

Mick Morris Rutherglen Liqueur Muscat (half bottle) 17 C

A miraculously richly textured pud wine of axle-grease texture and creamy figginess. Huge, world class.

Superior Oloroso Seco Sherry, Tesco (half bottle) 15 B

Superior Palo Cortado Sherry, Tesco (half bottle) 16.5 C

SPARKLING WINE/CHAMPAGNE

Asti Spumante, Tesco 13 C

Australian Sparkling Wine, Tesco 14.5 C

Blanc de Blancs Champagne, Tesco 13 G

Blanc de Noirs Champagne, Tesco 13.5 E

Cava, Tesco 16 C

Chapel Down Epoch Brut NV (England) 11 D

Goodness how it tries, and one aches to want to like it a lot, but it's a wine stretched to breaking point. It simply lacks the ease of classic bubbly. It is easier to like sparkling elderflower cordial than this.

Chapel Hill Sparkling Chardonnay (Hungary) 14.5 C

Lindauer Brut 13 E

Lindauer Special Reserve NV (New Zealand) 14 E

An echo of peach but it's essentially dry and very stylish.

Millennium Champagne 1990, Tesco 13 G

Nicolas Feuillate Brut NV 13.5 G

One of the more elegant and silkier champagnes. It has class. Top eighty-five stores only.

Premier Cru Champagne Brut NV 15 F

More finesse, more class, more delicacy (and thus great value) than many more expensive grand marque Champagnes. It has the distinctive dryness yet sensitive fruitiness of the breed at its best.

Rose Cava, Tesco 14.5 C

Seppelt Sparkling Shiraz 1992 16 E

South African Sparkling Sauvignon Blanc 1998, Tesco 14.5 C

Assured class and great value here. Dreadfully naff label but the fruit is well designed and neat.

Vintage Cava Brut 1994, Tesco 15 D

Superb dry bubbly with real class, liveliness and style. Much better than so many Champagnes.

Vintage Champagne 1990, Tesco 12 G

Yalumba Pinot Noir Chardonnay 16 E

Yalumba Sparkling Cabernet Sauvignon NV 16 E

WAITROSE LIMITED

DEAR OLD WAITROSE? NOT ANY MORE AS THE STORE GROUP GETS TO GRIP WITH MODERNITY AND VALUE!

Waitrose's accelerated efforts to join the twentieth century before the twenty-first arrives have resulted in the creation of its first marketing directorial position, filled by the charming Mr Mark Price, the engagement of one of the world's leading design gurus, my good friend Mr John McConnell, and the appointment of one of Britain's wittier, hairier ad agencies, Banks Hoggins O'Shea. What on earth has this to do with wine, you ask?

Well, for Waitrose to have coughed up £4 million for an advertising campaign (Sainsbury and Tesco probably spend over twenty times that between them as a point of comparison) was an explosive move. It overturned decades of conservative trading. It compares with the Papal recognition that Copernicus and Galileo were, after all, right on the ball re heliocentricity. Waitrose's new dynamism means that one day soon the store that has believed all its life that wine labels were the strict prerogative of the wine grower will recant; it will surely introduce a heretical, adventurous range of own-label wines to compare with the best and the most inexpensive around.

One can compare the charm of a wine tasting at Waitrose, with the urbane Mr Julian Brind MW managing matters and the rest of the buyers, all MWs (like the delightful Miss Dee Blackstock) or would-be MWs (like the enthusiastic roustabout Mr Joe Wadsak), agitating elegantly in the background, to a morning spent at a stately home where one is courteously shown the items of interest and, apart from the irreverential banter of the more vulgar wine writers who are intent only on the delicious free lunch provided, the only sounds, like those from incontinent exotic birds, come from the sniffage, the swillage, and the spittage of salivated wine into the tall silvery spittoons. What next, one feels obliged to ask? Will this essential, this ritual destination – a Waitrose training centre situated above the Finchley Road – be discarded?

Tesco tried a wine tasting on a Thames barge; Sainsbury hired an extremely trendy Bermondsey brasserie; Safeway rented a theatre in Piccadilly. What is in store for us at Waitrose? Personally, I hope the Finchley Road venue remains the one icon Waitrose does not blast. It is utilitarian and unpretentious.

Not so, however, some of the sites which Waitrose has been rumoured to be considering for certain new stores. 'Prestigious London locations including the City' said one report. Trend setting, though, is now in Waitrose's blood and I expect to see a Waitrose on the Isle of Dogs by 2010. More intelligently (speaking as a frequent and hungry rail passenger), Waitrose has been said to be considering opening stores in railway stations in the south-east.

On environmental issues, Waitrose also set trends. The store group used 32 million fewer carrier bags last year, following the introduction of its Bag for Life environmentally-friendly initiative in which customers buy a recyclable bag for 10p which lasts 10 times as long as a normal one and is then replaced by Waitrose for free. Waitrose did not, however, always get it right on sensitive issues. The wrath of crustacea protectionists fell on the store's head when it decided to stock live lobsters in one of its London stores as a trial. As far as I know no-one has ever protested about anyone selling live mussels, but then lobsters have eyes and French poets have been known to carry them around on the end of a lead.

But further dynamic moves at Waitrose went ahead. People working for ICL, the computer company, were able to shop from their desks (sorry, work stations) at Waitrose via an interactive home shopping scheme. It's a similar move to a scheme operated by Sainsbury's, but it does demonstrate Waitrose is nowhere near as fuddy-duddy as it used to be. Self-scanning is also being introduced in more Waitrose stores. The expectation that this year's financial results should push Waitrose over the £2 billion mark in terms of sales, is obviously not causing this retailer to take anything for granted.

Interestingly, with so much fascination with computers at Waitrose it was somewhat ironical to read that Waitrose would not be opening on the 1st January 2000. It has been claimed this was to give the staff 24-hours to recover from Millennium celebrations; it has nothing to do with any anticipated computer problems re the much-publicised forecast of the doom that will befall computers if they become flummoxed about the new date.

A day off work to get over a hangover? Waitrose is already picking up good ideas from its association with a trendy advertising agency.

Waitrose
Southern Industrial Area
Bracknell
Berks RG12 8YA
Tel: 01344 424680
Fax: 01344 862584
Customer Care Line: 0800 188884

ARGENTINIAN WINE RED

La Bamba Mendoza Shiraz 1997 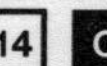

Interesting shiraz which might give the Aussies something to worry about, especially at this price, if the Mendozans can stretch the fruit more, add wood, and develop complexity.

La Bamba Tempranillo 1997 

Juicy and seemingly straightforward but as it quits the throat and descends a beautifully warm suffusion of custardy fruit, slightly toasty, impacts.

Santa Julia Bonarda/Sangiovese, Mendoza 1997 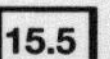 

Juicy, rich, soft, but finishing dry and deep. Impressive quaffing here.

Sierra Alta Cabernet Sauvignon/Malbec, Mendoza 1996 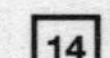 

Delicious, considerate, engaging.

ARGENTINIAN WINE WHITE

Bodega Lurton Pinot Gris, Mendoza 1997 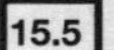 

Superb ring-a-ding fruit.

La Bamba Mendoza Sauvignon Blanc 1997 15.5 C

Great fun – has serious sauvignon attack but with that hint of southern warmth.

AUSTRALIAN WINE RED

Brown Brothers Tarrango 1997

Quite offensively slurpable and richly soft and near-gooey, this is a wine to chill and serve to recent divorcees.

Brown's of Padthaway T-Trellis Shiraz 1995

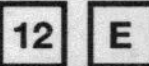

Juicy, jammy, soft, gooey – spread it on bread before you drink it. Or use it to dunk biscuits in.

Bushman's Crossing Dry Red

Oddly attractive: fresh, saddle-weary, ripe yet astonishingly dry.

Chateau Reynella Basket-Pressed Shiraz 1995

Cassis and tannins. What a recipe for heavenly quaffing. Pity the price has gone astronomic, though.

Nanya Vineyard Malbec/Ruby Cabernet 1997

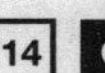

Drink it chilled with a salad of cos lettuce, garlic (a lot!), green olive oil and sherry vinegar, with fried blood sausage. What an adventure for the palate!

Orlando Jacob's Creek Shiraz/Cabernet 1995 13.5 C

Rosemount Cabernet Sauvignon, Hunter Valley 1996 14.5 E

Big, juicy, rich.

Rouge Homme Coonawarra Cabernet Sauvignon 1994 13.5 E

Jammy with nuts and biscuit. I can tolerate a small glass. You may take the whole bottle.

Southern Creek Shiraz/Cabernet Sauvignon, SE Australia 1997 13.5 C

Tatachilla Cabernet Sauvignon, McLaren Vale 1996 15.5 E

Vigorous, dry yet richly fruity and all-embracing, textured and handsomely tannic. A terrific Aussie red combining fine high and low notes.

Tatachilla Merlot, McLaren Vale 1996 14 E

Only just rates 14. It's young, fresh and frisky.

Wynn's Coonawarra Michael Shiraz 1994 17.5 H

This has come on immeasurably in bottle since I first tasted it. It is now one of the most deftly woven fruit-and-tannin Australians I have ever tasted. It is intensely concentrated but very warm, soft and aromatic, showing a cassis and toffee edge with the texture, divine, of crimped velvet. A magnificent beast. It will age with distinction but not beyond five or six years I believe (contrary to the maker's ideas of longevity). It is the height of luxury, this wine, for it has an impossibly smug hauteur and sense of superiority. I love it. Available at Inner Cellar stores (0800 188884 for details).

Yaldara Reserve Grenache, Whitmore Old Vineyard 1997 15 D

Soft, but saved from complete soppiness by some baked fruit edginess mixing firmly with the tannins on the finish.

Yarra Yering Pinot Noir 1991 12 H

Ludicrous pretentious price. Only available in the Inner Cellar Waitrose stores.

AUSTRALIAN WINE WHITE

Basedow Barossa Chardonnay 1996 16 E

Australia is making the best chardonnays in the world at this price when the fruit is so pure, rich (without blowsiness), clean (without tartness) and beautifully textured.

Brown Brothers Late Harvest Riesling 1995 (half bottle) 14 D

A deliciously different wine to go with rice pudding.

Brown's of Padthaway Non-wooded Chardonnay 1996 16 E

Just stunning richness of texture. It liberally oils the taste buds with fruit of utter simplicity, unpretentiousness and direct charm. A lovely wine.

Bushman's Crossing Dry White 13 B

Chateau Tahbilk Marsanne, Victoria 1996 15 D

A superb rich-fish-dish wine with its texture, ripeness, and thick flavoursomeness.

Currawong Creek Chardonnay 1997 14 C

Shows the impressive fatness-with-fitness fruit of this vintage.

De Bortoli Rare Dry Botrytis Semillon, SE Australia 1993 12 E

Ebenezer Chardonnay, Barossa Valley 1995 14 E

Henschke Semillon, Eden & Barossa Valley 1994 16.5 E

Astonishing texture and leafy, herby complexity. Terrific to put down for three to four years, if not more. It will become a massively characterful, quirky wine in time. Only available in the Inner Cellar Waitrose stores.

Houghton Gold Reserve Verdelho 1994 15.5 D

Classic Western Australia richness, reserve, balance, finesse and crab cake compatibility. Lovely stuff. Will go with Thai food, too.

Nanya Vineyard Chenin/Gewurztraminer 1997 15 C

Hints of spicy-to-ripe melon and mineralised fruit give the wine a measure of complexity surprising at this price.

Penfolds Bin 202 Riesling 1997 15 C

A crisp, clean, rather elegant wine for fish dishes which the cook has taken some trouble to prepare.

Penfolds Bin 94A Chardonnay 1994 15 G

Big, rich, woody, very pretentious, creamy, Meursault-meets-Napa style, with some age ahead of it to really show its individuality. It will probably rate 17 or 17.5 in two or three years when the vegetality has undercut the smoothness of the fruit and given the wine character. At twenty pounds, it's a lot to pay and Chilean chardonnays at a quarter of the price, whilst not possessing this wine's future, do offer some competitive stylishness. At its best after dinner with goat's cheese.

Penfolds Clare Valley Organic Chardonnay/ Sauvignon Blanc, 1997 16 E

Very calm, classy wine in complete command of its faculties: understated richness, firm acidity, delicate balance. Lovely tipple.

Penfolds Koonunga Hill Chardonnay 1997 15.5 D

The '97 Aussie whites are on song and no branded chardonnay hits a sweeter (yet drier) top note than this one. Gorgeousness of almost the drop-dead variety.

Tatachilla Sauvignon Blanc/Semillon 1997 13.5 D

Wynns Coonawarra Riesling 1996 15 C

Has only echoes of the rich riesling tones of Europe but it has these echoes resonantly in place and well held by the mountain-stream fresh acidity.

BULGARIAN WINE RED

Domaine Boyar Cabernet Sauvignon/ Merlot, Iambol 1996 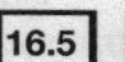 

Quite brilliant flavour. True, it's light on texture but the tannin and perfect alcohol balance cut the concentrated cassis fruit superbly. A magnificent *super* plonk.

Iambol Cabernet Sauvignon/Merlot 1996 

Oriachovitza Barrel-aged Merlot 1996 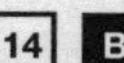

BULGARIAN WINE WHITE

Aligote/Rikat, Lyaskovets 1996  

CHILEAN WINE RED

Cono Sur Cabernet Sauvignon 1996  

Most approachable with its cherry/blackcurrant ferocity undercut by tannin and acid. Balanced, bonny, bouncy.

Cono Sur Pinot Noir Reserve 1996 12.5 D

Isla Negra Cabernet Sauvignon 1996 15 C

How is it possible to conjure texture like this from grapes? Compellingly soft and attractive – on all fronts (and as far as the tongue is concerned, back and sides also).

La Palma Merlot 1997 16 C

Gorgeous concentration of leathery softness and almost jammy sweetness but not in fact sugary because of the complexity of the finish. Lovely stuff.

San Andres Cabernet Sauvignon, Lontue 1997 15.5 C

Cabernet in the richly approachable vein of softness, ripeness and utterly sinful gluggability.

Stowells of Chelsea Chilean Merlot Cabernet (3-litre box) 10 C

Price bracket has been adjusted to show the bottle equivalent.

CHILEAN WINE WHITE

Isla Negra Chardonnay 1996 14 C

Montenuevo Sauvignon Blanc 1997 15.5 C

Brilliant fruit, has a versatility with food, a wittiness of finish and a lovely texture.

San Andres Chardonnay, Lontue 1997 16 C

Ooh . . . it's simply gorgeous: ripe, balanced, flavourful, young yet far from innocent, fruity, delightfully drinkable.

San Andres Sauvignon Blanc, Lontue 1997 14.5 C

Lovely sticky texture and crispness.

Stowells of Chelsea Chilean Sauvignon Blanc (3-litre box) 15.5 B

Price bracket has been adjusted to show the bottle equivalent.

Valdivieso Chardonnay 1997 16.5 C

Amazing depth and vibrancy for such youth. Has plump fruit with a hint of tropicality and a rich, almost toffee edge to it. Utterly ravishing.

ENGLISH WINE — WHITE

Chapel Down Summerhil Oaked Dry White 11 C

Denbies Surrey Gold 12 C

FRENCH WINE — RED

Beaujolais 1997, Waitrose 13.5 C

Ripe and ready.

Beaune 1er Cru Greves, Domaine Maillard 1992 13.5 G

Getting towards the tightness of definition pinot must have. Only available in the Waitrose Inner Cellar stores.

Beaune 1er Cru Teurons, Domaine Rossignal 1993 13.5 G

Close to being really good: texture, and aroma, but the fruit as an impactful presence seems wan. Only available in the Inner Cellar Waitrose stores.

Biovinum Organic Cotes du Rhone 1997

C

Nice touch of earth, light on the fruit.

Boulder Creek Red VdP du Vaucluse 1997

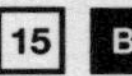

Absolutely no need to spend three times more on Beaujolais with this beauty on shelf.

Cahors Cotes d'Olt 1996

Real country goatskin fruit and rich quaffing here. Needs food.

Chateau de Grammont La Mejanelle, Coteaux du Languedoc 1996

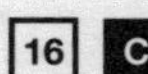

Tremendous! Great Italianate richness, ripeness, earthiness and texture. A very striking wine.

Chateau de Jacques Moulin a Vent 1996 10 E

Ludicrous price for a Moulin a Vent.

Chateau des Combes Canon, Canon-Fronsac 1996 16 E

Open several hours beforehand, jug it, and then let the dry, rolling, intensely fruity wine simply engulf the taste buds.

Chateau des Deduits, Fleurie 1997 13 E

Chateau Giscours, Margaux 1993 12 G

Chateau La Faviere, Bordeaux Superieure 1996 14.5 D

Real charcoal-edged fruit here. Were the grapes grilled first? Delicious richness here.

Chateau La Lagune Haut-Medoc 1993 13.5 H

Chocolate, coffee and tannins, rather sweet to finish. Lot of money, though.

Chateau La Pointe, Pomerol 1993 13 G

Chateau Laroque St Emilion Grand Cru 1994 16 G

Worth the money to catch a glimpse of what real Bordeaux is all about: woody, vegetal yet rich in deeply dry, cassis-tinged fruit, lengthy, witty, meaningful, uniquely potent.

Chateau Le Tertre Bordeaux 1996 14 C

Chateau Leoville Lascases, St-Julien 1981 13 H

Cheesy and ludicrously pretentiously priced. Only available in the Inner Cellar Waitrose stores.

Chateau Malescasse, Haut-Medoc 1994 13 F

Chateau Segonzac Premieres Cotes de Blaye 1995 14 D

Old style Claret classicism: tannic, dry, food friendly.

Chateau Senejac, Haut-Medoc 1993 13.5 E

Chateau St Auriol, Corbieres 1995 16 C

Coolly classy – indeed, almost casually so as the fruit takes time to gather on the tongue before it ripens and descends. Terrific finish.

Chateauneuf-du-Pape Bernadine, Chapoutier 1995 11 F

Disappointing at this price. Only available in the Inner Cellar Waitrose stores.

Chorey les Beaune Domaine Maillard 1996 12 E

Cigala VdP d'Oc, M Chapoutier 1995 13 C

Clos Saint Michel Chateauneuf-du-Pape 1996 13.5 E

Bit young perhaps but has a jammy edge which makes me question if it will age with distinction.

Cornas, Chapoutier 1995 15 F

Is it *really* worth thirteen smackers? To the Rhone enthusiast yes, not to the Aussie syrah lover. This wine is rich, soft, with a richness which will deepen over the next two or three years. But it's the texture which wins it.

Cotes du Rhone 1996, Waitrose 13.5 B

Very fruity, very.

Cotes du Ventoux, N. Butler 1997 14 B

Terrific cherry-ripe yet dry wine.

Crozes-Hermitage Cave des Clairmonts 1995 12 D

Domaine de Rose Merlot/Syrah, VdP d'Oc 1997 16 B

Richly fruity, dry, polished, textured, superbly energetic and charming.

Domaine de Serame Syrah VdP d'Oc 1996 14.5 C

Domaine du Moulin 'The Cabernets', VdP d'Oc 1995 16 C

I've tasted clarets less rich and dryly incisive than this terrific, personality-packed bargain.

Domaine Fontaine de Cathala Syrah/Cabernet Cuvee Prestige VdP d'Oc 1994 (half bottle) 13 A

Domaine Ste Lucie Gigondas 1996 14 D

Classy earth here – very high class soil.

Ermitage du Pic St Loup Coteaux du Languedoc 1996 15 C

Very classy and dry and rolling and rich. Youthful yet experienced.

Fortant de France Grenache VdP d'Oc 1997 15.5 C

Brilliant tone of voice for a rustic minstrel: soft, deep, rich, hints of sweetness. Lovely quaffing wine.

Gevrey Chambertin Chauvenet 1996 13 G

Has some texture.

Good Ordinary Claret Bordeaux, Waitrose 15 C

Still a wine which possesses better fruit than is implied by its name. This understatement is its theme. An excellent buy.

Hautes Cotes de Beaune Tete de Cuvee 1996 12 D

Almost sweet, but not sweetly priced.

James Herrick Cuvee Simone, VdP d'Oc 1996 16 C

I love the insouciance of the delicious fruit.

L de La Louviere, Pessac-Leognan 1995 14 E

Expensive but the tannins are as taut as a high guitar string.

L'Enclos Domeque Mourvedre Syrah VdP d'Oc 1996 14 C

A more sedate vintage for this gallant red.

Le Faisan Syrah Grenache VdP du Gard 1997 15.5 C

Lovely texture, rounded and ripely fruity, but with a warmth and dryness which is typical of the Midi. Thus, it has modernity with antiquity.

Merchants Bay Merlot/Cabernet Sauvignon, Bordeaux 1996 13 C

Merchants at bay, more like.

Merlot/Cabernet Sauvignon, VdP d'Oc 1996 13 B

Prieure de Fonclaire Buzet 1995 13.5 C

Red Burgundy JC Boisset 1996 13 D

Has its points. Also, alas, has its pennies.

Romanee St Vivant Grand Cru, T Regnier 1991 12 H

Only available in the Inner Cellar Waitrose stores.

Saint Roche VdP du Gard 1997 (organic) 15.5 C

The label to be seen with! The fruit? It's earthy, ripe, rich and most deliciously characterful. Black cherries, plums and earth.

Saint-Joseph Cuvee Medaille d'Or, Cave de Saint Desirat 1994 15 E

Lovely texture and rich, dark fruit finish. Only available in the Inner Cellar Waitrose stores.

Special Reserve Claret, Cotes de Castillon 1994, Waitrose  14 C

Curiously, it's most un-Claret-like. It substitutes prissy tannins for earthy characterfulness.

St Emilion Yvon Mau 13.5 D

Trinity Ridge VdP d'Oc 1996 13 C

Winter Hill Pinot Noir/Merlot VdP d'Oc 1997 14 C

Simple and unpretentious glugging of soft fruit.

Winter Hill Red VdP de l'Aude 1997 15.5 B

Earthy, dry, splendidly vulgar and enjoyable.

Winter Hill Reserve Shiraz 1997 15.5 C

My goodness! Australia had better look to its laurels! £3.89? It's a steal. Gorgeous stuff.

FRENCH WINE WHITE

Alsace Gewurztraminer Cave de Beblenheim 1996, Waitrose 16 D

Terrific stuff: has fruit (exotic, roseate, perfumed), texture, ripeness, wit and richness.

Alsace Pinot Blanc, Paul Blanck 1996 13.5 C

Bordeaux Blanc Medium Dry, Yvon Mau 12 B

Bordeaux Sauvignon 1997, Waitrose 13 B

Boulder Creek White VdP du Vaucluse 1997 14 B

Fresh and fruity.

Chablis Gaec des Reugnis 1996 14.5 E

Has some real freshness and impish humour, this wine.

Chablis Premier Cru Beauregard, Brocard 1996 13 E

Now if only it was half the price, Chablis would have charm.

Chardonnay VdP du Jardin de la France 1997

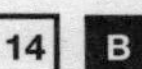

Brilliant bargain. Rich and textured.

Chateau Carsin Cuvee Prestige, Bordeaux 1995

One of the nattiest turned out white Bordeaux around. Rich yet controlled, delicate and beautifully balanced, it has style, flavour, limpidity and impact.

Chateau Climens Sauternes-Barsac 1991

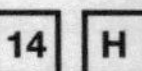

A real treat. It's the texture which lets the biscuity honey of the finish linger so long. Like creme brulee, a touch, with yogurt, raisins and herby honey.

Chateau Haut Gardere, Pessac-Leognan 1995

Chateau La Caussade Ste Croix du Mont 1994

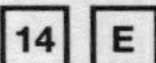

Not a big Sauternes style – more in the subdued Barsac vein. Good with fresh fruit.

Chateau la Chartreuse, Sauternes 1994 (half bottle) 16 E

The texture is so rich and waxy you feel you could chew it for ever. A wonderful pudding wine.

Chateau Terres Douces, Bordeaux 1995 13 D

Colombard Sauvignon Blanc, Comte Tolosan 1997 14 B

Decently biting and clean living.

Cotes du Luberon, Nick Butler 1996 13.5 C

Cuckoo Hill Viognier, VdP d'Oc 1997 14 C

Crisp apricot fruit with a hint of pineapple. Delicious aperitif.

Domaine de la Foret Tete de Cuvee Sauternes 1990 13 G

Domaine de Planterieu VdP de Gascogne 1997 15 C

Minerals, pears, pineapple and lemons – all freshly squeezed.

Domaine Petit Chateau Chardonnay, VdP du Jardin de la France 1997 14 C

Hints of Aussie texture and richness here.

La Baume Chardonnay/Viognier VdP d'Oc 1996 16.5 D

Lovely balance and flavour, clean and very controlled. Has knife-edge freshness yet the hints of oil and wood, skimming the surface, give the wine depth and vibrancy.

Laroche Grande Cuvee Chardonnay, VdP d'Oc 1996 13 D

Nice woody aroma and fruit. Wanders thereafter.

Le Pujalet VdP du Gers 1997 14 B

Delicious lilt of fresh pineapple on the finish.

Les Bateaux Terret/Chardonnay, VdP d'Oc 1997 

Interesting earthy tang to the ripe fruit.

Les Fleurs Chardonnay/Sauvignon VdP des Cotes de Gascogne 1997 

Now this is a clever paradox, and utterly delicious. On one hand it's rich and serious, on the other it's crisp and flirtatious. The result is louche, lovable, very fruity and deeply individual.

Macon Solutre Auvigue 1997 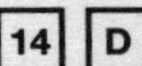

Mostly richly endowed with individuality, flavour and style.

Macon-Lugny Les Charmes 1996 14.5 

Solid, mineralised, rich-edged white Burgundy of no little distinction. Not grand or pompous but very friendly.

Merchants Bay Sauvignon Blanc/Semillon, Bordeaux 1996 

Meursault, Bouchard Pere et Fils 1996 11 G

Montagny Special Cuvee, Cave de Buxy 1996 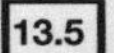 

Lemony beast but with some character – tough on the pocket, though.

Muscadet de Sevre et Maine sur Lie 1996, Waitrose 13.5 C

Muscat de Rivesaltes, M. Chapoutier 1996 (half bottle) 15.5 C

Superb with fresh fruit after a feast. Or, in this way, a feast in itself.

Pinot Blanc d'Alsace Blanck Freres 1996 14.5 C

Pouilly Fuisse Les Chailloux, Domaine Revel 1996 13 F

Only available in the Inner Cellar Waitrose stores.

Pouilly Fume, Domaine Masson-Blondelet 1997 12 E

Decent but indecently priced.

Puligny Montrachet 1er Cru Les Folatieres 1994 14 H

Lovely texture and vegetal richness. An impressive Puligny of great class. Only available in the Inner Cellar Waitrose stores.

Roussanne VdP d'Oc Ryman 1997 16 C

Curious blend of richness and freshness. Has a hint of sticky toffee to the texture; crisp pineapple and melon fruit, and a finish which lingers deliciously.

Saint Roche VdP du Gard 1997 (organic) 13 C

Finishes a bit wanly for a wine at this price.

Salmon Run, Bordeaux NV 13 C

Sancerre Les Hautes Rives 1996 13.5 E

Not quite knife-edge fresh. There's a spot of rust on it.

Sauvignon Calvet, Bordeaux 1997 13.5 C

Fresh and clean, touch of earth, should be fifty pence cheaper.

Terret/Chardonnay, VdP d'Oc Lurton, 1996 14 C

Tokay Pinot Gris d'Alsace, Cave de Beblenheiim 1996 13.5 D

Just fails to clinch a higher rating because of the uncertainty of the finish. But in two or three years . . .

Touraine Sauvignon Blanc 1997 14 C

Lovely lilt to clean, fresh gooseberry fruit.

Vouvray Le Haut-Lieu 1ere Trie Moelleux 1990 17 H

Great sinful richness. Sheer rot and ripeness. Only available in the Inner Cellar Waitrose stores.

White Burgundy, Boisset 1996 13 C

Winter Hill Dry White VdP de l'Aude 1997 15.5 B

Super class here: crisp, clean, rich, full, developed, engaging. Terrific value.

Winter Hill Reserve Chardonnay VdP d'Oc 1997 15 C

Has some plump fleshiness under the clean, fresh fruit. Has charm and precision.

Winter Hill Syrah Rose, VdP d'Oc 1997 14 

Charming richness and freshness.

GERMAN WINE WHITE

Avelsbacher Hammerstein Riesling Auslese, Staatsweingut 1989 15.5 D

Delicious aperitif. A perfectly mature specimen where the gentle honeyed nature of the fruit is coated in mineralised acidity. Lovely balance.

Bert Simon Serriger Wurzberg Riesling Spatlese, Saar 1990 16.5 D

Intense sherbet, lime, lemon and satsuma fruit of great richness yet aperitif delicacy. Gorgeous.

Domdechant Werner Hochheimer Riesling Spatlese, Rheingau 1990 13.5 E

Touch tart, rather than acidic. Needs time? It's had eight years.

Dr L Riesling 1996 15 D

Graacher Himmelreich Riesling Spatlese, JJ Prum 1994 12 G

Needs time to come around – five or six years. Only available in the Inner Cellar Waitrose stores.

Haardter Herrenletten Grauburgunder Auslese, Pfalz 1992 (50cl) 17 E

Great wine for Christmas. Waxy, honeyed apricot, sesame seeds and such sweet depth although it never drowns you in sweetness. A great wine. In five to eight years, a 19 point one.

Kirchheimer Schwarzerde Beerenauslese, Pfalz 1994 (half bottle) 15 C

Morio Muskat, Pfalz 1995 12.5 B

Ockfener Bockstein Riesling QbA, Dr Wagner 1996 13.5 D

Riesling Kabinett, Robert Weil 1996 12 E

Only available in the Inner Cellar Waitrose stores.

Schloss Schonborn Hattenheimer Pfaffenberger Riesling Spatlese 1989 16 D

A superb aperitif with its hint of rot subsumed under masses of mineralised acidity. Superb. Will last for ten to fifteen years.

Serriger Vogelsang Riesling Spatlese 1990 16 D

Quite brilliant acidity and richness here. Resounds with dry honey fruit with hints of wet wool, pineapple and lots of lime.

St Ursula Devil's Rock Riesling 1996 13.5 C

Improving fast.

St Ursula Dry Riesling 1996 13.5 C

Chile, South Africa and Italy crush it to death at this price level.

Urziger Wurzgarten Riesling Spatlese, Monchhof 1993 12 D

HUNGARIAN WINE RED

Deer Leap Dry Red Blauer Zweigelt 1997 16 B

Superb youth, suppleness, cherry/plum fruit, hint of tannin, ripeness and a touch of passion. Brilliant! Knocks Beaujolais for several sixes.

Deer Leap Sauvignon/Cabernet Franc 1996 14 C

Carroty aroma: that's cabernet franc for you, but the fruit gets there in the end.

HUNGARIAN WINE WHITE

Chapel Hill Irsai Oliver, Balatonboglar 1997 14 B

Delicious as a warm weather aperitif.

Deer Leap Gewurztraminer, Mor 1996 13.5 C

Deer Leap Pinot Grigio 1996 16 C

Terrific little quaffing bottle here: gentle, crisp, clean, an echo of apricot and a surge of refreshment on the finish. First class value for money here.

Deer Leap Sauvignon Blanc 1997 

The Magyars spit in the Kiwis' eye. Lovely grassy backbone and rich concentration of fresh mineral acidity.

Lakeside Oak Chardonnay, Balaton Boglar 1996 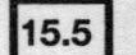

Matra Springs Pinot Gris/Muscat, Gyongyos 1997 

Touch of earth to the fresh muscat fruit. Most attractive aperitif.

Nagyrede Barrique-aged Chardonnay 1995 

Very lemony and tarty.

Szt Tamas Tokaji 5 Puttonyos 1991 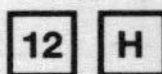

Ludicrously overpriced. The sheer sweetness overpowers everything. Cellar it thirty years to get something great out of the bottle. Only available in the Inner Cellar Waitrose stores.

Tokaji Aszu 5 Puttonyos 1988 (50cl) 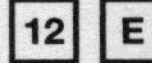

ITALIAN WINE RED

Amarone Classico, Vigneti Casterna 1992 (50cl) 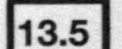 

Expensive treat for the lone lush: bitter cherries with a hint of almond.

Barolo Gomba 1994 14 F

Lot of money! Lot of wine! Licorice and cherries plus earth.

Chianti 1996, Waitrose 14.5 C

Chianti Classic, Rocca di Castagnoli 1996 15 D

Sweet and dry, earthy and ripe.

Copertino Rosso 1994 14.5 C

Delicious tobacco hints undertoning the ripe plum fruit. A real handsome quaffing bottle for pasta and a serious tipple for conversation (of the very fruity sort).

Laste Merlot Atesino 1997 15.5 C

Lovely! It really coddles the taste buds in rich, textured, soft fruit.

Merlot Atesino, Concilio 1996 13.5 C

Montepulciano d'Abruzzo, Umani Ronchi 1996 13 C

Negroamaro del Salento Le Trulle 1996 13 C

Poggio a'Frati Chianti Classico Riserva 1993 15.5 E

Earthy, ripe, very forward yet mature and manicured. A lovely chianti.

Sangiovese di Toscana, Cecchi 1996 15.5 C

Superb value here. More sweet fruit and friendly baked earthiness than many an expensive Chianti. Has improved enormously in bottle since I tasted it last year.

Teroldego Rotaliano, Ca'Vit 1997 16 C

Gorgeous ripe texture, plump and cherry/blackcurrant deep. Very polished but far from all surface.

Vino Nobile di Montepulciano, Avignonesi 1994 15.5 E

Nuts, black cherries, earth, hedgerow fruits – they're all there more or less fighting to get out of the bottle.

ITALIAN WINE WHITE

Alasia Cortese Piemonte, 1996 15.5 C

An excellent shellfish wine. Superb individuality and rich, balanced fruit here. Terrific texture, depth of flavour and finish.

Avignonesi Il Marzocco Chardonnay di Toscana 1993 13.5 E

Nice texture. Fruit is a touch dumb and inexpressive, even though a certain nuttiness lingers. Only available in the Inner Cellar Waitrose stores.

Catarrato/Chardonnay, Firriato 1996 (Sicily) 15 C

Unusually double-edged impact of oily texture with clear crisp fruit of clinical cleanliness. Delicious.

Lugana Villa Flora, Zenato 1996 15.5 D

This is one of those crisp Italians which have such distinct Germanic leanings in their manners they offer the best of both worlds.

Marche Trebbiano, Moncaro 1996 14.5 B

Mezzo Mondo Chardonnay 1996 14 C

Very Italian in that it's difficult to conceive of its makers, putting this fresh, nutty wine together, that they weren't licking their lips and thinking of the food it would go with (shrimp risotto for one).

Pinot Grigio VdT delle Venezie 1997 14 C

Delicious calmness and concentration here. Unusually compact and juicy yet very classy pinot grigio.

San Simone Sauvignon, Friuli Grave 1997 15 C

Lovely – better than many a Sancerre.

Soave Classico, Vigneto Colombara 1996 14.5 C

Catch it whilst it's young. Always one of the tastiest Soaves, when it's young it has a joyous crispness and rich liveliness.

Verdicchio dei Castelli Jesi, 1997 15.5 C

Gorgeous richness of texture and crisp fluency of fruit and acidity. A lovely Verdicchio. Gorgeous fish wine.

LEBANESE WINE RED

Chateau Musar 1989 12 E

MOROCCAN WINE — RED

Domaine Cicogne Grenache/Cinsault 1996

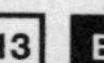

Light, drinkable.

NEW ZEALAND WINE — RED

Church Road Cabernet Sauvignon/Merlot 1995

Got something for the money. Coffee, tea, cassis, leather, texture and tannin. Who minds nine quid when you come back with a complete spice cabinet?

Church Road Merlot/Cabernet Sauvignon, Hawkes Bay 1995

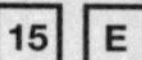

Real class here. Expensive, yes, but the value's there.

Church Road Reserve Cabernet Sauvignon/Merlot 1995

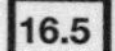

Most impressively Bordeaux-like in the most classical sense of the word. Except for that rich dryness, there is a hint of Antipodean warmth and down-to-earth wit.

NEW ZEALAND WINE — WHITE

Cooks Chardonnay, Gisborne 1997

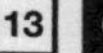

Lawson's Dry Hill Sauvignon Blanc, Marlborough 1997 16 E

Its best manifestation yet? Gorgeously controlled, rich, herbaceousness and finesse here.

Millton Vineyard Barrel-fermented Chenin Blanc 1996 13 E

Has some wry elegance, but lacks depth and energy for £8.

Tiki Ridge Dry White, Montana 1997 14 C

Villa Maria Private Bin Chardonnay, Marlborough 1997 14 D

Young (and it will improve) but very rich and ready to provide lingering fruity pleasures.

Villa Maria Private Bin Sauvignon, Marlborough 1997 16.5 D

Superbly greasy grassiness which thunders across the palate with silken hooves; such stealth and purpose here.

PORTUGUESE WINE RED

Falcoaria Almeirim 1995 16.5 D

Quite superb figgy richness with hints of cherry/plum/blackberry and a touch of cream. But earthy with it – that's the brilliant bit.

ROMANIAN WINE RED

River Route Limited Edition Merlot 1996 15 C

Lovely soft texture, rich fruit with hints of the hedgerow and a lingering, polished finish. Delicious.

Willow Ridge Merlot 1996 15.5 B

Delightful little wine. Has aroma, depth, flavour and style with true hints of merlot leatheriness and impact. Delicious bargain for food or mood.

SOUTH AFRICAN WINE RED

Avontuur Cabernet Sauvignon/Merlot 1997 15 C

Very soft and plush, aromatic and pleasingly textured. Well worth anyone's fiver.

Avontuur Pinotage 1997 15 D

Pinotage as a marriage of Barolo and Beaujolais: delicious!

Benguela Current Merlot, Western Cape 1996 12.5 C

Not a lot of character but pleasant enough.

Clos Malverne Pinotage, Stellenbosch 1997 16 D

The essence of great pinotage, to be drunk young whilst it is also unselfconsciously warm, soft, natural and very cherry/plum rich.

Culemborg Unwooded Pinotage 1997

Treat it like Beaujolais! Chill it, swig it, bathe in it. Lovely stuff.

Diamond Hills Pinotage/Cabernet Sauvignon 1997

Solid but soft, approachable yet with some tannins, fruity but dry.

Diemersdal Pinotage 1997

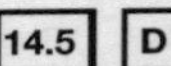

Juicy rubberised fruit with a hint of gun-barrel. Delicious pasta wine.

Du Toitskloof Cabernet Sauvignon/Shiraz 1997

Fairview Cabernet Franc/Merlot, Paarl 1995

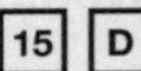

Fairview Cyril Back Shiraz Reserve 1996

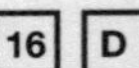

Coffee, blackcurrant, tea, plums, hint of tannin – a recipe for ambrosia.

Fairview Zinfandel, Paarl 1997

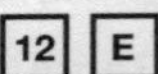

Curiously OTT for a Fairview wine. Only available in the Inner Cellar Waitrose stores.

Grangehurst Cabernet/Merlot, Stellenbosch 1994

Fruit juice and light tannins. Perhaps the egg white fining was a mistake. Only available in the Inner Cellar Waitrose stores.

Kudukop Cape Dry Red 1997 13 C

Kumala Ruby Cabernet/Merlot 1996 14.5 C

La Motte Millennium 1993 14 E

Fancy assemblage of rich grapes, handsomely balanced, ripe, and deliciously textured.

Simonsvlei Cabernet Sauvignon 1996 15.5 C

A most engaging and individual cabernet with a warmth of personality and rich concentration of fruit which is ripe yet dry and mature in feel.

Steenberg Merlot, Constantia 1996 15 E

Gorgeous, individual, highly textured, pretty, very powerful concentration of complexity. An unusually advanced, tannic Cape red. Available at Inner Cellar stores only (call 0800 188884 for details).

Warwick Estate Old Bush Vine Pinotage, Stellenbosch 1996 15.5 E

Hearty brew of huge depth and flavour. A terrific pinotage of texture and complexity. Serious/fun wine. Only available in the Inner Cellar Waitrose stores.

SOUTH AFRICAN WINE WHITE

Avontuur Chardonnay 'Le Chardon' 1997 16 D

Lovely elegance and silky textured fruit here. Not a big buttery job but a sly, soft-yet-crisp, subtly nutty wine with an echo of ripe melon.

Blue Ridge Barrel-fermented Chenin Blanc 1997 14 C

Bouchard Finlayson Kaaimansgat Chardonnay 1996 14.5 E

Finishes very richly and ripely. Great for goat's cheese dishes.

Cape Sauvignon Blanc NV 14.5 D

Good grapefruit aroma, very keenly taut and knife-edged. A wine for raw or smoked fish and crustaceans.

Culemborg Unwooded Chardonnay, Western Cape 1997 13.5 C

Odd sort of chardie.

Diamond Hills Chenin Blanc/Chardonnay, Western Cape 1997 14 C

Has some ripeness well balanced by the freshness. Nice effect.

Fairview Barrel-fermented Chenin Blanc 1997 15.5 C

Terrific dryness and richness, style, flavour, and a lovely cheeky finish.

Fairview Chenin Blanc, Paarl 1996 14 C

Kudukop Cape Dry White 1996 13 B

Kumala Colombard/Chardonnay 1997 13.5 C

Good, soft, rich fruit. Needs food to wake up.

KWV Chardonnay 1996 14 C

Landema Falls Chenin Blanc 1996 13 B

Springfield Estate Chardonnay, Robertson 1996 14.5 C

Springfield Sauvignon Blanc Special Cuvee 1997 14 D

The mineral, zippy style of sauvignon. Great with shellfish. I wouldn't be surprised if this developed very nicely in bottle over the next six months.

Steenberg Semillon 1997 13 E

Available at Inner Cellar stores (0800 188884 for details).

SPANISH WINE RED

Agramont Tinto Tempranillo/Cabernet Sauvignon Crianza, Navarra 1994 15.5 C

Chivite Coleccion 125 Reserva, Navarra 1993 15.5 D

Smooth, classy, and with an uplift of sweet cherry on the finish. Delightful quaffing.

Cosme Palacio y Hermanos Rioja 1996 14 D

Rich and ripe, dry rather grouchy tannins.

Enate Tinto, Somontano 1995 15.5 C

Marques de Murrieta Ygay Reserva Especial 1991 13.5 F

The juiciness, which is highly slurpable, suggests a wine at less than half the price. Only available in the Inner Cellar Waitrose stores.

Stowells of Chelsea Tempranillo (3-litre box) 14 B

Price bracket has been adjusted to show the bottle equivalent.

Vina Fuerte Garnacha, Calatayud 1997 15.5 C

What a swinger! Moves superbly well to the beat of fruit, acid and a touch of tannin. Has character and charm.

SPANISH WINE WHITE

Agramont Blanco, Navarra 1996 14 C

Las Lomas Moscatel de Valencia 16 C

Fabulous ice-cream and creme brulee wine.

Solana Torrontes and Treixadura 1996 13 C

Vina Dorana Pardina, Tierra de Barros 13 B

USA WINE RED

Fetzer Valley Oaks Cabernet Sauvignon 1995 15 D

Perfumed, ripe, gently vegetal and very warming. Every time I taste it, it seems to have improved a little more in bottle.

Mondavi Carneros Pinot Noir, California 1992 13 G

Only available in the Inner Cellar Waitrose stores.

Redwood Trail Pinot Noir 1996 14.5 D

Excellent, if slightly sulphurous, on first opening, but the texture and ripeness and sheer class of pinot are obvious.

Ridge Lytton Springs Zinfandel 1995 16.5 G

Exuberant, rich, complex, deeply fruity yet dry, polished and incredibly well textured wine. Has a gorgeous sweet/dry finish of black cherry. Impossible to feel indifferent about a wine this good (and pricey).

Stone Bridge Cellars Zinfandel 1995 13.5 C

Very juicy and medicinal. Might suit bedridden geriatrics.

Yorkville Cellars Cabernet Franc 1994 (organic) 14 E

Expensive, dry (but with a sweet, almost raspberry-like finish) and with some attractive tannins. I do feel it is expensive for the style, however, but feel organicists should know of it.

USA WINE — WHITE

Fetzer Sundial Chardonnay 1996 14.5 D

Impressive finesse yet fullness here. Rich and warm yet crisp and beautifully balanced. Has great elegance.

Fetzer Viognier, California 1996 15.5 E

A beautiful, serene, apricot-fruited wine. Only at twenty-eight branches.

Redwood Trail Chardonnay 1996 15.5 D

Gorgeously rich texture and ripeness yet, in the end, it shows power and class on the finish.

FORTIFIED WINE

10 Year Old Tawny, Waitrose 14 F

Apostoles Palo Cortado Oloroso (half bottle) 15.5 E

Fruit cake vinified and then laid out in the sun to become as dry and wrinkled as a raisin.

Churchill's Dry White Port 13 E

Comte de Lafont Pineau des Charentes 15 D

Worth it! Try it! As a chilled aperitif.

Dow's 1977

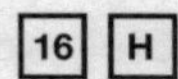

Magnificent port at a magnificent price. Shows licorice, prunes, cassis and chocolate, never so sweetly expressed as to be merely a confection, and the texture is lush yet finely wrought, mature and beautifully knitted. Only available in the Inner Cellar Waitrose stores.

Dow's LBV 1990 13.5 F

Dry Fly Amontillado 12 D

Fino, Waitrose 15.5 C

Lovely texture to this rich yet bone dry wine.

Fonseca Traditional LBV 1983

Warm yet far from sweet. It has power, richness, texture and a capacity to delight.

Gonsalez Byass Matusalem Oloroso Dulce Muy Viejo (half bottle) 16 E

The ultimate Everest for the taste buds. Can they climb the peaks of this hugely rich, fruity, acidic, bursting-with-flavour sherry? Or will they wilt?

Harveys Isis Pale Cream Sherry 13 D

Jerezana Dry Amontillado, Waitrose 16 D

A wonderful cold weather cockle warmer. Not remotely austere or molly-coddley fruity, it's simply blood arousing.

Late Bottled Vintage Port 1991, Waitrose 13.5 E

Oloroso Sherry, Waitrose 13 C

Pando Fino, Williams and Humbert 14.5 D

Red Muscadel 1975 14.5 D

Rich Cream Sherry, Waitrose 13 D

Very rich and ripe.

Solera Jerezana Dry Oloroso, Waitrose 16.5 D

Fabulous chilled as an aperitif. Dry toffee fruit with a hint of almond.

Southbrook Farm's Framboise (half bottle) 15 E

Vintage Warre Quinta da Cavadinha 1986 17 G

Gorgeous ripeness yet hugely concentrated acid and tannin, compacted and fully ameliorated, so that the final texture is magnificent.

White Jerepigo 1979 (South Africa) 14 D

SPARKLING WINE/CHAMPAGNE

Bohemia Regal Sparkling Red (Czech Republic) 12 D

Brut Rose NV, Waitrose 13.5 G

Attractive in all but price.

Brut Vintage 1989, Waitrose 14.5 G

Expensive but a real treat. Shows its maturity and richness and it finishes superbly.

Canard Duchene Brut NV 12.5 G

Cava Brut, Waitrose 16 D

Superb blend of character-forming, crisp grapes making a mockery of Champagne prices.

Champagne Blanc de Blancs NV, Waitrose 14 G

Again, class from Waitrose where classic bubbly is concerned. This specimen really shows its all-chardonnay pedigree.

Champagne Blanc de Noirs NV, Waitrose 15 F

Makes a case for Champagne. It's rich, well-priced, fresh, nicely balanced.

Champagne Bredon Brut, F. Bonnet 14 E

Mature, soft, a touch coy.

Champagne Brut NV, Waitrose 12 F

Chapel Down Century Extra Dry (England) 13.5 D

Clairette de Die Tradition (France) 14 D

Brilliant fruity, off-dry aperitif. Great for evenings in front of the telly.

Cremant de Bourgogne Blanc de Noirs, Lugny 14 D

Deliciously classy fruit and finish.

Cremant de Bourgogne Brut Rose 13 D

Cremant de Bourgogne Rose, Cave de Lugny 15 D

Charm, personality and wit. How many champagnes have it?

Cuvee Royale Blanquette de Limoux 13 D

Green Point Vineyards Brut, 1994 (Australia) 13.5 F

Lovely fruit with a gently bready edge.

Krone Borealis Brut 1994 (South African) 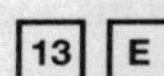

Put it down. Keep it for another two years. The only wine on Waitrose's shelves, as far as I know, without any sulphur whatsoever.

Le Baron de Beaumont Chardonnay Brut (France) 15 C

Lindauer Brut (New Zealand) 13.5 E

Getting a touch pricey in comparison with Cavas – and not so vivid.

Quartet NV, Roederer Estate (California) 14 G

Very stylish and fresh.

Saumur Brut, Waitrose 16 D

Superb, better than champagnes three times the price. Class, richness, dryness.

Seaview Brut 14 D

Seaview Brut Rose 14 D

Engaging rosiness without flushness.

Seppelt Great Western Brut (Australia) 13.5 D

Still a bargain. Elegant and dry.

Silver Swan Chardonnay (Hungary) 14 C

Perfectly charming and fresh bubbly.

STOP PRESS

ASDA

ARGENTINIAN WINE — WHITE

Argentinian Chenin Blanc 1997, Asda 15 B 

This has improved immeasurably in bottle since I tasted it in the spring of '98 and now offers delicious crisp, nutty fruit – elegant, calm and terrific value.

AUSTRALIAN WINE — RED

Landskroon Cabernet Franc/Merlot 1998  14 C

Very soft and sweet with a hint of earth.

Oxford Landing Cabernet Sauvignon/Shiraz 1997 15.5 C

Impressively spicy and rich, yet dry. Terrific stuff.

AUSTRALIAN WINE — WHITE

Oxford Landing Sauvignon Blanc 1997 14 C

Very cool and dry.

Penfold's Organic Chardonnay/Sauvignon Blanc 1997 16 E

Quite superb level of fruit here: fresh, deep, dry, layered and lush without being remotely ungainly or blowsy.

Peter Lehmann Riesling 1997 15.5 D

Sherbety riesling of rich classiness and texture, improving nicely in bottle (as I suspected it would when I tasted it earlier this year).

CHILEAN WINE WHITE

35 Sur Sauvignon Blanc 1998 16 C

Superb! The grassiness of the acidity and the richness of fruit, still classic dry sauvignon, makes for a wonderful crisp mouthful.

Araucano Chardonnay, Lurton 1997 16 E

Remarkably Californian style Chilean (i.e. elegant and very classy).

FRENCH WINE RED

Chateau Lahore Bergez, Fitou 1996 15.5 C

Delightfully earthy fruit here. Real characterful fruit of considerable gruff-voiced charm. Very polished.

Chenas NV, Asda

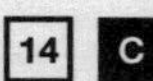

Has a pleasant hammy undertone.

Gigondas Chateau du Trignon 1995

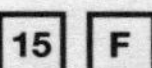

A big, dry, meaty, savoury treat with a hint of beef gravy and tobacco on the finish.

ITALIAN WINE RED

Allora Primitivo 1997

Gorgeous smoky tannins, clods of dry earth-coated cherries/plums/blackberries, and a zippy freshness on the finish. Terrific food wine and quaffing companion.

Barolo Veglio Angelo 1994

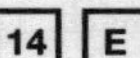

A real treat: hugely dry and teeth tingling, ripe and festively fruity. The fruit has licorice and a hint of almond. The finish is of vineyard soil and rich fruit. Expensive but very engaging.

---

d'Istinto Nero d'Avola Sangiovese 1997

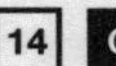

Rich cherries and plums – smooth and polished.

La Vis Trentino Oak Aged Merlot 1997

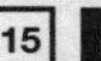

Great rich throughput of fruit on the tastebuds. Has great character and charm; elegant dishevelment (i.e. modern and baggy).

Montepulciano d'Abruzzo 1997, Asda 14 B

Terrific characterful quaffing: earth, ripe cherries, balance and a rich dry finish.

Puglia Toggia Rosso 1997, Asda 15.5 C

Great quaffing here, very elegant and gently weighty, character and style, deliciously fruity and dry – and it's all topped off with a fault-free plastic cork.

Valpolicella Classico San Ciriaco 1997 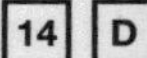

Juicy, ripe, raisiny, forward, and flush with fruit.

ITALIAN WINE — WHITE

Chardonnay Garganega 1997, Asda 14.5 C

Very dry and fresh where underripe melons and apples mingle with a steely acidity.

Cori 1997, Asda 14 B

Clean, fresh, touch austere (an austerity fish will mollify) and some glint of charm.

---

d'Istinto Catarratto Chardonnay 1997 (Sicily) 14 C

Combines some fleshiness of fruit with a taut acidity of finish.

La Vis Aldadige Pinot Grigio 1997, Asda 14 C

Interesting fatness which is made more lithe by the pertness of the acidity. It's sort of an echo of apricot with crisp melon juiciness.

La Vis Trentino Chardonnay 1997, Asda

Superb warmth, nuttiness, freshness and flavour. Works on several levels including refreshment and repast.

Orvieto Classico 1997, Asda

Lovely hint of lushness to the melony crispness. Terrific quaffing here.

Puglia Chardonnay 1997, Asda

Very prim and proper: nuts and a hint of vegetality with a suggestion of fish knives. Delicious with crustacea.

PORTUGUESE WINE RED

Bright Brothers Baga 1997

Very dry, hint of earthiness, and hedgerow alert richness. Great with food.

PORTUGUESE WINE WHITE

Bright Brothers Atlantic Vines Fernao Pires/Chardonnay 1997

Superbly vegetal, rich, slightly oily, beautifully balanced and classy. Terrific value.

SOUTH AFRICAN WINE — WHITE

Cape Muscat de Frontignan NV, Asda 14 C

A sweetie for fresh grapes after a meal.

SPANISH WINE — RED

Hecula Monastrell/Cabernet Sauvignon/ Merlot 1996

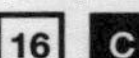

Superb richness, really long, elegant, classy and deep, with great tannins and fruit in perfect hedonistic harmony. A lovely under-a-fiver wine.

Jumilla Monastrell 1997, Asda

Great house red. And a posh residence this can be for this specimen of brick work is solid and rich.

Jumilla Tempranillo 1997, Asda

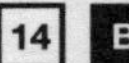

Fruit juice with attitude. Great little quaffer here.

Oaked Tempranillo 1997, Asda

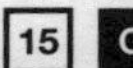

A very impressively rich and raisiny red of character and charm. Real style here and handsome build.

Valdepenas Reserva 1993, Asda

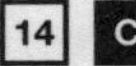

Very mature and ripe at the peak of its drinkability. Good price for such well-toned fruit.

Vina Albali Gran Reserva 1989

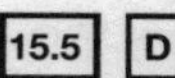

Superb maturity and raisiny richness and soft, textured complexity: plums, blackcurrants, almonds and a hint of anise and vanilla.

SPANISH WINE WHITE

Jumilla Airen 1997, Asda 14.5 B

Earthy yet plump and ripe. Comforting glug and also a wine for rich food.

La Vega Verdejo/Sauvignon Blanc 1997 14.5 C

Lovely cool sauvignon of class and clout. Great shellfish wine.

Oak Aged Viura 1997, Asda 15 B

Brilliant restraint and elegance here.

SPARKLING WINE/CHAMPAGNE

Vintage Cava 1996, Asda 15 D

Interesting complexity of mineralised, pebbly acidity and a hint of fruit.

BUDGENS

ITALIAN WINE RED

Primitivo Puglia Torrevento 1996 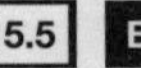

Superb value here with fruit as bold and dashing as the exuberant label. Has tannins, texture, depth and rich fruit on the finish. Hint of spice, too.

MARKS & SPENCER

CHILEAN WINE RED

Sierra Los Andes Cabernet/Merlot 1997 16.5 C

What marvellously well integrated fruit and tannins here. It strikes deftly yet richly, with soft fruit and spice, loads of vim and personality, and with a finish of stylish wit and warmth.

Sierra Los Andes Merlot/Cabernet Reserve 1997 17 D

More compacted, extruded, concentrated, and ineffably elegant than its non-reserve sister, it has more soupy and lingering richness – a touch. It is extraordinarily posh and vivid in feel. The texture is world-class.

CHILEAN WINE WHITE

Sierra Los Andes Chardonnay 1998 16 C

Impressive balance and richness of tones, ripe yet intensely well formed and elegant, and the texture is crisp yet yielding.

Sierra Los Andes Chardonnay Reserve 1998 15 D

Curiously, not two quid's worth of more impressive fruit here, though there is undoubtedly a woody feel, very subtle, of creaminess and distant vegetality. But these effects have to be searched for.

FRENCH WINE RED

La Tour de Prevot 1997

15 C

Such warmth and very gentle tannic deliciousness (never coarse or one whit cloddish too aggressive). It has soft fruity charms. It soothes rather than bludgeons.

La Tour de Prevot Reserve 1997

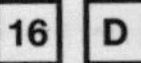

Classic posh Cotes du Rhone (I've tasted Chateauneufs less accomplished), this has richness and depth in full control of the tannins. The finish is stylish and very concentrated. A wine of considerable style.

La Tour du Prevot Cuvee Speciale 1997

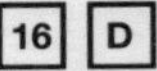

Very youthful, its character and depth have to be searched for. And time will help. It is ripe and responsive now, with classic Hermitage-like plumminess, but I think given a couple of years cellaring an 18-point wine might emerge. It has charm already and is rated thus, but the patient drinker (or, more accurately, non-drinker) may acquire an even greater treasure.

Vin de Pays des Collines Rhodaniennes 1997

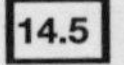

C

Intensely likable strawberry/cherry fruit of charm and persistence. It has a sweet nature it is impossible to condemn.

SOUTH AFRICAN WINE RED

Bin 121 Merlot Ruby Cabernet 1998 15.5 C

Perfumed, spicy, rich, hugely fruity and soft, this is a terrific Indian food wine. There's a terrific baked fruit edge of dry, rubbery, almost smoky richness.

Oaked Ruby Cabernet 1997 15 C

Unlike the '96 (see the main M&S entry in this book), the wood seems to put this vintage in a straitjacket so that it's unable to express its essential exuberance and unfettered fruitiness. However, this is still a plumply elegant wine if somewhat stiffer and more formal than its predecessor.

Rock Ridge Cabernet Sauvignon 1998 16.5 

Magnificent bargain here. The tannins and fruit offer smelliness (tobacco-edged), savouriness and a hint of spice, and that luxurious texture of ruffled corduroy. A smashing wine – good enough to grace the poshest and most highly polished of dinner tables.

SOUTH AFRICAN WINE WHITE

Cape Country Chenin Blanc 1998 15 

Drier, more concentrated than the colombard, this has some delicious sour gooseberry touches to its modernity.

Cape Country Colombard 1998 

Very pert and fresh, hint of lime to the richness and it's a highly agreeable quaffing bottle.

McGregor Chenin Chardonnay 1998 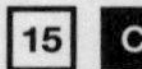

Combines some chardonnay ripeness with some mineralised chenin freshness. Makes for a handsome double whammy of styles on the finish.

SPARKLING WINE/CHAMPAGNE

Sparkling Chardonnay Vin Mousseux de France NV 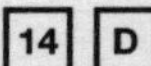

Fun bubbly this. Hint of mango helps and this is never strident or too soppy. There is some dry sophistication here.

SAFEWAY

ARGENTINIAN WINE RED

Diego Murillo Malbec, Patagonia 1997 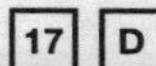

Fabulous Christmas fowl wine. Combines rich baked spicy fruit and evolved tannins. Incredible richness.

Fantelli Barbera/Cabernet, Mendoza 1998 

Bargain bonny red combining ripe, textured fruit and structured richness.

AUSTRALIAN WINE RED

Hardys Coonawarra Cabernet Sauvignon 1995 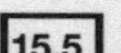

A rich jammy treat – great with game dishes – with blackcurrant savoury softness.

McPherson Croftwood Vineyard Shiraz, SE Australia 1998 

Juicy (by any other name it would be called squashed grapes).

Penfolds Clare Valley Shiraz/Cabernet 1996 (organic)

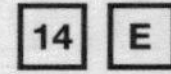

Aromatic, rich (very rich), ripe, and extremely generous with its charms. It might be great with spicy vegetables and melted cheese and it's gluggable enough. Eight quid's a lot of money, though.

AUSTRALIAN WINE WHITE

Annie's Semillon, Clare Valley 1996

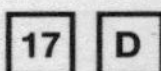

Absolutely hums with multi-layered flavours (peaches, plums, hint of strawberry).

Australian Dry White 1998, Safeway

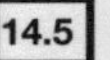

Now this is riesling at the level of intriguing fruitiness and price the Germans must attain.

Australian Oaked Colombard 1998, Safeway

Not much woodiness here, chips are such insubstantial things anyway, but a good deal of fruit.

Chardonnay/Colombard 1998, Safeway

Ripe melon and gooseberries with appley/lemonic acids. This new vintage will be coming into store as this book comes out.

Oxford Landing Estate Viognier 1996 15.5 D

Lovely apricot fruit with a hint of nut, lime and modern freshness.

Rothbury Estate Verdelho, Hunter Valley 1998 16 D

Makes a wonderful case for the grape as a spicier version of chardonnay. Great stuff.

BULGARIAN WINE RED

Huntman's Red 1997 15.5 B

Brilliant value here: cherries, wild strawberries and lead pencils.

CHILEAN WINE RED

35 Sur Cabernet Sauvignon, Lontue 1997 14.5 C

Has some tannins to relieve the plummy softness.

Chilean Cabernet Sauvignon 1998, Safeway 16 C

It's not classic and peppery but it is cabernet. But cabernet as soft, rich, deep and utterly quaffably delish.

Concha y Toro Casillero del Diablo Cabernet Sauvignon, Maipo 1997 16 C

Motors in top gear across the whole sensory system: has such gorgeous tannins!

Errazuriz Syrah Reserve, Aconcagua 1997 17.5 E

Big, berried fruit, rugged yet immensely soft, huge depth, flavour and commanding richness. This is even better than it was in the summer of '98 when I first tasted it.

Vina Morande Merlot 1998 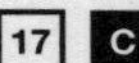

This has fruit so textured and rich it surprises like fluid grease. Incredible leathery lushness here.

CHILEAN WINE — WHITE

Chilean Sauvignon Blanc Lontue 1998, Safeway 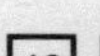

Combining great nuttiness and gooseberry, nettle-fresh fruit. Huge charm and subtle richness.

Chilean Semillon/Chardonnay 1998, Safeway 

Baked fruit mixed with fresh. Wonderful stuff!

Chilean White, Lontue 1998, Safeway 

What a price for such depth, elegance, freshness and flavour.

Terra Mater Chardonnay, Maipo 1997 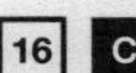

Astonishing richness yet charm (of relaxed manners) here. Selected stores.

FRENCH WINE RED

Domaine Chris Limouzi, Corbieres 1996 

Very juicy but has hints of tobacco and the Midi scrub.

Domaine des Bruyeres, Cotes de Malepere 1996 

Delicious modernity of manners with a hint of sunny soil.

Domaine des Lauriers, Faugeres 1995 

Fabulous vibrancy and richness here with huge depth, beautifully modulated tannins, and finish. Brilliant stuff.

FRENCH WINE WHITE

Wild Trout VdP d'Oc 1997 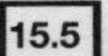

Gorgeous ring-a-ding fruit combining freshness and fullness. Has elegance and bite. Improving nicely in bottle, this wine, since I tasted it earlier this year.

HUNGARIAN WINE — WHITE

Nagyrede Oaked Zenit 1997 14.5 

Apples and pear, hard and soft – tickles the palate.

ITALIAN WINE — WHITE

Casa di Giovanni Grillo 1997, Safeway (Sicily) 16 C

Utterly gorgeous fruit! Terrific opulence and gently toasty lemon.

Tenuta 'Pietra Porzia' Frascati Superiore 1997 15 

Class act here. A real fresh Frascati of nuttiness, fruitiness and elegance. Balanced and bonny, this is a Frascati to revise the prejudiced mind.

MEXICAN WINE — RED

L A Cetto Malbec 1997 15.5 

Great texture here, and it clings to the teeth seemingly without tannins. The finish is very deep and rich.

L A Cetto Petite Syrah 1997 

The perfect depth of fruit and tannin, ripe and deep. Indian lamb and vegetable dishes suit it.

NEW ZEALAND WINE WHITE

Oyster Bay Sauvignon Blanc, Marlborough 1998 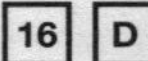

Dry honey edges to the warm gooseberry-fool fruit, and a fresh finish. Selected stores.

Villa Maria Private Bin Sauvignon Blanc, Marlborough 1998  

Elegant and chic, beautifully designed. The tongue rarely wears such perfectly fitted fruit. This new vintage will be replacing the '97 about the time this book comes out.

SOUTH AFRICAN WINE RED

Kleinbosch Young Vatted Pinotage, Paarl 1998  

So vibrant and perky it shakes one's teeth to their roots! Lovely ripe fruit here.

Landsdowne Cinsaut/Pinotage 1998 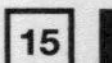 

Big, rich, juicy, softly spicy – brilliant for Asian food.

Landskroon Cinsaut/Shiraz, Paarl 1998 16 C

What an improvement on the '97 (see the main Safeway section of the book)! This is jammy, spicy and soft (yet fresh) but with good tannins. A masterly food wine.

Plantation Ruby Cabernet, Stellenbosch 1998 15.5 C

So modern, rubbery, juicy and jaunty, anyone over seventy will find it obscene.

The Pinotage Company Selected Bush Vine Pinotage 1998 16 D

Tasted the morning after Bill Clinton's televised squirmings, I found this wine fruitier by far.

SOUTH AFRICAN WINE WHITE

Arniston Bay Chenin Chardonnay 1998 15 C

Interesting fluidity of fullish fruit which finishes in a pleasing gush of freshness.

Delaire Chardonnay, Stellenbosch 1997 17 E

Toasted nuts, hint of gunsmoke, tight gooseberry and melon fruit, gently viscous texture, terrific finish. A very convincing wine.

Kleine Zalze Sauvignon Blanc 1997 15.5 C

Apples, kumquats and plums with a hint of pebbly crispness. Gorgeously thirst-quenching and utterly non-classical.

Namaqua Colombard, Olifantsrivier 1998 

Plump, fresh, young, slightly erotic – great Thai food wine.

South African Chardonnay 1998, Safeway  C

Soft yet hard, fresh and young yet mature in feel, rich yet refreshingly unpretentious.

SPANISH WINE — RED

El Leon Mencia, Bierzo 1997  C

Interesting quaffer with hints of cherries and ripe plums. It's the surprise of the delayed spice on the finish which makes it most charming.

Santara Cabernet/Merlot, Conca de Barbera 1996 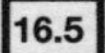 

One of the great under-a-fiver reds of supermarketing and Spain. Rich, mature, Claret-like aroma, big, dry, cassis-edged fruit with a hint of chocolate and tobacco and a roaring, handsomely dishevelled finish. A smooth rough diamond of deliciousness.

SPANISH WINE — WHITE

El Velero Rose, Valdepenas 1997 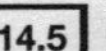 

Superb little rose for food. Has dryness, character and a lingering earthy cheeriness.

USA WINE RED

Fetzer Barrel Select Cabernet Sauvignon 1994

Great opulence and richness here. Coats the teeth like emulsion. Has bite and backbone.

USA WINE WHITE

Fetzer Viognier 1997

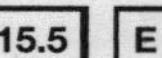

Pebble dash fruit, gently chewy and full of flavour. Hint of dry apricot and nuts.

Ironstone Vineyards Chardonnay 1997 17 D

Such calm hauteur and unaggressive yet rich fruit. Superb structure and modernity.

FORTIFIED WINE

LBV 1992, Safeway 15 E

Rather splendid in its richly figgy fulsomeness. Great value.

Warre's Vintage Port, Quinta da Cavadinha 1986 17 G

A most unusually complete port where alcohol, sugar, acid and tannin meld in mouth-watering harmony.

SPARKLING WINE/CHAMPAGNE

Seaview Pinot Noir/Chardonnay 1995 

Some interesting plumpness to the fruit.

SAINSBURY'S

AUSTRALIAN WINE RED

Saltram Classic Cabernet Sauvignon 1996

An aromatic soupy wine of great softness and lively, gently plummy fruit. Extremely slip-downable.

AUSTRALIAN WINE WHITE

Rosemount Semillon/Chardonnay 1997

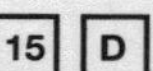

Very calm and collected, elegant and unruffled. The fruit is fresh, underripe and classy. Not at all stores.

CHILEAN WINE RED

Villa Montes Gran Reserva Cabernet Sauvignon 1995

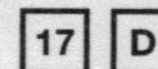

Highly polished, almost luxuriously soft and ripe, aromatic, gently leathery and hugely approachable. It has a little pepperiness and supple tannicity. It is utterly at its drinkable peak.

FRENCH WINE RED

Chateau Fourcas Hosten, Listrac Medoc 1995 16 E

Dry, tobaccoey, very rich, beautifully harnessing the fruit and tannin to pull the whole construct elegantly yet robustly across the tastebuds. Great class here. Limited distribution.

Merlot VdP d'Oc NV, Sainsbury's (1.5 litre) 15.5 D

Brilliant taint-free value here. This superb plastic bottle of magnum capacity (and screw-cap accessibility) is fat with plummy fruit but has rustic manners. It's warm, old leather bootish, highly polished and thus untypical.

Volnay Chateau Genot-Boulanger 1995 14 G

At first all that strikes is a pleasant perfume and then some meat to the savoury fruit. But class pinot? Almost. It does flaunt a classically cheeky price tag of high dimensionality, and this may be worth it for the dry, cherry (almost bitter before an hour or so of breathing) fruit, and the really impressive tannins. Nothing feral or gamey here, but has some real classy texture. Limited distribution.

FRENCH WINE WHITE

Chenin Blanc, VdP du Jardin de la France 1997 15.5 C

Beautifully pert lemon fruit, ripe, fresh, soft and not remotely too lush or simpering. Terrific little quaffing wine. Not at all stores.

ITALIAN WINE — WHITE

Anselmi Soave 1997 15 D

Real class here and for once Soave means what it says – suave. This is a superb, nutty, rich, textured wine of great class.

SOUTH AFRICAN WINE — WHITE

Mont Rochelle de Villiers Chardonnay 1997 15.5 D

Big, rich, buttery and oily – the usual roll call for a chardonnay but this also has a creamy toffee edge.

USA WINE — RED

Black Ridge Carignane/Grenache 1997 14 C

Hugely soft and jammy – like toffeed plums – but great glugging, and not so soppily, by virtue of its edgy dryness and warmth.

E & J Gallo Ruby Cabernet 1996 14 C

Not at all bad considering the address of the grape. A soft, ripe wine with some character and likeability.

FORTIFIED WINE

Pale Dry Fino Sherry, Sainsbury's 

A fino of finesse, flavour, fanciful nuttiness and texture, and that tight, saline finish.

SOMERFIELD

ARGENTINIAN WINE — RED

Argentine Red 1998, Somerfield 14.5 B

Juicy and rich and very fresh but the tannins confer weight and richness. Brilliant value (even better than the '97 which appears in the main Somerfield section in this book).

AUSTRALIAN WINE — RED

Basedow Barossa Shiraz 1996 16 E

Brilliant richness, helped by tannins, and the overall structure is stern yet all-enveloping. Lovely stuff.

AUSTRALIAN WINE — WHITE

Basedow Barossa Chardonnay 1997 15.5 D

Excellent, controlled richness and well-textured feel. Has some fat to it, some muscle, and some suppleness. Not a big wine but certainly bonny. Top 150 stores.

Penfolds The Valleys Chardonnay 1996 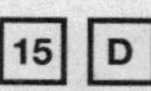

Always turns in a nicely tailored performance, this wine. Expensive? A touch. But it does show some class. This vintage has improved in bottle since I first tasted it.

BULGARIAN WINE RED

Domaine Boyar Special Reserve Cabernet Sauvignon, Oriachovitza 1993 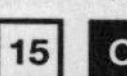

Amazingly vigorous considering its age. Fresh blackcurrant and soft tannins.

Iambol Bulgarian Merlot 1997 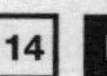 

Ripe and juicy and very earthy on the finish. Good if not elegant glugging.

BULGARIAN WINE WHITE

Domaine Boyar Barrel Fermented Chardonnay 1996  

Remarkable value and liveliness – considering the price and the age of the wine. It has texture and fruit and poise on the finish. A simple construct, true, but effective.

CHILEAN WINE RED

Canepa Reserve Merlot 1995

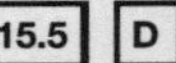

A juicy merlot but it does have mouth-watering juiciness.

Chilean Cabernet Sauvignon 1997, Somerfield

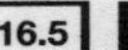

Oh what nerve! It offers all of a great Bordeaux's tannins but none of the austere fruit. It's simply terrific.

Chilean Merlot 1998, Somerfield

Lovely rich warmth to the texture, ripeness to the fruit and a whiplash clean fruity finish of elegant leather.

Cono Sur Pinot Noir 1997

Raunchier than many a Volnay at four times the price. Has great pongy length and savour. This has improved immeasurably in bottle since I first tasted it. Top 150 stores.

CHILEAN WINE WHITE

Valdivieso Reserve Chardonnay 1996

Classy, ripe (yet sophisticated), rich, deep, deliciously accomplished as a fruity artefact of some considerable style. *This* is the vintage which will be in the shops come Christmas '98 – I'm now told that the '97 vintage (which appears in the main section of the book, because I tasted it before that went to press) won't be coming in to replace it until next spring. Top 150 stores.

FRENCH WINE RED

Beaumes de Venise Carte Noire, Cotes du Rhone Villages 1997 

Brilliant earthy fruit. Loads of hedgerow personality and purposeful finishing power.

Buzet Cuvee 44 1997 

Best vintage yet!

Chateau Blanca, Bordeaux 1997 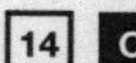

Delicious hints of charcoal and blackcurrant. Has a suggestion of classic young claret.

Chateau Cazal-Viel Cuvee des Fees Vieilles Vignes, St Chinian 1997 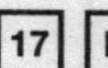

No fairy tale, this. Has wonderful savouriness, herbiness, cigar-edged fruit of elegant tannicity, and richness. Top 150 stores only.

Chateau Saint Robert, Graves 1996 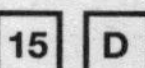

Has some haughty classiness and great tannins. Top 150 stores.

Chateau St Benoit Minervois 1996  

This matches in quality the previous vintage (which appears in the main Somerfield section of this book). The lushness is beautifully controlled by the tannin. Very impressive. Top 150 stores.

Chateau Valoussiere, Coteaux du Languedoc 1996 16 C

Like a minor claret of a great year (plus a herby undertone of savoury richness).

Cotes du Rhone Villages 1997, Somerfield 14 C

Gouts et Couleurs Syrah Mourvedre VdP d'Oc 1997 14 C

Modern, modish, ripe, fresh and very dry. Has a nice hint of underdeveloped quirkiness.

Vacqueyras Domaine de la Soleiade 1997 15.5 C

Pleasant pong of the distant *fumier* gives the wine something other than fruit and earth, sun and herbs, to flaunt.

Winter Hill VdP de l'Aude 1997 15.5 B

Lovely polished richness and ripeness. Gorgeous plump texture and svelteness of fruit.

FRENCH WINE WHITE

Bordeneuve Blanc VdP des Cotes de Gascogne 1997, Somerfield 14 B

Fresh pineapple and Cox's Orange Pippin hints here. Fun quaffing.

Les Marionettes Marsanne, VdP d'Oc 1997 14.5 C

Richness, plumpness, apricot fullness and juiciness, and real class.

GREEK WINE — WHITE

Samos Greek Muscat NV (half bottle) 15.5 B

This continues to be a terrific pudding wine, and fabulous value under £3. Selected stores.

HUNGARIAN WINE — WHITE

Hungarian Chardonnay, Szekszard 1997, Somerfield 14 B

Crisp and appley and best beside a fish dish.

ITALIAN WINE — RED

Amarone della Valpolicella Veneto 1994 16 E

Immensely classy with great spicy cherries and figs. Lovely tannins which mingle so marvelously with the fruit. Top 150 stores only.

Caramia Primitivo Barrique, Puglia 1996 16 D

Gorgeous fresh-faced fruit yet has a worldly-wise, rich air. Terrific tannins. Top 150 stores only.

Le Trulle Primitivo del Salento 1997 16 C

Most engaging for the teeth (though the throat is soothed well) as it lingers lushly yet dryly like a fruity cigar smoke.

Mimosa Maremma Sangiovese 1997 

I love the dark chocolate edge, tight but tasty, and the hint of earthy cherry. Wholly fresh and fulsome.

Monrubio Sangiovese, Umbria 1997 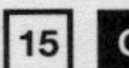

Not remotely like the Tuscan example of this grape, this has richness, gripping tannins, and subdued hedgerow fruit. Top 150 stores.

Montepulciano d'Abruzzo Madonna dei Miracoli 1997, Somerfield 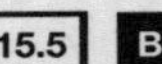

I love that juicy freshness combined, as only Italian wine can, with a dry, rich-edged finish.

Montepulciano d'Abruzzo, Riparosso Illuminati 1996 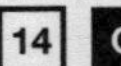

The new vintage is the essence of Italian jamminess and drinkability. Yeah, it's frivolous but it's lush and lovable. Top 100 stores.

ITALIAN WINE — WHITE

Chardonnay delle Venezie NV, Somerfield 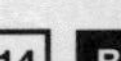

Simple, cheeky and highly gluggable. Would do fish and chips a favour.

Le Vele Verdicchio Classico, Le Marche 1997 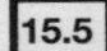

Superb plumpness to the fruit and the finish combines weight and wit. Terrific food wine and quaffing companion.

Sicilian White Settesoli 1997, Somerfield 14.5 B

Crisp, clean, cheerful (and cheap) and engaging. Good with fish and makes for confident sipping unaccompanied.

PORTUGUESE WINE RED

Bright Brothers Trincadeira Preta, Ribatejo 1997

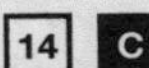

Has developed some character and bite. Top 150 stores.

PORTUGUESE WINE WHITE

Fiuza Bright Chardonnay, Ribatejo 1997

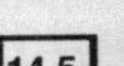

Gets there in the end but it seems shoulder shrugging and difficult at first quaff – then it runs at the throat and delivers rich, fresh, melony fruit. Top 100 stores.

ROMANIAN WINE RED

Pietrossa Young Vatted Cabernet Sauvignon 1997

Great interest to the palate with its dry, peppery fruit. Good with food and for dry wine tipplers (although this new vintage rates slightly lower than the '96 which appears in the main Somerfield section of the book).

SOUTH AFRICAN WINE RED

Bellingham Pinotage 1996 16 D

Smoky, tobaccoey, rich, fresh, eager, deep, full yet never blowsy. Top 100 stores.

SOUTH AFRICAN WINE WHITE

Hoopenburg Chardonnay 1997 15.5 D

Delicious, woody, creamy, ripe and ready. Gushes with eager fruit which is tempered by its vegetality. Classy.

Simonsvlei Hercules Pillar Chardonnay, Paarl 1997 14.5 D

Nice chewy edge to the fruit (wood) and the fruit is in good trim. Not altogether elegant but it would be very effective with food. Top 150 stores.

South African Colombard 1998, Somerfield 14.5 C

Has a good steely backbone and firm flesh.

SPANISH WINE RED

Bright Brothers Old Vines Garnacha NV 15.5 C

Terrific richness, earthiness and soft fruitiness harnessed to a fresh, dry, gushing edge. Makes for striking tippling.

SPARKLING WINE/CHAMPAGNE

Pierre Larousse Chardonnay Brut NV (France)

Steely and dry. Good value.

TESCO

USA WINE — WHITE

Fetzer Barrel Select Chardonnay 1997

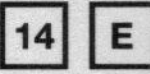

Somewhat more subdued than the '95 (c.f. the main section of the book), this is a dry, lemon and woody-melon chardonnay with a pleasant nut and cream finish. Hints at elegance rather than flaunting it. Available at the thirty Wine Advisor Stores only.

DON'T MISS:

STREETPLONK 1999

Gluck's Guide to High Street Wine Shops

Britain's best-loved wine writer is back with his comprehensive annual assessment of the best-value wines available through our top high street wine shop chains: Fullers, Majestic, Oddbins, Spar, Thresher, (including Wine Rack and Bottoms Up), Unwins, Victoria Wine and Wine Cellar. All come under Gluck's scrutinous nose in his quest for the best bottles at the bonniest prices.

* Completely rewritten every year

* The most up-to-the-minute wine guide on the market

* 'An impressive and accessible guide to what's really worth drinking' *Observer*

COMING SOON:

SUMMERPLONK 1999

Gluck's Guide to Summer Supermarket Wine

* Easy-to-follow, bang up-to-date and brimming with value-for-money recommendations

* The essential guide to the new summer wines available on our supermarket shelves

* Compiled in response to the overwhelming popular demand of *Superplonk* readers

Asda, Booths, Budgens, Co-op, Kwik-Save, Marks & Spencer, Morrisons, Safeway, Sainsbury's, Somerfield, Tesco and Waitrose are all checked out by Britain's best-loved wine-writer in his continuing quest for the very best bargain bottles.

'Gluck's illuminating descriptions and humorous comments will have you running to the nearest supermarket. Essential for a summer of pleasurable quaffing at an affordable price'
Daily Express